Saving the Big Thicket

From Exploration to Preservation, 1685–2003

James J. Cozine, Jr.

Foreword and Afterword by Pete A. Y. Gunter

Number 4 in the Temple Big Thicket Series

Big Thicket Association
University of North Texas Press
Denton, Texas

10 9 8 7 6 5 4 3 2 1

Permissions:
University of North Texas Press
P.O. Box 311336
Denton, TX 76203-1336

The paper used in this book meets the minimum requirements of the American National Standard for Permanence of Paper for Printed Library Materials, z39.48.1984. Binding materials have been chosen for durability.

Library of Congress Cataloging-in-Publication Data

Cozine, James.
  Saving the Big Thicket : from exploration to preservation, 1685-2003 / James J. Cozine, Jr. ; foreword and afterword by Pete A.Y. Gunter.
    p. cm.
  "Number 4 in the Temple Big Thicket Series."
  Includes bibliographical references and index.
  ISBN 1-57441-175-6 (cloth : alk. paper)
  1. Environmental protection—Texas—Big Thicket. 2. Historic preservation—Texas—Big Thicket. 3. Big Thicket (Tex.)—History. 4. Big Thicket (Tex.)—Environmental conditions. 5. Big Thicket National Preserve (Tex.) I. Title. II. Series: Temple Big Thicket series ; no. 4.

F392.H37C695 2004
333.72'09764'14—dc22
                                                          2004005846

Saving the Big Thicket is Number 4 in the Temple Big Thicket Series

This book was made possible by a generous grant from the T. L. L. Temple Foundation and the assistance of the Big Thicket Association.

The Foreword and Afterword by Pete A. Y. Gunter are based upon work supported by the National Science Foundation, Grant CNH BCS-0216722 under Biocomplexity in the Environment, Coupled Natural and Human Systems program.

DEDICATION

This dissertation is dedicated to my wife Sharon,
for her encouragement, support, and understanding.

CONTENTS

FIGURES

PHOTOGRAPHS FOLLOWING PAGE 134:

1) A bear hunt, early 1900s
2) Longleaf pine stumps, circa 1920s
3) Dearborn Sawmill
4) R.E. Jackson, 1880–1957
5) Justice Douglas and Dempsie Henley on Thicket tour
6) Dempsie Henley, Texas Indian Commissioner, at
    Alabama-Coushatta event, 1966
7) Representative Bob Eckhardt
8) Rep. Emmett Lack, Gov. Price Daniel, and Dempsie Henley
9) Archer Fullingim at Senate hearings, February 1974
10) Senator Ralph W. Yarborough and Lorraine Bonney,
    Senate hearings, February 1974
11) James Webster, Kirby Lumber Company, at Senate hearings,
    February 1974
12) Edward C. "Ned" Fritz at Senate hearings, February 1974
13) Geraldine Watson at Senate hearings, February 1974
14) Arthur Temple honored by Big Thicket Association
    luncheon, 1976
15) The Preserve's first Superintendent Thomas E. Lubbert
16) Professor Claude McLeod with Howard Peacock
17) Congressman Charles Wilson
18) Lance Rosier
19) Pete Gunter giving keynote address at Visitor Center dedication

FOREWORD

When *Saving the Big Thicket* (then called "Assault on a Wilderness") reached completion, in 1976, the dust had just settled on a ten-year-long struggle between conservationists and timber companies. The upshot of this controversy was the creation, in 1974, of a sprawling southeast Texas Big Thicket National Preserve of 84,550 acres: the first such biological preserve in the history of the National Park Service. In giving an account of this conflict, the author, James J. Cozine, had his work cut out for him. To achieve an overview, Cozine found it necessary to work his way through a long paper trail of newspaper and magazine articles, to read the many books and pamphlets staking out positions on both sides, and, finally, to interview personally political, conservationist, and industry leaders. The result was a story of movement and counter-movement, protest and response. As such, however, the project was incomplete. It was only a beginning (or rather, an end) of a much longer history.

The conservationist struggle that culminated in the creation of the Big Thicket National Preserve had been preceded more than a decade earlier by another conservationist movement with its own problems and goals. It, in turn, had been preceded by the unprecedented development of railroads and cut-and-get-out timber operations and of oil field development in the swampy, biologically rich area. Prior to oil booms and large-scale timbering loomed legends of bear hunting backwoodsmen, escaped slaves, and outlaws. These reached back into a not well worked-out past. Before the pioneer epoch lay yet another, peopled by Spaniards and Frenchmen who quarreled over an area that neither was quite able to settle or to conquer. Before the struggles of the French and the Spanish was a time in which journals were not kept or history recorded: a time when Native Americans lived along the margins of the Big Thicket and hunted and camped there. All this had to be recorded, too, and made into historical perspective.

Like many writers who chose to write history in depth Cozine was to find that his subject matter had a history as tangled and dense as the vegetation that had given the Big Thicket its name. The Native Americans who once lived there are no more. The Bidais and Akokisas were wiped out by illness, presumably contracted from European traders. The Hasinais (termed "Tejas" or friendly by the Spanish, and from whom Texas was to get its name) were similarly decimated, the remainder joining with their Caddo relatives to the north. The author describes the intertribal relations and the agricultural, sedentary way of life of the Native Americans, drawing on notes by explorers and the studies of anthropologists. Probably his most surprising conclusion concerns the way in which the Native Americans, though they hunted in the Thicket, chose as a rule not to live there. Clearing the Thicket forest, he speculates, would have been harsh and unrewarding labor.

Like the Indians, the author reports, the Spaniards chose to skirt the Big Thicket and had little effect on it. They built their missions and other settlements along the margins of the forbidding wilderness, locating the missions next to the major Indian villages. The same was true of the French, who, though they hoped to exploit trade with Native Americans in order to get a foothold in Texas, left little in the way of settlements, locating these too outside the Thicket's dense forest walls. The brief Mexican interregnum between Spanish and American domination had a similar non-effect.

From the time of the earliest Indian settlement, then, little had changed. The French and the Spanish, as described by Cozine, played out their geopolitical fantasies spasmodically and with little foresight. Move followed countermove in a vast chess game, which never seemed to achieve checkmate.

The coming of the Americans changed everything.

The author describes the American onslaught in three stages: first, an early period, starting in the 1820s, represented by backwoods settlers who worked around fifty acres of farmland each and who largely lived off the land. These early settlers did some timbering, floating logs down area rivers in the wet season to small lumber mills downstream. Second came a middle period, beginning in the 1870s, in which a complex of logging railroads and often mobile timber mills radically transformed the region, leaving extensive patches of scalped forest. To the ruthless onslaught of the timber operations was added, after 1900, a period of oil discovery which transformed sleepy villages into roaring boomtowns, compared to which the cattle-kingdom railhead towns of Kansas were prim and proper New England townships. The author's descriptions of the boomtowns captures their excitement and danger, just as his description of the corporation-owned lumber towns captures their top-down paternalism.

The third period, which reaches well into the twentieth century, is described by the author as a time of relative isolation and stability, in which portions of the forest were able to regrow and capture some of their former luxuriant depth, and in which the first stirrings of an environmental conscience began to emerge. Those stirrings were, though at first intermittent, gradually to grow into the first environmental movement in the area. Associated with the name of R. E. Jackson, a Santa Fe railroad conductor from Silsbee, Texas, this movement began in the late 1920s, peaked in the period just before World War II, and then declined, dying out in the late 1950s without achieving its goals. The emergence on the scene of a new cadre of environmentalists (Bill and Price Daniels, Dempsie Henley, Charles Wilbanks, and others) heralded the founding of the second—and present—Big Thicket Association and the eventual creation of the Big Thicket National Preserve.

This brief account of *Saving the Big Thicket* scarcely does justice to either the author's knowledge of detail or to his capacity to write. What might have been a list of statistics or a series of graphs becomes through his skill an engrossing narrative. It is, as newspaper reviewers like to put it, a "good read." It is also effective history.

Pete A.Y. Gunter
Past President
Big Thicket Association

# PREFACE

The Big Thicket of East Texas, which at one time covered over 2,000,000 acres, served as a barrier to civilizations throughout most of historic times. It was an inhospitable, inaccessible region, uninhabited even by the Native Americans until the early 1800s. The Indians who lived on its fringes only ventured into the Thicket to hunt. Early Spanish colonists in East Texas also avoided this region. The Spanish instead established their missions on the northern and southern extremes of the Thicket.

The Big Thicket became something of a no man's land in the early nineteenth century. Fugitives from justice, runaway slaves, and the rugged hunters and trappers who resented civilization, all sought refuge in the Thicket. But over the next half-century an assault on this virgin wilderness began in earnest. First came the great migration of American settlers, followed by the railroads, timber companies, and oil producers. Each group whittled away a portion of the Big Thicket.

By the 1920s, much of the Big Thicket wilderness had been destroyed by timber firms and oil producers. Fortunately in 1927, R. E. Jackson, a railroad conductor whose daily route carried him through portions of the Big Thicket, formed the East Texas Big Thicket Association with the specific purpose of saving over 400,000 acres of the region. However, a lack of funds and the timber demands of World War II killed the project. Jackson's Association limped along and eventually expired in the 1950s.

For a few years the movement to preserve a portion of the Big Thicket was moribund. However, spurred on by the continued destruction of the wilderness, a new group called the Big Thicket Association organized in 1964, to carry on the fight to save the Thicket. These wilderness advocates argued that the Big Thicket was a unique botanical region worthy of preservation because of the wide variety of plant life within its confines. Over the next several years the Big Thicket Association enlisted the aid of scientists, politicians, and other preservationist societies in an attempt to persuade the federal government to save the Thicket. Eventually the United States Congress reacted to the pleadings of the preservationists and moved to save a small portion of the remaining thicket. On October 11, 1974, President Gerald Ford signed a bill authorizing an 84,550-acre Big Thicket National Preserve. These 84,550 acres are not confined to one large tract. Rather, the preserve is composed of several small tracts scattered among seven counties of East Texas. Representative samples of the wide variety of flora within the Big Thicket will be preserved by utilizing this technique.

The present work evolved from my dissertation in the field of American History at Texas A&M University. It was completed in 1976, just two years after President Gerald Ford signed the bill that summoned the Big Thicket National Preserve into being, and its content reflects the research material available at the time. Since the heart of the story concerns the effort to create the Preserve, I have not attempted to trace the subsequent course of the Big Thicket's history. I leave that task to future historians, and to Pete Gunter, whose Afterword brings the reader through the political twists and turns from 1974 to 2003.

ACKNOWLEDGMENTS

Several people were critical to the completion of this work. Particular thanks are due Dr. Henry Dethloff who first suggested the topic; his comments and suggestions added immeasurably to the completed work. I am also grateful to Dr. Herbert Lang, Dr. Lloyd Taylor, Dr. Allan Ashcraft, Dr. Gary Halter, and Dr. Emil Mamaliga, for their constructive criticisms.

Numerous people aided me in my research. Mr. James Webster of the Kirby Lumber Corporation allowed me to pilfer his company's Big Thicket files. Mrs. Francis Ferguson, Special Collection Librarian at Stephen F. Austin State University, placed her knowledge of the Kirby Lumber Company Records at my disposal. Congressman Bob Eckhardt was kind enough to allow me to research the Big Thicket files at his Houston office. Also, Dr. Charles Schultz and Mr. David Chapman of the Texas A&M University Archives constantly furnished me with new and valuable primary material for this study.

I am also grateful to the numerous politicians, preservationists, and timber company officials who granted me a few hours of their time for informative and valuable interviews. Very special thanks are due the National Parks and Monuments Association for furnishing a generous grant that allowed me to complete the project.

Finally, I would like to acknowledge the support of my family. My mother and father offered both moral and monetary support that helped me to complete four years of graduate school. My wife, Sharon, and son, Steven, gave constant encouragement, and displayed patience and understanding beyond the call of duty.

CHAPTER I

Introduction

When the first European pioneers landed on the North American coast, they were greeted by a primeval forest of seemingly limitless proportions. To many, the prospects of living in such a wilderness were frightening beyond comprehension. These would return to the safety of the Old World. Those who remained set about the task of carving a new life in this great forest. There were occasional openings in the woods where settlers could travel with relative ease.

> But elsewhere the earth was covered with a thick tangle of berries and shrubs . . . saplings and ferns, and the debris of trees that had fallen to rot. . . . Grape trunks as thick as a man's thigh flung themselves from the ground to grip the treetops. . . . and the interlocking branches in beech or hemlock woods shut out the sun by day and the stars by night.[1]

From the very beginning of settlement through the twentieth century, this immense forest—which stretched from the Atlantic seacoast to the second tier of states west of the Great River—has been under a sustained assault by man. The forest, the settlers believed, was an obstruction to civilization, an enemy to man. Where it existed, farms could not. It hid

1

the aborigines and allowed them to ambush those pushing West. It harbored the wild animals that preyed upon livestock. Clearly, if this new country was to survive and flourish, the wilderness must be conquered. The pioneers set about this task with an evangelical zeal. Over the next three centuries they toiled in a struggle with the forest. Improvements in the axe and saw, coupled with a burgeoning influx of settlers moving westward, spelled doom for the vast woodlands.

Most of the great forest gave way to the yeoman farmer, but a few remnants managed to survive into the twentieth century. One such region is the Big Thicket of East Texas. At one point, the Big Thicket had nearly succumbed to man's assault. The timber companies of the late nineteenth century and early twentieth century, following a "cut-out and get-out" practice, cut most of the Thicket, leaving behind only stumps and stunted trees. However, by the 1920s, the Texas Forest Service, the state agency charged with protecting Texas' forests, began to convince the more progressive timber firms to reforest the region. The practices of scientific forestry, coupled with the healing powers of abundant rainfall and favorable soils, quickly rejuvenated the Thicket. By the 1950s much of the Big Thicket resembled a pristine wilderness. In 1968, a journalist visited the area, and his description of the Big Thicket is hauntingly similar to the type of environment encountered by those first, hardy pioneers. The Big Thicket, he exclaimed, was,

> a forest floor of fallen trees swamped with brush and briar, an understory of holly and dogwood and gum and oak and maple and hawthorn trailing vines and Spanish moss, and a soaring pillared canopy of beech and magnolias and loblolly pine. There was no sky, no sun, no sense of direction. . . . There were no landmarks.[2]

The survival of the Big Thicket is a small miracle, for it has withstood the assaults of five civilizations: the Native Americans, the Spanish, the French, the Mexicans, and finally the Americans. The first four civilizations it survived with relative impunity. However, the Thicket was slowly being destroyed by the last group until a small nucleus of determined preservationists halted the attacks.

Because of its very nature it is extremely difficult to assign any definition to the Big Thicket. What is it, where does it begin, and where does it end, are all questions that people have tried, with varying degrees of success, to answer for many years. Some critics of the region attribute the difficulty in arriving at a consensus definition to the fact that the Big Thicket is nonexistent. It is, according to these unbelievers, nothing more than a "gullible state of mind."[3] These individuals maintain that at best the area is simply the western extension of the Southeastern Evergreen Forest, which begins in Virginia and extends across the entire South.[4]

Even those who recognize the existence of the Big Thicket differ widely on its location. John Henry Kirby, an early Texas timber baron, claimed that the Big Thicket was located only in Hardin County. *The Handbook of Texas*, however, states that the name originally applied to the entire area encompassed by the Old San Antonio Road on the north and the coastal prairies on the south. The eastern boundary was the Sabine River, and the western extreme touched the Brazos River. *The Handbook of Texas* does point out that as settlement progressed, the people viewed the Trinity River as the western edge of the Thicket.[5]

Dr. Frederic W. Simonds, professor of geology at the University of Texas in the early twentieth century and one of the pioneer geographers of the state, set the Big Thicket within a ten- to fifteen-mile area in the lower part of Hardin County. Vernon Bailey in his United States Department of Agriculture bulletin entitled *Biological Survey of Texas* stated that the Big Thicket extended into Texas from the lower Sabine River and ran west to the San Jacinto River. Elmer H. Johnson, a noted industrial geographer at the University of Texas, published a study entitled *The Natural Regions of Texas* in 1931, which offered yet another definition for the area. In this work, Johnson did not give any firm boundaries for the Thicket. However, he claimed the Big Thicket centered in Hardin County. None of these men had made a careful survey of the Big Thicket area; their references to the region were nothing more than tangential remarks within their larger works.[6]

The first concerted effort to give scientific definition to the area occurred in 1936, when Hal B. Parks and Victor L. Cory of the Texas Agricultural Experiment Station directed a biological survey of the Big Thicket region.

Strangely enough, Parks and Cory defined the region not on botanical or biological grounds but on a geological basis. According to them, the Big Thicket tract was formed during the Pliocene Age. The original Big Thicket, they claimed, spread an emerald canopy over 3,350,000 acres of southeast Texas and covered all or portions of fourteen counties in southeast Texas. They contended that the boundaries of the region ran from the towns of Huntsville to Weirgate on the north, and from Orange to Houston on the south. The eastern boundary was the Sabine River while the western extension followed a line from Houston to Huntsville.[7]

Two years after the biological survey, Parks published an article in *Texas Geographic Magazine*, in which he expounded his geological theory concerning the formation of the Big Thicket. The entire region, he now maintained, owed its origin to the continued expansion and retreat of the Gulf of Mexico during the Pleistocene Age.[8] As the water of the Gulf of Mexico swept inland, it brought sand from the underwater floor, and as the Gulf receded, this sand was deposited to help form the soils of the Thicket. As one author stated, "It was the transgression and regression of the sea that created the area known as the Big Thicket."[9]

Claude McLeod, a botany professor at Sam Houston State College in Huntsville, is the author of a book that gives the most recent scientific definition to the area. Writing in 1972, McLeod maintained that the original Big Thicket was a region totaling over two million acres. McLeod based his definition on ecological factors. He believed the Thicket could be delineated from the surrounding areas of East Texas because of its ecological uniqueness. McLeod's ecological definition makes it almost impossible to give any true geographical boundaries to the Thicket region, for the ecology of the area does not follow any hard and fast position on the map. Roughly, the ecological Thicket follows a twisting path from the Sabine River on the east to Conroe on the west. Its northern border follows a winding path across portions of Newton, Jasper, Tyler, Polk, San Jacinto, and Montgomery counties, while its southern extreme follows an equally tortuous route across Hardin and Liberty counties until it joins with the northern border just west of Conroe in Montgomery County.[10] (See Map 1.)

One more definition must be added to this montage, and that is the hunter's Thicket or traditional Thicket. This region, encompassing

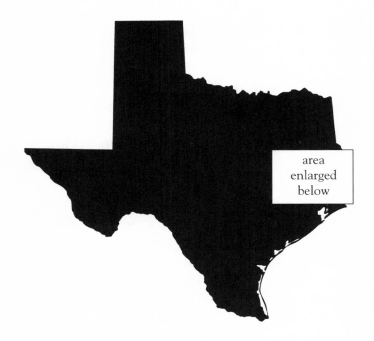

area
enlarged
below

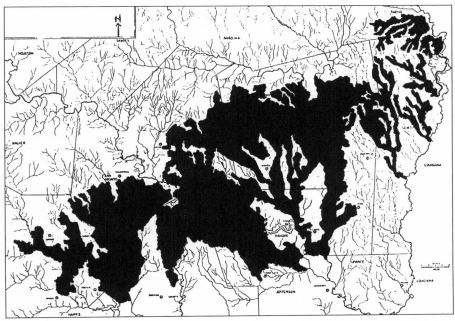

Claude McLeod's Ecological Big Thicket

5

northwestern Hardin and southeastern Polk counties, was once heavily populated with bear and panther as well as all the conventional game native to East Texas. One author maintained that this hunter's Thicket might be viewed as the heart of the Big Thicket region.[11]

Since there is no consensus definition for the location of the Big Thicket, any person writing about the region is relatively free to set his own particular boundaries. For the purpose of this study, the Big Thicket region will be interpreted as being situated in Tyler, Polk, and Hardin counties as well as the southern half of Jasper and Newton counties and the northern portion of Liberty County with slight spillovers into adjacent counties. Admittedly, this is an imperfect definition, but it does offer a few advantages. First, it gives the region some firm geographical definition. Hopefully, this geographic concept will make it simpler to understand the human impact on a specific area of land. The second advantage is that it encompasses nearly all of the areas that other writers have defined as the Big Thicket. In short, it offers a composite of the varied descriptions set forth by other authors.

Just as complex and confusing as the question of the location of the Big Thicket, is the question of the definition of the Big Thicket. Once again, there is a wide variety of opinions. Those who deny that the Thicket exists proclaim that there is nothing within the East Texas pine forest to distinguish one area from another. They maintain that anything within the so-called Big Thicket can be found elsewhere in a forest environment.[12]

However, others claim that the Big Thicket possesses unique features, which distinguish it from adjacent woodlands. Parks and Cory in the 1936 biological survey describe the Big Thicket as a "temperate zone mesophytic jungle."[13] Put more succinctly, it is a region where plants grow under medium conditions of moisture. The survey admitted that smaller areas of similar vegetation are scattered about the flatwoods of the southern United States. Parks and Cory maintained, however, that the Big Thicket differed from these similar areas by being much more extensive and being less affected by large-scale timber operations. In short, its uniqueness rested on size and not on the wide varieties of flora within the confines.[14]

McLeod's ecological survey gives a much more detailed picture of the Big Thicket. He describes it as an "edaphicmesophytic climax forest type, predominantly a loblolly pine-hardwood association, abounding in a rich understory of both evergreen and deciduous shrubs, a variety of climbing vines, and both annual and perennial herbs."[15] The term "edaphic" simply means that the plants are more influenced by soil factors than climatic factors while "mesophytic" refers to a medium moisture level. Thus, a particular combination of soil and moisture level has created a loblolly pine-hardwood association that possesses a definable type of undergrowth.[16]

In attempting to give further definition to the region, McLeod divided the area into two sections, designated simply as the upper thicket and the lower thicket. The northern, more elevated portion called the upper thicket is characterized in its climax form by a mixture of loblolly pine, white oak, beech, and magnolia. The primary difference between the upper and lower thicket is the presence of beech in the upper area. There it is a co-dominant with the loblolly pine. In the lower thicket, which is flat land, beech is almost totally absent. In its place is a new co-dominant for the loblolly pine: the chestnut oak.[17]

Further complicating this ecological description is McLeod's insistence that certain subordinate trees and lower understory plants must also be present if an area is to be classified as part of the Big Thicket region. The list of subordinate trees includes, but is not limited to, red maple, cherry laurel, and American holly, while the understory plants can be composed of such species as red bay, sweetleaf, yaupon, or witch hazel. Only a few of the many varieties of subordinate trees or understory plants need be present in any one location to qualify an area for inclusion into the Big Thicket region.[18]

Although McLeod's study was based on meticulous research, his ecological description was not totally accepted. Timber company officials claimed that the Big Thicket never extended to Conroe, Texas, while some preservationists maintained that the absence of certain understory plants or subordinate trees did not disqualify an area from being part of the Big Thicket.[19]

Other definitions of the region have centered around the wide variety of plant life in the area. Some environmentalists call the region the "Biological Crossroads of North America."[20] Those adhering to this concept always emphasize the wide varieties of plants, shrubs, wildflowers, and fungi found within the region, proclaiming that the Thicket is the meeting place for plant life from the four major regions of the United States. These naturalists cite a report of the National Park Service as authority for their claims of biological uniqueness of the region. The report stated that the Big Thicket contained "elements common to the Florida Everglades, the Okefenokee Swamp, the Appalachian region, the Piedmont Forest, and the open woodlands of the coastal plains."[21]

Indeed, the plant community within the Big Thicket is impressive and lends credence to the claims of the naturalists. Within its realm are ferns from the New England section such as the Christmas fern and the cinnamon fern, coexisting with plants generally associated with an arid environment, the mesquite, tumbleweed, and cactus. Trees commonly associated with a northern climate such as elm, beech, and sugar maple, mingle with the magnolias and cypress of the South.[22]

Additionally, environmentalists have identified eight major plant associations that thrive within the Big Thicket. Preservationists claim that these eight plant associations, growing in ecological harmony, contribute to the uniqueness of the region. The plant associations encompass such diversified vegetation as prairie land, giant palmettos growing alongside hardwood trees, longleaf pineland, pine savannah wetlands, and stream floodplain plant life. The beech-magnolia-loblolly pine plant association, and the acid-bog and baygall association, are also represented in the Thicket. The final plant association is the arid-sandyland group of xerophetic plants normally found in the drier sections of the Southwest. The preservationists were determined to save at least a small representative sample of each of the plant communities.[23]

To further press their claims of biological uniqueness, naturalists have compiled extensive lists of the flora of the Big Thicket. They claim that four of the five types of carnivorous plants in America thrive within the Thicket. They point with pride to the 2,000 species of fungi and the fifteen national champion trees inside its boundaries. They boast of the more than 400 species of wildflowers, including forty species of orchids that bloom within its confines. To cap their claims of biological uniqueness, the naturalists refer to the Big Thicket as a "region of critical speciation." This simply means that plant species that have reached the range of their geographical limits in the region of the Big Thicket have adapted to their unique environment and may differ significantly from species of their own kind growing in a different section of the nation under different environmental stimuli. In certain cases these differences may become so great as to warrant segregating the plants into a new species.[24]

Several factors are responsible for the tremendous varieties of flora within the Big Thicket. Some species from the North were brought into the Big Thicket by flood waters of the Mississippi during the Pleistocene Age, while plants from the South were supplied by the periodic wash of the Gulf of Mexico over the Big Thicket region. The soils and climate of East Texas are also responsible for the luxuriant plant growth of the Big Thicket. The area has an average temperature of 60 to 68 degrees. The surface soils of the Big Thicket consist mainly of fine sand or fine sandy loam, while the subsoils range from clay to sandy clay. When it rains, water, which easily penetrates the surface soils, often backs up to the surface upon meeting the tightly packed subsoils. This condition is more characteristic of the loblolly pine soils.[25]

The subsoils of the longleaf pine portion of the Big Thicket differ significantly from the loblolly area. Here the subsoils are more porous and this quality allows the water to pass freely through them. As a result, during the summer months these subsoils dry out to great depths. Fortunately, the longleaf pine is characterized by an extremely long tap root which enables it to reach down great distances to find its water supply. Since the other trees of the Big Thicket do not possess this ability, the longleaf pine is generally found growing alone without any co-dominant trees within its realm. Thus a fortunate combination of soil, temperature, rainfall, and a growing season of 250–260 days contributes to an environment that allows the Big Thicket plant life to flourish and grow.[26]

The name Big Thicket is a misnomer. It conjures up an image of a vast region so dense that travel is impossible. This is not the case. There are, of course, areas that qualify as thickets, but interspersed within the region are open woodlands such as the longleaf pine forest of Newton and Jasper counties. Also inside its realm are low-lying swampy areas called baygalls as well as open prairie lands. One of the most unusual facets of the region is the presence of large sand mounds covered with desert vegetation. These mounds are several feet tall and vary from a few square feet to several acres in size. These mounds might have been coastal dunes during the age when gulf waters traversed the region. The Big Thicket is well watered by the Sabine, Neches, and Trinity Rivers as well as innumerable streams and bayous. As might be expected, the areas of greatest densities, which give the region its name, are located along these waterways.[27]

Although the definition of the original Big Thicket is still disputed, the size, location, and botanical content of the Big Thicket National Preserve have been designated by an act of Congress. On October 11, 1974, President Gerald Ford signed Public Law 93-439 creating a Big Thicket National Preserve. The Preserve consists of 84,550 acres scattered among Tyler, Hardin, Polk, Liberty, Jasper, Jefferson, and Orange counties. Since the Big Thicket contains such a diversified plant life, the 84,550 acres is not confined to one large block of land. Rather, the Preserve is composed of several small unconnected tracts. Representative samples of several of the original Thicket's plant communities were preserved by utilizing this technique.[28] (See Map 2.)

The largest unit in the Big Thicket Preserve is the 25,024-acre Lance Rosier Unit. Named after one of the leaders of the preservation movement, the unit is located in southwestern Hardin County between the cities of Saratoga, Sour Lake, and Kountze. The area is characterized by large stands of loblolly pine, swamp chestnut, and laurel oak trees. It contains five of the plant associations the environmentalists hope to preserve. The Rosier Unit is the heart of the old hunter's Big Thicket. Preservationists had hoped that the region would be a sanctuary for the ivory-billed woodpecker, but that species was declared extinct after the formation of the Preserve. The second unit, the Pine Island Bayou Corridor, sweeps across lower Hardin County and connects the Rosier Unit with the Neches River. The corridor covers 2,100 acres and is fourteen miles long. Pine Island Bayou contains excellent specimens of the palmetto-hardwood plant association.[29]

Big Sandy Creek Unit in southeast Polk County, a few miles east of Livingston, covers 14,300 acres. The unit's plant associations range from pine-upland forest to the streambank, baygall, and beech-magnolia-loblolly pine groupings. Since the unit adjoins the southern edge of the Alabama-Coushatta Indian Reservation, the Big Sandy Creek tract should attract a relatively large number of tourists. The Menard Creek Corridor Unit is attached to the southwest flank of Big Sandy Creek. The corridor, which is twenty miles long and covers 3,359 acres, follows a serpentine path from Big Sandy Creek Unit to the Trinity River to the west. The corridor will function as a connecting link for the plant associations of the Preserve with the Trinity River region.[30]

Comprising 668 acres, the Hickory Creek Savannah Unit is the second smallest unit in the Preserve. Located in southwest Tyler County a few miles south of Warren, the Hickory Creek Savannah Unit contains a multitude of herbaceous plants and stands of longleaf pine. The smallest unit in the Preserve is the 550-acre Loblolly tract located east of the tiny hamlet of Moss Hill in northeast Liberty County. As the name implies, the unit is composed of one of the few remaining stands of virgin loblolly pine in the state. The pines in this unit are of fairly recent origin. Prior to 1900, much of this unit was prairie land, but over the intervening years, the aggressive loblolly pine seeded the area and produced a new virgin forest. This rather unique area managed to escape the timber firms because the land had been entangled in litigation since the turn of the century. Since the unit has not reached its climax form, it offers botanists an opportunity to study the ecological succession of the region.[31]

Turkey Creek Unit, an elongated strip covering 7,800 acres, spills across the Tyler-Hardin County line in a north–south axis. Situated east of Warren in Tyler County, the Turkey Creek Unit contains the greatest diversity of plants in the Preserve. Five of the seven major plant associations are found in the unit. Orchids, carnivorous plants, and a wide variety of wildflowers grow in this tract. Additionally, the unit contains a small sample of the xerophytic plants generally found in desert environments. The northern-most section of the Preserve is the Beech Creek Unit. Covering 4,856 acres near Woodville in Tyler County, the Beech Creek Unit contains the finest remaining specimen of the beech-magnolia-loblolly pine plant association. In 1967, the unit contained a fifty-acre tract of virgin forest; however, when the Preserve was established in 1974, the virgin forest had shrunk to only five acres. Since the region is close to the Neches River and the Sam Rayburn Reservoir, Park Service officials believe this unit will have heavy visitation for hiking, backpacking, and nature study.[32]

The remaining units of the Preserve are all located along the Neches River. A corridor stretches the entire length of the Neches River from Dam B in Jasper County to the northern boundary of Beaumont. Although the corridor is 39 miles long, it only encompasses 6,375 acres. The bill creating the Preserve divided the corridor into two separated units called the Upper Neches and Lower Neches Units; but in reality they comprise one unbroken unit. The Neches River corridors were included in the Preserve primarily for their recreational values. Park officials believe that the fishing and canoeing opportunities of the Neches River will constitute some of the prime attractions of the entire Preserve.[33]

Two other units, the Neches Bottom and Jack Gore Baygall, and the Beaumont Units, are situated along the course of the Neches River. The Neches Bottom and Jack Gore Baygall section covers 13,300 acres and is located a few miles north of Evadale. Bisected by the Neches River, a portion of the unit is in Hardin County, while another section is situated in Jasper County. This unit boasts a variety of hardwood trees such as bald cypress, water tupelo, and birch. Acid bogs and baygalls are also present in this tract. The final tract, the Beaumont Unit, is perhaps the wildest area within the Preserve. The unit, which covers 6,218 acres, is located just north of Beaumont at the confluence of Pine Island Bayou and the Neches River. Since the Beaumont Unit is surrounded by water most of the year, the area escaped timber operations. It is a superlative example of the hardwood forest of southeast Texas, and represents the streambank plant association. Additionally, the region, which is subject to saltwater intrusion from the Gulf of Mexico, boasts a wide variety of aquatic life.[34]

The 84,550-acre national Preserve contains the only remnants of the Big Thicket wilderness that will survive man's assault. The remaining portions of the Big Thicket that are outside of the Preserve will eventually give way to civilization.

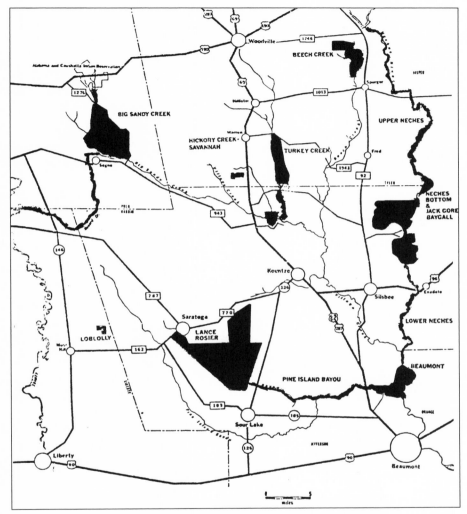

Big Thicket National Preserve

13

The Indians' Assault

The first group to assault the virgin wilderness of the Big Thicket were the Native Americans. None of the indigenous peoples of Texas lived within the Big Thicket. However, three principal tribes—the Hasinai, Bidai, and the Akokisa—lived on its fringes. The Hasinai Indians, who were members of the Caddoan linguistic stock, lived in several villages scattered along the upper Trinity and Neches rivers just beyond the northern boundary of the Big Thicket.[1] The Hasinai customarily called their friends or allies by the name "Tejas."[2] The Spanish, in turn, applied this name to the Indians of the region. These Tejas Indians were sedentary and followed agricultural pursuits. Maize, pumpkins, watermelons, and peas constituted some of their primary crops. Some writers have hinted that the Tejas and other tribes were too frightened of the Thicket to live within its confines. This was not the case. The Tejas Indians never established permanent villages in the Big Thicket because the region was ill-equipped to support their agriculture-based society. The redlands where they lived were much more fertile than the sandy soils of the Thicket.[3] Also, the Indians would have been required to spend years of arduous labor clearing the Thicket for planting.

Remarking on the richness of the Indians' soil, a Spanish priest declared that the fertility of the lands of the Tejas was superior to Spain. The land, according to the priest, had but one fault :"that of being thickly covered with a great variety of trees."[4] The Indians, however, settled in the numerous open spaces interspersed within the forest. The priest bemoaned the thick woods, for it made it more difficult to gather the Indians into large groups. Such action was desirable because it would have allowed the priest greater control over the Tejas.[5]

The Akokisa Indians lived along the southern fringes of the Big Thicket. Their settlements lay between the Trinity and Sabine Rivers. The Akokisas were members of the Attacapan language group, and possessed the unsavory reputation of being cannibals. Like the Hasinai Indians on the north, this tribe had no reason to live within the Big Thicket. The Akokisa's entire culture centered around the sea. In fact, according to their legends, the first Akokisa came from the sea. The Gulf furnished them with both their primary diet and articles of value to barter with other tribes.[6]

The Bidai Indians, relatives of the Akokisa, lived primarily to the west of the Big Thicket along the western bank of the Trinity River. Their name is derived from a Caddo word meaning brushwood, which implies a close connection with the Big Thicket region. The Bidai lived in fixed dwellings, and, like the Tejas, cultivated the soil.[7] Apparently the Bidai, like their Akokisa relatives, possessed a very low culture for one authority described the habitat of these two tribes as "a kind of ethnological sink."[8]

Although all these tribes were separated by the Big Thicket, there was an active trade among them. The Akokisa furnished the Tejas with decorative items such as shark teeth and feathers from plumed coastal birds. Archaeologists inspecting Tejas burial sites have found conch shells and pearls, which confirmed commercial intercourse between the Tejas and Akokisa. Contacts between the Bidai and Tejas were frequent, for the Tejas believed that the Bidai medicine men could cure most infirmities.[9]

White contact with these three tribes was devastating. Before the Spanish settled in the region in 1690, the Tejas population was 4,000 while the Akokisa and Bidai each numbered 500. In 1691, an epidemic of unknown character ravaged the Tejas and the other East Texas tribes. A smallpox epidemic in 1776–1778 further decimated the three tribes. By 1907, both the Bidai and Akokisa were extinct and the Tejas had merged with their northern relatives, the Caddos. Combined, they totaled only 555, and probably fewer than half that number were Tejas Indians.[10]

Ironically, the Indians most closely associated with the Big Thicket were not natives of Texas, but migrated to the area in the early 1800s. These were the Alabama and Coushatta tribes. The Alabama and Coushatta Indians, who originally inhabited northwest Mississippi and northeast Alabama, were separate but related tribes of the Muskhogean language group. Their first contact with white men occurred when the DeSoto expedition passed through their native land in 1541. Later, the French, after establishing their post at Mobile, won the allegiance of the two tribes. When the French withdrew from this region after the end of the French and Indian War in 1763, the Alabamas moved west into Louisiana. The migration was precipitated by two factors. First, the French warned the Alabamas that the English, who now controlled the Indians' homelands, would exterminate them. Also, the virgin hunting grounds of the West appealed to the Alabamas. The Coushatta tribe followed them in 1790.[11]

While in Louisiana, the Alabama Indians split into two groups. One group settled on the upper Red River near the Caddos, while the other remained in the Opelousas area of south Louisiana. The Coushatta tribe also split in Louisiana. One band lived along the southern portion of the Sabine River, while the others joined their Alabama relatives along the Red River.[12]

These Indians enjoyed cordial relations with the Spanish officials in Louisiana, but when the United States acquired the Pelican State in 1803, the affinity between the Indians and whites rapidly deteriorated. Murders by both the Indians and the Americans inflamed the growing friction between the two groups. Finally, in 1807, some Coushattas accepted the invitation of Spanish officials and migrated to Texas. The Alabamas followed suit a few years later. The Spanish had invited the Indians to East Texas, hoping that they would serve as a barrier to American settlers pushing west.[13]

In Texas, the Coushattas first settled near the village of Salcedo on the Trinity River, north of the Big Thicket. However, the Alabama Indians moved directly into the Big Thicket along the Neches River and established Fenced-in-Village in present-day Tyler County. Later, they moved to Peach Tree Village in the same county.[14] The Alabama Indians were thus the first people to settle permanently in the Big Thicket. Their decision to live in the Big Thicket was no accident, for their name in Choctaw means "I open or clear the Thicket."[15]

In their new homeland, the Alabama and Coushatta Indians managed to maintain amiable relations with the Anglo settlers who migrated into East Texas in the 1820s. These Indians ingratiated themselves to the Anglos by their actions in the Texas Revolution. During this critical period, the Indians could have joined the Mexican forces and inflicted severe losses on the lightly garrisoned settlements in East Texas. Instead, they remained neutral. The Alabamas merely moved into Louisiana until the war ended. After the conflict they returned to Fenced-in-Village. The Coushattas, however, remained in Texas, and aided the settlers fleeing the invading army of Santa Anna.[16]

In 1840, both tribes petitioned the Texas legislature for grants of land between the Neches and Trinity rivers. The Texas legislature eventually responded, and provided each tribe with two leagues of land near their old villages. However, an unfortunate set of circumstances prohibited either tribe from receiving titles to the land. Finally in 1854, the Texas state government purchased 1,280 acres of land in Polk County just seventeen miles from the town of Livingston, and deeded it to the Alabama Indians. The state then, in 1855, granted the Coushattas 640 acres but this plot was never located. Eventually, the Coushattas' settlements disintegrated, and some moved back to Louisiana. Others, however, remained in Texas, and joined their Alabama kin on the reservation in Polk County.[17]

When the Civil War began, the Alabamas and Coushattas volunteered to serve the Confederate cause. Their offer was accepted, and on April 11, 1862, twenty members of the tribes enlisted as Company G of the 24th Texas Cavalry. The company was ordered to report for duty in Arkansas. Upon arriving in Arkansas, the Indians, much to their chagrin, learned that they were to be converted to infantrymen and assigned garrison duty at El Dorado. The strict camp life added to their disenchantment. Since the Indians had trouble adjusting to military regimentation, they eventually returned to Texas.[18]

Again in 1864, the Alabama-Coushatta Indians volunteered to serve. Their company became part of the 6th Brigade, 2nd Texas Infantry Division. Their duties involved constructing and transporting flat-bottom boats, laden with produce, down the Trinity River to the Confederate forces along the Gulf Coast. The Indians continued their river route until the end of the conflict.[19] After the Civil War, Governor James W. Throckmorton wrote the Commissioner of Indian Affairs, asking that the federal government assume guardianship of the tribe. According to Throckmorton, Texas was too impoverished to properly care for the Alabama-Coushatta Indians. In 1873, a bill which would have moved the Alabamas and Coushattas to a federal reservation was introduced in Congress, but it failed. The tribe continued to eke out a living by working on farms for their white neighbors, and by laboring in the sawmills of the surrounding area. The diminishing amount of game in the Big Thicket, one of their primary food supplies, added to their plight. The succeeding years brought little improvement to the tribe.[20]

In 1896, J. C. Feagin, a concerned neighbor of the Indians, wrote Congress requesting federal aid for the Alabama-Coushatta tribe. However, no relief legislation was passed. Investigations by the Department of the Interior in 1910 revealed that the greatest needs of the Alabama Coushattas were more land, and a vocational education program to train them for jobs. Unfortunately, the 1910 investigation failed to generate any congressional action.[21]

Again in 1912, Feagin wrote Texas Senator Charles A. Culberson pleading for relief of the tribe. Feagin asked Culberson to use his influence to wring some federal funds from the Department of the Interior. Culberson dutifully contacted Samuel Adams, the Acting Secretary of the Interior, asking him to aid the Indians.[22]

Adams replied that the Alabama-Coushatta could claim an allotment of land under the Dawes Severalty Act of 1887, but he warned that this option would entail moving the Indians from Texas to land set aside for allotment purposes. Adams also stated that the Indian Office was considering asking Congress for a $10,000 appropriation to aid the Alabama tribe.[23]

Adams' reply did not satisfy Feagin, for he knew that the Indians would never move to allotment land, and he also believed that $10,000 was not enough to secure the reforms. Once again, Feagin contacted Culberson, urging him to exert additional pressure on Adams for more aid. He added that the government should purchase at least two to three thousand additional acres of land for the Indians and provide some type of job training on the reservation. Feagin also suggested that Culberson enlist the aid of Texas Congressman John H. Stephens, a member of the House Committee of Indian Affairs.[24]

Stephens proved receptive to the idea, and he approached Adams, asking for aid. Adams reiterated that the Indians could apply for land under the Dawes Act, but now he stated that he was opposed to the $10,000 appropriation for the tribe. Adams claimed to have changed his mind for a number of reasons. First, he said $10,000 would be useless, because it was not sufficient to relieve the plight of the Alabama-Coushatta tribe. Apparently Adams did not believe in the old proverb that half a loaf of bread is better than none. Adams also stated that if he made such a request for the Alabama-Coushattas, then other tribes who were not receiving federal aid would clamor for a share of the spoils. In short, he believed that the plight of the Indians was a Texas problem that should be solved by Texas money.[25] Feagin's pleas had failed.

However, in 1918, the federal government finally moved to ease the condition of the tribe. Congress appropriated $7,000 for educational aid. This was the first federal aid to the Indians. It was not until ten years later that the Indians received their first large federal aid. In 1928, Clem Fain, Indian agent for the Alabamas, together with several tribal members, traveled to Washington to plead for more money. The group appeared before the House Committee of Indian Affairs and also met with President Calvin Coolidge and several members of the Cabinet. The trip was a great success. Congress appropriated $102,000 designated to purchase additional land and to make improvements on the reservations. With part of this money, the government purchased 3,071 acres adjoining the old reservation to be held in trust for the tribe. In 1955, the federal government deeded this 3,071 acres to the Texas government. Once again, Texas was totally responsible for the Alabama-Coushatta land.[26]

Ten years later, in 1965, the Texas legislature created the Commission of Indian Affairs to develop the economic potential of the tribe. The efforts of the commission coupled with the self-help projects of the tribe have transformed the Alabama-Coushatta reservation into an outstanding tourist facility.[27] As might be expected, one of the major attractions is a tour of the Big Thicket.

The Indians' assault on the wilderness was not destructive. Their mere presence did, of course, alter the Big Thicket, but to no significant degree. Their foraging and hunting caused no lasting damage. They, of all the civilizations that assailed the Big Thicket, altered the environment the least. The only monument to the Indians' assault is a small reservation in a corner of Polk County.

The Spanish Assault

The white man's assault on the Big Thicket region began as a small part of the great struggle between Spain and France for supremacy of the southern regions of what is now the United States. Prior to 1685, the area encompassing the region of present-day Texas was uninhabited by white men. Spain, who claimed Texas, had not attempted to colonize the region. Indeed, only a few Spanish adventurers, such as Cabeza de Vaca and Luis de Moscoso, had traversed even a small portion of the realm. However, in 1685, an event occurred that would drive the Spanish to establish permanent settlements in East Texas.

In that year, Robert Cavelier, Sieur de La Salle, established an ill-fated French colony of 180 settlers in Texas. The settlement was located on the banks of the Garcitas River about five miles inland from Matagorda Bay. Even the founding of this small colony in the vast unexplored region of Texas was an accident. La Salle had intended to plant this colony at the mouth of the Mississippi River, which he had explored just a few years earlier. Such a colony would have established French supremacy over the fur-rich Mississippi Valley. Unfortunately, a navigation error caused the French colonists, who were traveling by sea, to miss their intended destination and land on the wild Texas coast. The settlement, called Fort St. Louis, was immediately beset with hardships. A series of disasters left the colonists without supplies, and the one ship that could have been used to relocate the colony was lost in a wreck off the coast. The situation seemed so hopeless that several men deserted the colony to live with the Indians of the area.[1]

Faced with this situation, La Salle attempted to march overland from Fort St. Louis to Canada where he hoped to obtain the needed supplies to ensure the survival of the colony. La Salle made three attempts to reach Canada by this overland route. On one of these attempts he penetrated into the realm of the Tejas Indians living along the Trinity and Neches Rivers above the Big Thicket area.[2]

On his third desperate attempt to reach Canada, La Salle was ambushed and killed by some disgruntled members of his own expedition. The survivors of this third expedition then continued the journey. As had La Salle before them, these men reached the land of the Tejas Indians. Here, those associated with the assassination remained to live among the Indians. A few hardy souls pushed on and eventually reached Canada. Those who had been forced to stay behind at Fort St. Louis either perished from disease or were killed or captured by the Indians living around Matagorda Bay.[3] Despite the pathetic demise of this little colony, it set in motion a vigorous reaction by the Spanish that would lead them to establish a series of settlements around the northern fringes of the Big Thicket region.

The Spanish in Mexico had learned of La Salle's colony shortly after it was established. They first heard of the colony from Denis Thomas, a sailor who at one time had been a crew member on one of the four ships that carried La Salle and his colonists to Texas. A Spanish ship had captured Thomas' vessel, the *St. Francois*, off the coast of Yucatan in 1685. Thomas told the officials in Mexico about La Salle' s colony, but he could not give them the precise location.[4]

Both sea and land expeditions were dispatched to discover and destroy the French intruders, but the colony could not be located. Six expeditions searched for the colony between 1686 and 1689, but to no avail. One of the sea expeditions found the wreckage of La Salle's ship, but no colonists were sighted. Since they had been unable to find the settlement, the Spanish began to doubt its existence. Perhaps, they mused, it was nothing more than a manifestation of Thomas' imagination. But then, Juan Enrique, a deserter from La Salle's colony who had been living among the Indians, appeared in Coahuila, Mexico, and told the startled Spanish officials that Fort St. Louis did indeed exist.[5]

After hearing Enrique's story, the viceroy of Mexico ordered Alonso de León, governor of Coahuila and captain of the presidio at Monclava, to mount another expedition to find the French interlopers. This time the Spanish discovered their long-sought goal, but they found Fort St. Louis completely deserted. While at the fort, de León received a group of Tejas Indians, who were down in this region hunting buffalo. These Indians informed de León that some survivors of the colony were living among them on the upper Trinity and Neches rivers. Father Damian Massanet, a priest accompanying the expedition, spoke to the Tejas, and managed to secure the Indians' permission to establish a mission among the tribe.[6]

Having completed his task, de León returned to Mexico and reported his findings to the viceroy. After hearing the evidence, the viceroy decided to send de León on yet another expedition. The viceroy instructed de León to find the French survivors, and to assist Father Massanet in establishing a mission in East Texas to Christianize the Tejas. The mission was also to serve as a buffer against further French intrusion into Texas.[7]

On March 28, 1690, de León, leading an expedition of soldiers and priests, set out for the land of the Tejas. First, they stopped and burned Fort St. Louis to remove all traces of the hated French invaders. After accomplishing this task, the group resumed its march toward northeast Texas. Finally after an exhaustive trip, this little band reached the land of the Tejas in May 1690, but failed to find the reputed French survivors. On June 1, 1690, they established the Mission San Francisco de los Tejas on San Pedro Creek just six miles from the Neches River. Having accomplished his task, de León returned to Mexico, leaving three priests and three soldiers to man the mission. This frail outpost was the first of many missions that would be built just beyond the northern border of the Big Thicket.[8]

During the ensuing 131 years of Spanish rule, the pattern of settlement in East Texas followed the direction laid down by the viceroy in 1690. Missions and presidios were established only where Indians dwelled or where the French attempted to penetrate into Texas. Inasmuch as Indians did not live within the Big Thicket, and because the French efforts to penetrate Texas occurred in areas north and south of the Big Thicket, the Spanish were never compelled to establish settlements within its confines. They did, however, erect a ring of settlements around the Big Thicket region.

Mission San Francisco de los Tejas survived only three years. The Indians did not readily convert to the Christian religion, nor were they pleased with the advances of the soldiers toward their women. In addition, the Indians blamed the priest for the failure of their crops. Faced with the mounting hostilities of the Indians, the priest burned the mission in 1693 and returned to Mexico.[9]

It was not until 1716 that the Spanish forces reoccupied the land of the Tejas. The reawakened interest of Spain was due to the aggressive commercial activities among the Tejas by the French from their newly established post at Natchitoches, Louisiana. The Spanish countered the French incursions by establishing six new missions. The two most important included Mission Nuestra Señora de Guadalupe, near the site of present-day Nacogdoches, and Mission San Miguel de Linares in a region called Los Adaes near modern Robeline, Louisiana. The other missions, Nuestro Padre San Francisco de los Tejas, La Purisima Concepcion, Nuestra Senora de los Ais, and San Jose, were strategically placed to control the various Tejas tribes. The Spanish also established a presidio, garrisoned by a few troops, near Mission Nuestro Padre San Francisco de los Tejas to protect the priest and to serve as an additional bulwark against French interlopers.[10]

The missions and presidio lasted only a few years. In 1719, war broke out between Spain and France, and it spilled over to their colonies in America. When news of the war reached the French in Louisiana, the governor, John Baptiste Le Moyne, Sieur de Bienville, ordered M. Blondel, commandant of Natchitoches, to attack the Spanish in northeast Texas. Actually Blondel, with a diminutive invasion force of six men, raided only the mission at Los Adaes. At the time of the raid, the post was almost deserted. Only one lay brother and a crippled soldier were manning the mission, and they were easily captured. However, the lay brother managed to escape and warn the other missions and presidios. Unfortunately for the Spanish, the frightened lay brother exaggerated the size of the French force. In his hysteria, he declared that 100 well-armed men were marching from Louisiana. Since the Spanish could only muster a fighting force of twenty-five soldiers, most of them boys without guns, the commander decided to retreat. The priest followed the example of the soldiers, and once again East Texas was totally abandoned.[11]

Spanish officials in Mexico were angered at this retreat and ordered the immediate re-establishment of the missions and presidio. The viceroy selected the Marquis de San Miguel de Aguayo to lead the task force. Aguayo's expedition, consisting of 500 soldiers and settlers, 4,000 horses, 600 cattle, 900 sheep, and 800 mules, was the most ambitious undertaking by the Spanish to settle the eastern portion of Texas. Like his predecessors, Aguayo failed to penetrate the Big Thicket. He simply re-established the abandoned mission and established a strongly garrisoned presidio in the Los Adaes region near Natchitoches. He took no punitive action against the French, for peace had already been declared. From these vantage points, the Spanish were able to reduce French commercial activities among the Tejas, but they never completely eradicated French influence in the region.[12]

Inasmuch as the Spanish had developed a commanding position in northeast Texas, the French shifted their attention to the Indians dwelling along the southern rim of the Big Thicket. As had occurred in the north, this French activity led to a reaction by the Spanish and the ultimate establishment of Spanish settlements in the southern regions. By 1745, rumors of French intrigues among the Indians of the lower Trinity River region became so strong that the governor of Texas ordered Captain Joaquin Orobio y Basterra, commander of the presidio at La Bahia, to investigate the reports.[13]

Orobio y Basterra visited the Bidai and Akokisa villages located on the Trinity River. Although he found no French settlement, Orobio y Basterra observed signs of French commercial activities among both tribes. He then returned to La Bahia and sent his report to the governor. Apparently, Basterra had impressed the Akokisa Indians, for tribal representatives journeyed to La Bahia and requested that a Spanish mission be established in their land. Subsequently, Orobio y Basterra was ordered to explore the region and select a suitable site for a mission.[14]

He left La Bahia in May 1748, and followed a course approximately fifteen miles inland from the coast. He arrived at the Akokisa village on the Trinity River on June 13, 1748. At the camp were Akokisa chiefs from villages further east on the Neches and Sabine Rivers. These chiefs invited Orobio y Basterra to continue his explorations eastward, and he consented. The Indians guided him along a trail that they claimed ran from the Trinity to the Sabine River and beyond. The first two leagues along the trail followed open and level country. Subsequently, the group encountered a region of heavy pine trees and thick underbrush. The Indians announced that the remainder of the journey would be through similar vegetation until the troop reached an area about one day's march east of the Sabine River. Faced with the prospects of such a harsh journey, Orobio y Basterra turned back, but not before noting that the country was swampy and unfit for settlement.[15] Orobio y Basterra had just encountered the southern extension of the Big Thicket.

Although Orobio y Basterra recommended the establishment of a mission among the Akokisa, typical Spanish procrastination forestalled settlement in the region for years. Finally in 1754, renewed rumors of French activities among the Akokisa Indians spurred the governor of Texas to dispatch Lieutenant Marcos Ruiz to investigate. This time the rumors proved to be true, and Ruiz captured a Frenchman, Joseph Blancpain, two white associates, and two black slaves. This little group had built a cabin on the lower Trinity River and were engaged in a brisk fur trade with the natives. Blancpain informed his captors that there were plans to establish at least fifty French families close to the mouth of the Trinity.[16]

To suppress any such plan, the Spanish established a mission and a presidio just two leagues from the mouth of the Trinity in 1756 or 1757. Collectively the two outposts were called El Orcoquisac after the Akokisa Indians. Fifty settlers were sent to populate the area. El Orcoquisac was a hell-hole. Lack of a proper source for drinking water and the mosquito-infested swamp near the outpost made life intolerable. On several occasions, plans proposing to move the settlements to a place known as El Atascosita, about nineteen leagues further north on the Trinity River, were submitted to the authorities, but for various reasons the move was never approved.[17]

Although the Spanish authorities never sanctioned a government-sponsored outpost at Atascosita, settlers moved into that region in the late 1750s or early 1760. They were probably settlers from the Orcoquisac region searching for a more salubrious environment. Atascosita became the first Spanish settlement within the Big Thicket region. Eventually in 1831, Atascosita's name was changed to Liberty.[18] Thus in 1760, Spain could only boast of a string of missions and presidios north of the Big Thicket and one inconsequential settlement resting on its southwestern flank.

The transfer of Louisiana to Spain in late 1762 foreshadowed the demise of the missions and presidios in East Texas. The removal of the French threat, coupled with the generally unsuccessful attempts to convert the Indians of East Texas, reduced the need to man the region. However, the final blow to their existence did not fall until three years later. In 1765, the Marques de Rubi, a Field Marshall in the Spanish Army, received orders from King Charles III to inspect all presidios in the Viceroyalty of New Spain. After the inspection, Rubi was to report on the conditions of the presidios and make any recommendations to improve frontier defense. Upon receiving his orders, Rubi immediately left Spain, arriving in Mexico in February 1766. Fortunately, Nicholas de La Fora, a captain of engineers accompanying Rubi, maintained a diary of the trip that included a description of their route.[19]

Rubi first inspected the presidios in California, Arizona, and New Mexico. He finally reached the presidios of northeast Texas in 1767. After inspecting these sites, he set out for the Orcoquisac presidio on the lower Trinity River. Instead of taking the trail leading around the western edge of the Big Thicket, Rubi followed a course that carried him through the center of the Thicket. From Nacogdoches, he struck out due south. For the entire journey he stayed between the Trinity and Neches Rivers: the heart of the Big Thicket.[20] In his diary, La Fora described the hardships they encountered in the Thicket. He wrote,

> On the 5th [Oct. 1767] we traveled twelve leagues southwest along a middle course over ground like the preceding. At four

leagues is La Parida. For the eight remaining leagues we traveled through thick woods that were almost impenetrable on account of the great amount of chaparral which chokes up that narrow path. The way is obstructed by fallen trees and branches lying across it, making passage very difficult because one has to avoid the brush and climb over the trunks. To this inconvenience another was added. At intervals the rain fell all day until five in the afternoon. At that hour the downfall became steady and the road impracticable, and we were forced to make camp on an almost imperceptible and nameless rise.[21]

At this time, Rubi's expedition was approaching the area east of the present-day city of Livingston in Polk County. Traveling further south, La Fora exclaimed that flood waters reached the bellies of their horses. Continuing their southerly excursion, La Fora mentioned that on October 8 they camped at a place called El Atascoso (Atascosita), the site of a small rancho. Finally on October 9 the weary group reached El Orcoquisac.[22]

After completing this arduous inspection tour, Rubi submitted his recommendations to the King. His report called for the abandonment of all the missions and presidios in East Texas. Rubi's report documented several reasons for his recommendations. With the French threat from Louisiana removed, Rubi maintained that Spanish troops in East Texas could be more profitably used against the Comanches on the West Texas frontier. A small force in Natchitoches would be sufficient to maintain a Spanish presence among the Indians of the region. Rubi also wished to consolidate the defense line of the frontier of New Spain. He envisioned a string of presidios stretching from the California coast, through Arizona, New Mexico, and across the southern half of Texas, terminating at La Bahia. The East Texas missions were far outside this defensive perimeter, and, therefore, were useless from Rubi's point of view.[23]

In 1772, the King of Spain issued the order to abandon East Texas. By 1773, all missions and presidios in East Texas were closed, and the settlers around Nacogdoches and Atascosita were forced to move to San Antonio. East Texas, both north and south of the Big Thicket, was now uninhabited except for the Indians and a few stoic settlers who decided to live among the Native Americans instead of obeying the imperial order.[24]

Some settlers who had been forced to withdraw from northeast Texas were unhappy in San Antonio. Led by Gil Ybarbo, they petitioned the governor to allow them to return to their farms. At first the governor refused, but in 1774, he allowed them to establish the village of Bucareli at the junction of the San Antonio Road and Trinity River in the upper portion of present-day Walker County. The experiment with Bucareli was a disaster. The hostility of the Comanches coupled with the ravaging flood waters of the Trinity River doomed the little settlement. In 1779, under the direction of Gil Ybarbo, the settlers abandoned Bucareli and returned to the area around Nacogdoches. Nacogdoches prospered, and by 1790, boasted a population of 480 people.[25]

The purchase of Louisiana by the United States in 1803 transformed Nacogdoches into one of the most strategic cities in the Spanish Empire. Now the town served as the first barrier against the spread of American influence into Texas. The Louisiana Purchase also spurred the re-establishment of Atascosita in the south. By 1805, a number of settlers, many of them Frenchmen from Louisiana dissatisfied with the transfer of their homeland to the United States, had moved into the region around Atascosita. Spanish troops were sent to re-enforce the settlement and to guard against American encroachment into southeastern Texas.[26]

The Louisiana Purchase also ignited a boundary dispute between the United States and Spain which would rage for fifteen years. President Thomas Jefferson proclaimed that the western boundary of Louisiana was the Rio Grande River. Jefferson based his claim on La Salle's exploits in Texas. To his line of reasoning Texas had belonged to France and now it belonged to the United States. The Spanish, of course, disputed this claim, and announced that the boundary between the two nations was actually several miles east of the Sabine River.[27]

Neither country was willing to abrogate its claim to the disputed territory; however, the two nations managed to cope with the situation by establishing a modus vivendi for the contested ground until the issue could be permanently settled. Don Simon de Herrera, commandant of the Louisiana frontier, and General James Wilkerson, commander of the United States

Army in the West, signed this so-called "neutral ground" agreement in 1806. According to this document, the Sabine River on the west and the Arroyo Hondo and Calcascieu River on the east were to serve as the boundaries for the neutral ground. The agreement stated that neither Americans nor Spanish troops could penetrate the neutral ground. However, civilians of both nations were free to settle in the disputed area. Since forces from neither sovereign were allowed to enter the area, it became a hideaway for all manner of unlawful enterprises. Outlaws, filibusters, and fugitive slaves all used the neutral ground for their sometimes-nefarious purposes.[28]

While the diplomatic maneuvering between the United States and Spain to resolve the boundary dispute was in progress, Spanish officials were once again forced to react to a new French threat in Texas. In 1817, a group of disgruntled and defeated Bonapartists originated a grand scheme to re-establish an empire in the New World. This band, formed by Charles and Henri Lallemand, French generals who had fought with Napoleon, planned to establish a colony in southeast Texas. This colony was to serve as a springboard for an invasion of Mexico. These visionaries believed that if they could conquer Mexico, then Napoleon would be released from St. Helena and join them in their new domain.[29]

The promotional literature in the French press masked the true purpose of the colony. The newspapers claimed that the colony was to offer French military and political exiles an opportunity to pursue a pastoral life in the New World. The first shipload of these so-called colonists, numbering approximately 150 people, reached Galveston Island on January 21, 1818. Here they met with Jean Lafitte, the infamous buccaneer who used Galveston Island as a base of operation for his raids on Caribbean shipping. From Lafitte, the soldier-settlers received some supplies and several small boats. These Bonapartists then rowed thirty miles up the Trinity River and established a fort, which they called Champ d'Asile, near the Spanish settlement at Atascosita. These freebooters were ill-equipped for the rigors of frontier life in Texas. Discipline was almost nonexistent, and disputes frequently ended in duels. A chronic shortage of supplies forced the men to reduce their rations to one biscuit per day.[30]

Spanish officials soon heard of the settlement, and they dispatched a force under Captain Juan de Castaneda to expel the interlopers. The French, learning of the approaching Spanish troops, fled to Galveston Island seeking refuge with Lafitte. Some joined the forces of the buccaneer while others returned to France or sought a new life elsewhere. The attempt to re-establish the grandeur of Napoleonic France in the New World lay crumbled in the undergrowth of the Big Thicket of East Texas. Champ d'Asile existed only five months.[31] With this last French threat removed, the Spanish devoted their full attention to the solution of their boundary dispute with the United States.

Eventually, in 1821, the United States Senate ratified the Adams-Onis Treaty, which settled the territorial dispute between Spain and the United States. Under its terms, the Sabine River was established as the border between Louisiana and Texas. With the entire neutral ground now under American control, many of the lawless elements drifted across the border into Texas.[32] Doubtless some sought refuge in the Big Thicket.

Eighteen twenty-one was a propitious year in Texas history. The eastern border was firmly established, and Mexico, newly independent from Spain, now exercised jurisdiction over Texas. Spain's assault on the wilderness had ended. The 131 years of Spanish rule had scarcely touched the Big Thicket. Only the struggling settlement of Atascosita remained as a monument to Spain's attack on the Thicket.

The Anglo Assault

The Big Thicket had survived the assaults of the Indians, French, and Spanish with relative impunity. However, beginning in the 1820s the Texas wilderness was subjected to the onslaught of a more vigorous civilization. Land-hungry Americans, at the invitation of the Mexican government, swarmed into Texas by the thousands. At first these early Anglo settlers avoided the heavily wooded Big Thicket in favor of more open land. However, in later years they began nibbling at the Thicket's flanks. Eventually a few hardy souls entered the region to hunt, trap, or eke out a frugal living from the soil. By the mid-1830s, the Anglos' assault on the Big Thicket had begun.

The Anglo migration, which doomed the Texas wilderness, was initiated by the fertile imagination and perseverance of one man: Stephen F. Austin. In 1820, Stephen F. Austin's father, Moses Austin, a citizen of Missouri who had suffered a series of financial setbacks in the United States, obtained permission from Spanish officials in Mexico to establish a colony of 300 Anglo-American families in Texas. In return for colonizing the region, Austin was to receive a large grant of land, which he hoped would relieve his personal financial crisis. The colony was to be established on a grant of land mutually agreeable to both parties. Austin's plan held great appeal because it offered the government an inexpensive method of populating and developing the Texas wilderness. Unfortunately, Moses Austin died in June 1821, before he fulfilled his dream. The task of colonization fell to his son. Stephen F. Austin traveled to Texas and selected a suitable site for the colony on the lower Colorado and Brazos rivers, west of the Big Thicket.[1]

However, before any large-scale colonization commenced, Mexico won its independence from Spain, and the new government promptly suspended the colonization plan of the Spanish regime. Austin was informed that he would have to curtail settlement of his grant until the new Mexican government formulated its own colonization law. Due to the political turmoil in Mexico following independence, passage of a comprehensive colonization law was delayed. However, on April 14, 1823, the Mexican government, without waiting for passage of a permanent colonization law, approved Austin's petition and issued instructions for land distribution within his colony.[2]

Eventually, in August 1824, the Mexican government approved a colonization scheme. While it stipulated that each state should pass its own particular colonization law, the national document outlined a few general policies. For example, the Mexican government reserved the right to prohibit the entrance of any foreigner as a colonist if "imperious circumstances" required such action. In short, the government could curtail American immigration at any time.[3]

In accordance with the national decree, the state of Coahuila and Texas passed its own colonization law on March 24, 1825. This state law, as well as the national decree, institutionalized the empresario system. An empresario was an individual who contracted with the Mexican government to settle at least 100 families on a specific grant of land. In return for his labors in establishing a colony, the empresario was to receive a bonus of five leagues of grazing land and five labors of farming land for every one hundred families he settled within his colony. (A league equals 4,428 acres and a labor 177 acres. See Barker, *The Life of Stephen F. Austin*, 138.) The empresario could not receive bonus land for settling more than 800 families. If by the end of six years the empresario had failed to establish one hundred families within his colony, the contract was cancelled. These two laws closely paralleled the instructions the Mexican government had given

Austin, the first empresario, in 1823. Those who emigrated to an empresario's colony received a generous portion of land at a very moderate price. Additionally, the settler had six years to pay for his land.[4]

The lure of cheap land proved irresistible, and streams of Americans headed for Austin's colony. The two overland routes to the colony by-passed the Big Thicket. The San Antonio Road or Camino Real, which stretched from Natchitoches, Louisiana, to the Alamo City, ran to the north of the Thicket, while the Opelousas-Atascosita Road, which ran from Opelousas, Louisiana, to Laredo, Texas, skirted its southern fringes. Others coming by sea disembarked at the mouth of the Brazos River before proceeding to their land.[5]

Although Austin's grant did not include any of the Big Thicket region, he was aware of the lawless nature of that area. In fact, Austin might have inadvertently contributed to the lawlessness of the Thicket, for he instructed officials of his colony to give any desperado fifty lashes and to "seize sufficient of his property to pay a guard to conduct him beyond the Trinity River."[6] On one occasion Austin wrote the governor of Coahuila and Texas protesting the "perverseness of turbulent persons" along the Trinity and Neches rivers who were harassing settlers camped in that region while awaiting permission to settle in his colony.[7]

In 1825, Baron de Bastrop, a confidant of Austin, estimated that at least 1,000 desperate criminals from the United States had moved into Texas along the Sabine River.[8] A letter from the governor of Louisiana, Henry S. Johnson, to Austin seems to substantiate de Bastrop's claim. Johnson wrote Austin complaining that a number of slaves and horses in Louisiana had been stolen by "lawless banditti" and "dishonest debtors" and spirited into East Texas.[9] Some men did indeed enter the Big Thicket region just one step ahead of the gallows. In 1825, the Hardin brothers from Tennessee settled in the Big Thicket on the Trinity River just north of Atascosita. Two of the brothers, Benjamin and Augustine, were wanted for murder in their native state. Apparently the Hardins reformed, for they rose to a position of prominence in southeast Texas. In fact, Augustine Hardin was one of the signers of the Texas Declaration of Independence.[10] The lawlessness of East Texas did not deter the resolute settlers from traveling to Texas, and they continued to pour into Austin's grant.

Since Austin's colony prospered, several other men petitioned the Mexican government for empresario contracts. Among these were Joseph Vehlein and Lorenzo de Zavala. Joseph Vehlein was a German merchant living in Mexico City. In December 1826, he received his first contract to settle 300 families in his grant. In 1828, he received a second grant, which was contiguous to his original land, with the obligation of settling 100 families in the new land. Lorenzo de Zavala, a native of Mexico and a man of considerable political influence, received his contract in March 1829. According to his agreement, Zavala was to settle 500 families within his colony. Taken together, Vehlein's two grants coupled with Zavala's encompassed the entire Big Thicket region and beyond. The boundary of the land of the two empresarios ran from the Sabine River on the east to the San Jacinto River on the west. The San Antonio Road served as the northern border while the Gulf of Mexico marked its southern extreme.[11]

Unfortunately, neither Vehlein nor Zavala was particularly successful in inducing settlers to come to their colonies. Apparently, both men lacked the capital to undertake such an ambitious colonization scheme. Adding to their woes, the Mexican government passed a law on April 6, 1830, forbidding further emigration of settlers from nations adjacent to Mexico. It was a move designed to stop the Americanization of Texas. Thus, the most immediate source of colonists for their grants was effectively suppressed. Faced with these difficulties, Vehlein and Zavala combined with David G. Burnet, another empresario whose grant north of the San Antonio Road ran contiguous with their land, and all three men transferred their contracts to a group of New York and Boston capitalists who organized the Galveston Bay and Texas Land Company in October 1830.[12]

Anthony Dey and George Curtis of New York, with William H. Sumner of Boston, served as trustees and attorneys of the company. The enterprise also consisted of a board of directors, plus the three empresarios, as well as stockholders. The Galveston Bay and Texas Land Company boasted that their land encompassed fifteen million acres. The company began selling land scrip to prospective settlers at a price ranging from one to ten cents per acre. Unfortunately, many of those purchasing the scrip believed they had gained title to the land. This was not the case. The scrip merely entitled the holder to settle within the company's domain. Only the Mexican government could confer title. In reality the scrip was worthless in Texas, for the empresarios would grant land to immigrants whether they possessed scrip or not. Nevertheless, it was estimated that by 1834 the company had sold scrip amounting to 7,500,000 acres.[13]

Since Texas was closed to Americans at the time the company began its colonization efforts, the trustees turned to Europe for potential settlers. In late 1830, Zavala sailed for the Old World hoping to procure settlers from Germany, France, and Switzerland. The company also attempted to bring settlers from England, Ireland, and Scotland. The company's first boatload of emigrants left New York for Texas on December 29, 1830. The group, according to one account, consisted of thirty-four men, women, and children, mostly Germans, who had recently immigrated to the United States. A number of company agents, who were to take possession of the company's land, accompanied this pioneer party.[14]

When the ship landed at Galveston Bay, General Manuel de Mier y Teran, the commander of the Eastern Department of the Mexican Republic, refused to allow the emigrants to take possession of their land. Teran based his decision on two primary reasons. First, he claimed that the entrance of these colonists would violate the law of April 6, 1830. Secondly, he stated that the Mexican government had not recognized the Galveston Bay and Texas Land Company as a legitimate colonizing agency. Teran's decision rested on the fact that no empresario contract could be transferred without the consent of the Mexican government. In this case, neither Vehlein, Zavala nor Burnet had received permission to transfer their contracts to the company.[15]

Although Teran refused to allow the settlers to take possession of the land, he did permit the agents to erect some huts, which provided temporary shelter for the emigrants. He also assigned them an acre and one-half plot as a garden. After being provided with this temporary food and lodging, the settlers and agents awaited instructions from the company. However, when they received no further directions from the trustees, the emigrants began to believe that they had been used as a sham to promote the sale of scrip and that the company had no intention of planting a colony in Texas.[16]

One American, who claimed to have purchased 20,000 acres in scrip, had accompanied this first party. He gave a dismal account of the emigrants' existence in Texas. He wrote,

> Ignorant of everything, especially of the country, they had gone blindly into a wild expedition, committed themselves to the hands of a company, bound themselves by their signatures, and received in return papers which they could not read, under the firm belief that they thus acquired good title to little estates, though they in fact obtained what was of no value whatever. Here they were, hutted under leaky boards, some with their wives and little children, in a strange land, without any means of providing for the future, and believing that they had been made dupes by persons whom they had never injured or provoked, and whom they had scarcely seen.[17]

The Americans, however, believed the company acted out of ignorance and had not intentionally deceived the settlers. This seemed to be the case, for upon learning of Teran's action, Vehlein protested to the Mexican government and claimed that the emigrants should be allowed to settle on the land. Unfortunately for the company, the authorities sided with Teran. This decision temporarily suspended the colonization plans of the company.[18]

Eventually, on May 26, 1834, the Mexican government once again opened Texas to American settlers and in the same year recognized the Galveston Bay and Texas Land Company. These two events spurred the company to redouble their colonization efforts. However, before the company began to move colonists into the region, the vice president of Mexico, fearing that a revolt was brewing in Texas, dispatched Colonel Juan Almonte on an inspection tour of Texas. Almonte was to ascertain the best routes for a military invasion from Mexico in case the Texans revolted. At the time Texas was divided into three departments: Bexar, Brazos, and Nacogdoches. Almonte spent May, June, and half of July in 1834, inspecting the Nacogdoches department, which encompassed the company's colony. His report gave an excellent picture of the isolation of the Thicket area. According to Almonte, the only settlements of consequence were Anahuac, Beeville (Bevil), Teran, Tenaha, Nacogdoches, San Augustine, Johnsburg, and Liberty. Liberty, formerly Atascosita, was still the only settlement in the Big Thicket region. Unfortunately Almonte did not give any population figures for the city, but an earlier census in 1826 revealed that 331 people, mostly Americans, were living in the vicinity of Liberty. Of the other towns mentioned in Almonte's report, all, with the exception of Anahuac located at the mouth of the Trinity River, were situated north of the Big Thicket.[19]

In the report Almonte criticized the operation of the Galveston Bay and Texas Land Company as well as the three empresarios. He believed the colonies had not prospered because the empresarios had failed to fulfill their contracts. In fact, he mentioned that most of the people in the region were settlers who had obtained their land directly from the government without the aid of the empresarios. Almonte suggested that the government stop the "pernicious stock-jobbing" of the company, for it had stirred discontent among the settlers.[20] The Mexican government failed to act on Almonte's suggestion and the Galveston Bay and Texas Land Company resumed operation.

In 1835, Gideon Lincecum, a resident of Columbus, Mississippi, searching for a homesite in Texas, journeyed into the company's colony. On his trip, he passed through the Big Thicket. Fortunately, Lincecum maintained a journal of the trip, and he furnished one of the first descriptions of the Thicket.[21] On February 10, 1835, he wrote,

> This day passed through the thickest woods I ever saw. I[t] perhaps surpasses any Country in the world for brush there is 8 or 10 kinds of ever green undergrowth, privy, holly, 3 or 4 sorts of bay, wild peach tree, bay berry & etc, and so thick that you could not see a man 20 yards for miles, the soil is pretty good and the water the very best.[22]

Although Lincecum seemed impressed with the Big Thicket, he eventually settled in another colony.

To entice emigrants to their colony, the company embarked on a grand publicity campaign. Part of this propaganda campaign was a book entitled

Guide to Texas Emigrants, which extolled the virtues of the company and of its Texas holdings.[23] Like many such propaganda tracts, this book was a combination of truths, half-truths, and lies. The author made the land sound like a paradise. At one point he exclaimed, "Unlike the pioneer settlers in the western wilds of the United States, emigrants to Texas will not have to encounter years of arduous labor in subduing heavy and obstinate forest. . . ."[24] The author continued his description, stating, "No sturdy forest here for months defies the axe but smiling prairies invite the plough."[25] He never mentioned that the heart of the company's land was the Big Thicket. In another passage he proclaimed that the rivers of the region— the Sabine, Neches, and Trinity—seldom overflowed their limits.[26] In reality the region was subject to yearly inundations from these streams.

The efforts of the company worked and settlers began to seek land within the colony. One employee of the colony boasted that in 1835, 300 families had settled in Zavala's grant, while 185 families had located in Vehlein's realm. However, this short-lived prosperity ended abruptly with the outbreak of the Texas Revolution in the fall of 1835. In November 1835, the Provisional Government of Texas ordered all persons concerned with the location of the lands to cease operations. The company was naturally apprehensive about this order and its possible effects on their holdings. After Texas won its independence at the Battle of San Jacinto, the trustees of the company wrote President David G. Burnet—the same man who had transferred his empresario contract to the company in 1830. After explaining that the company had expended $70,000 on its colonization efforts, the trustees claimed they were willing to surrender their grant. However, the trustees maintained that the company, by virtue of establishing colonists in Texas, was entitled to receive bonus land amounting to 500,000 acres. Apparently the trustees realized they would never receive such a substantial tract, so they stipulated that they would accept a minimum amount of 276,000 acres.[27]

Even if Burnet had desired to further the aims of the company, he was powerless to act. In June 1837, the Republic of Texas declared that all empresario contracts had ceased to exist on March 2, 1836: the date of Texas' Declaration of Independence. The company, through one of its agents, waged a short court fight to salvage some of their former land. The

Texas courts, however, ruled against the company. With this decision the Galveston Bay and Texas Land Company ceased to exist.[28]

The colonization efforts of the company had not been entirely in vain. Under company auspices, a few families did move into the Big Thicket. Unfortunately, the locations of settlers within the Thicket are uncertain, but several were located along Big Sandy Creek, one of the major waterways in the Big Thicket, while others were on Menard Creek in the heart of the region. Nonetheless, penetration into the area had been minimal. A perusal of original land titles in the Big Thicket region revealed that in 1837, the year the company ceased operations, only twenty land titles had been issued in Newton County, thirty-seven in Tyler County, and forty-seven in Jasper County. Hardin and Polk counties boasted only sixty and eighty-four land titles respectively, while Liberty County recorded only 127 titles. Although land titles do not indicate total population, such a small number suggests that the entire region was still sparsely inhabited. A few hamlets such as Beaumont, Jasper, and Huntsville had sprung up on the flanks of the region during the 1830s, but the major assault on the Big Thicket was still in the future.[29]

The establishment of the Texas Republic paved the way for a mass migration of Americans into Texas. A number of "guide books" appeared in the post-revolution era that offered the prospective settlers some descriptions of the different regions of Texas. The publication of such books explains, in part, why this wave of settlers bypassed the Big Thicket. Namely, the authors' descriptions were not flattering to the region.

One of the first "guide books," published in 1840, bore the impressive title *Topographical Description of Texas; to Which is Added an Account of the Indian Tribes*. The author was George W. Bonnell, publisher of the *Texas Sentinel* newspaper. Most of Bonnell's descriptions centered around the land adjacent to various river systems. Bonnell left little doubt that much of the land along the Neches and Trinity Rivers within the Big Thicket was undesirable. He described the region as being little more than one huge pine barren. Also in 1840, Francis Moore, editor of the *Telegraph and Texas Register* newspaper, published another in the growing list of "guide books" on Texas. Moore's book, entitled *Map and Description of Texas*, gave a rather dismal description of the Big Thicket region. He proclaimed that

Jasper County was the poorest county in Texas. His description of Liberty County was more favorable, but he tempered his praise by stressing that the northern part of the county along the Trinity Riger was subject to inundation.[30]

The most voluminous "guide book" of that era appeared in 1841. The author was William Kennedy, an Englishman who had traveled extensively in Texas.[31] His two-volume work, entitled *Texas, the Rise, Progress and Prospect of the Republic of Texas*, was written to inform an inquisitive English public about opportunities in Texas. It was the most descriptive of the early guide books, and it was also the most devastating to the Big Thicket region. Kennedy warned prospective settlers that both the Neches and Trinity rivers were prone to extensive overflow. He also proclaimed that emigrants should avoid the heavily forested regions. To emphasize his point, Kennedy warned his English readers that,

> To hew out a farm from the heart of the primeval forest is a ponderous and life-consuming task, even for the American backwoodsmen, accustomed to wield the axe from boyhood, and to trust for subsistence to the unerring rifle. Alas! for the European, if above the condition of a daily Labourer, who is constrained to engage in the unwonted and depressing toil! Years may follow year, and find him struggling with difficulties which he is destined never to overcome. By dint of the severest and most irksome drudgery, he is enabled to reclaim a mere patch from the wilderness, and that overspread with unsightly stumps, and encircled by the burned and blackened trees. In this disheartening pursuit he wastes the flower of his manhood.[32]

To this depressing scenario of life in the forest, Kennedy added the specter of disease. He proclaimed that it was unhealthy to live on land which had been recently cleared of trees. According to Kennedy, in newly cleared areas

> where the vegetable accumulation of ages are suddenly exposed to the beams of a scorching sun, and where heaps of levelled tim-

ber are left to rot upon the ground. . . . the atmosphere is inevitably tainted with noxious inhalations, which soon blanch the ruddiest cheek and palsy the most vigorous arm.[33]

To those reading these and the numerous other guide books, the Big Thicket region must have appeared to be an inhospitable and undesirable place to settle. After reading these books, certainly any judicious emigrant would first attempt to locate on the prairie lands of Texas before committing his life to the bone-wearing task of clearing a virgin forest. Interestingly, none of the guide books referred to the area as the Big Thicket. Apparently the region had not sufficiently impressed the early writers to justify distinguishing it from the surrounding woodlands.

Over the ensuing years, a number of factors would eventually lure settlers into the Big Thicket region. By the late 1840s, much of the open prairie land of Central Texas adjacent to the Big Thicket had been settled. Migration into West Texas was blocked by the twin nemeses of Indians and lack of water. Therefore, new waves of settlers were forced by this unhappy combination of circumstances to disregard the "guide books" and seek their future in the Big Thicket area. The organization of the Big Thicket region into counties during the late 1840s and early 1850s was doubtlessly another factor that enticed settlers into the area. Previously, there had been only two organized counties in the Big Thicket region, Jasper and Liberty. In 1846, Tyler and Polk counties were carved from Liberty County; Newton County, also organized in 1846, was the offspring of Jasper County. Hardin, the last of the Big Thicket counties, organized in 1848, was the child of Liberty and Jefferson counties.[34]

The first reliable census of the Big Thicket region was tabulated in 1850. In that year, the entire area could claim only 10,200 people. Of this number, over 3,000 were slaves.[35] In the decade before the Civil War, a number of small villages began cropping up both within and along the fringes of the Thicket. By 1850, Woodville in Tyler County and Livingston in Polk County had been established in the heart of the Thicket. In 1851, Saratoga, a mineral spring resort in Hardin County, joined these villages. Magnolia Springs in Jasper County and Hardin in Liberty County were added to the region in the late 1850s. Although the region was beginning to attract settlers, on the eve of the Civil War the region's population was still a paltry 24,000 people. Most of these were settlers who farmed fifty acres or less.[36]

During the Civil War, the Big Thicket escaped the widespread devastation that mangled much of the South. The Civil War, however, gave rise to one of the most colorful stories to come out of the Big Thicket. Most of the people in the area supported the Confederate cause, but according to the story several men in the region vowed they would never fight for the slaveholders. Consequently, when the Confederate government enacted a conscription law, many of those unwilling to fight headed for one of the densest portions of the Big Thicket near the Hardin-Polk County line. For most of the war these so-called "Jayhawkers" remained in hiding, only venturing out of the Thicket to obtain provisions from their relatives.[37]

In the waning years of the war, the South desperately needed additional manpower. Faced with this situation, the Texas government decided to capture the Jayhawkers and force them to serve in the Confederate Army. In the fall of 1864, Captain James Kaiser was dispatched to the Thicket with orders to subdue the Jayhawkers and press them into service. To accomplish this goal, Kaiser attempted to burn the men out. According to the story, Kaiser burned over 2,000 acres of virgin pine in his attempt to dislodge the Jayhawkers. Estimates on the number of men trapped by the blaze range from zero to 100 depending on who tells the story. Not a single Jayhawker was captured. With this abortive effort, the Confederate government ceased harassing the draft-dodgers of the Big Thicket. For years the charred remains of the pines reminded local inhabitants of the incident, but in the 1930s a timber company reseeded the area, and the "Kaiser burnout" faded from view.[38]

The Civil War and its aftermath dramatically curtailed migration into the Big Thicket region. By 1870, the population was just under 26,000, an increase of only 2,000 from the last decade.[39] Life for most of the people in the post-war Thicket remained unchanged. The region was still isolated and poor. One man traveling through the Big Thicket during this period, commenting on the isolation of the area, stated,

Traveling through the deep piny woods of this part of Texas, you often find grown men and women that have never seen a prairie country, mountain or valley, railroad or steamboat. They grow to manhood and womanhood in the heart of the thick pine woods and are contented and happy in their log cabins.[40]

The poverty of the region limited many settlers' diets to such standard frontier fare as cornbread, bacon, potatoes, and venison. One wayfarer in the Big Thicket, who was forced to eat an evening meal at a settler's cabin, recalled, "My digestive organs after the inspection of the supper spread before me, rebelled and contracted supper was corn-bread, very fat bacon, and clabber."[41]

Another observer of the poverty in the region noted that while visiting in Newton County he saw only two women who were not barefoot: the sheriff's wife and a storekeeper's wife.[42]

In 1876, an event transpired that was destined to end the isolation of the region and to alleviate, to a small degree, the poverty of the Big Thicket. In that year, construction began on the Houston East and West Texas Railroad. This railroad, which skirted the western fringe of the Big Thicket, opened the area to large-scale commercial timber operations.[43] The construction of the railroad marked the true beginning of the devastating assault on the wilderness: an assault that would not end for nearly 100 years.

CHAPTER V

A Timber Bonanza

Although the development of bonanza timber operations in the Big Thicket only began when railroads traversed the region in the 1880s, lumbering activities had been a part of the economic life of the Thicket almost from the beginning of the Anglo settlement of Texas. Stephen F. Austin quickly recognized the importance of the lumbering industry to the growth and development of his adopted home. As early as 1828, Austin predicted that timber operations would be very extensive throughout all of East Texas within a few years. One sawmill was already operating on Buffalo Bayou, while another was being constructed on the east bank of the San Jacinto River.[1]

Austin's expected timber boom in East Texas failed to materialize for several years. Inadequate transportation retarded lumbering activities. Mill machinery had to be shipped up the waterways and then dragged over land to the construction site by a team of oxen: a costly and time-consuming operation. The absence of transportation facilities also made it extremely difficult to ship the lumber from the interior to the markets on the Texas coast. Early timber operators in the region depended almost entirely on river transportation. Steamboats and flatboats were used to haul lumber and firewood to the cities on the Gulf. Other operators in the Thicket region floated logs down the Neches River into Beaumont where sawmills had been established in the 1830s.[2]

Timbermen used a two-wheeled ox-cart, with huge wheels, measuring eight to five feet in height, to move their logs to the river. Although cumbersome in appearance, the carts easily rolled over fallen logs and passed above stumps without becoming stuck. Logs attached to the carts were hauled to an assembly area near the water. During the spring, the rising river picked up the logs and floated them downstream to Beaumont.[3]

One method of floating logs to market employed a technique known as the circle-boom. Several logs were chained together into the shape of a donut. Other logs were then placed in the "hole," and the entire circle-boom was floated down the river to the sawmill. This tactic allowed independent loggers to keep their supply together and insured that their logs would not become entangled with the logs of rival operators. Some lumbermen branded their timbers to identify them from the logs of other operators floating their product to market.[4]

Unfortunately, using the rivers was never a dependable method of shipping logs to the mills in Beaumont and to those that later developed along the lower Sabine River at Sabine Pass. The rivers and streams of Texas, particularly those traversing the Big Thicket, were ill-suited to handle year-round logging. Rivers were often wild and unpredictable during the rainy seasons of the later winter and early spring, and too shallow during the dry summer months. Oxen offered an alternative system of transporting logs to the coast, but this method proved too expensive.[5]

Even with the difficulties of building mills and transporting lumber and logs to market, some men dared to start timber operations in the Big Thicket region. By 1836, there was a sawmill operating at Liberty, Texas. On his sojourn through Texas in 1857, Frederick Law Olmsted, the noted abolitionist and landscape architect, reported that three steam sawmills were operating along the Trinity River near Liberty. Also in the 1850s, John Carr established a mill on Menard Creek, one of the main waterways in the Big Thicket. Another sawmill was reported operating in the little town of Moscow in Polk County during 1855.[6]

Despite the mills operating at Beaumont, Sabine Pass, and in the Big Thicket, in the late 1850s Texas suffered from a lumber shortage. In 1858,

Texas imported lumber to meet domestic needs. Most of the imported timber originated from Mobile, Alabama; however, lumber was imported from as far away as Maine. Texans found it cheaper to import lumber than to pay the exorbitant transportation cost required to ship timber from the wooded portion of the state.[7]

By 1860, the Texas lumbering industry had taken a few faltering steps forward. At this point, Texas boasted 192 lumbering establishments. The industry was capitalized at $1,272,380, and employed approximately 1,200 people. Sawmills employed one-third of all factory workers in the state. Within the Big Thicket region, Jasper County claimed four lumber firms, followed by Liberty and Newton counties with two each. Polk, Hardin, and Tyler counties were devoid of mills. However, by 1878, twenty mills were operating in Polk County. Of these, eight were steam powered, while the others were powered by water.[8] Even with these increases, the tremendous growth of the lumber industry in the Big Thicket did not begin until the 1850s when a spiderweb of railroads penetrated the region.

Railroads were chartered as early as 1848, specifically to tap the timber resources of the region.[9] The Big Thicket was a particular target of these railroads. One writer, supporting the proposed Houston and Great Northern Railroad, proclaimed, "at a distance of twenty miles from Houston, it enters what is known as the 'Big Thicket', a most magnificent body of timber, consisting of white oak, cypress, pine, post oak, ash, mulberry, wild cherry & etc."[10] This road, like many others, failed to materialize. Lack of capital, the Civil War, and the machinations of reconstruction politics, blunted such plans. When these obstacles were removed, Texas businessmen began a determined effort to push railroads into the rich timber area of southeast Texas.[11]

On March 11, 1877, the Texas state legislature approved a charter for the construction of a railroad from Houston to Texarkana with branches to the Sabine River by way of Jasper and Shelby counties. This route would carry the railroad into the western region of the Big Thicket. Paul Bremond, a wealthy Houston businessman, was the driving force behind the project. Bremond possessed a wealth of experience in the transportation industry. Prior to the Civil War, he had been one of the incorporators of the Galveston and Red River Railroad, and also one of the chief stockholders in the Brazos Plank Road. He was convinced that a railroad into the piney woods would be an extremely profitable venture. Bremond named his line the Houston, East and West Texas Railroad. The HE & WT was a narrow gauge road only three feet wide. Bremond had been converted to the narrow gauge after viewing a railroad display at the Centennial Exposition in Philadelphia in 1875.[12]

The route was surveyed, and construction began in July 1876. In April 1877, Bremond reported that twenty miles of track, stretching from Houston to New Caney in Montgomery County, had been laid. An additional forty-three miles were added by the fall of 1878. The railroad finally penetrated the Big Thicket in 1879 when it was completed to Livingston in Polk County. The next year it connected with Moscow in the same county. The predictions that railroads in the pineries would stimulate the lumber industry proved to be true. In October 1880, the *Houston Post* reported that 376 cars of lumber poured into Houston via the HE&WT. By 1882, no fewer than twelve sawmills were operating along its right of way.[13]

Unfortunately, Bremond did not live to see the completion of the road. He died in 1885, and the road was not completed to the Sabine River until the next year. At the Sabine, it joined with the Houston and Shreveport Railroad, the Louisiana portion of the HE&WT system. The bone-jarring ride of the narrow gauge road won it the sobriquet "Hell Either Way Taken." Its propensity to jump the track also garnered it the nickname "The Rabbit."[14]

In 1894, the road was converted to the standard gauge of four feet, 8 1/2 inches. The conversion was a masterpiece of engineering. One thousand workers, lining the tracks from Houston to Shreveport, performed the task in one day.[15] Eventually in 1894, the HE&WT became part of the Southern Pacific System. Bremond's desire to stimulate timber operations in the piney woods had succeeded. As one authority on the HE&WT exclaimed, "By the time of the First World War lumber companies were so thick along the right of way that a traveler was seldom out of the sound of a sawmill whistle."[16]

Several other railroads followed Bremond's lead and began laying tracks to develop the timber resources of the Big Thicket. In April 1880, J. F. Crosby, P. B. Watson, and J. J. Owen, all of Houston, received a charter to construct the Sabine and East Texas Railroad Company. These men secured additional financial aid from Herman and Augustus Kountze, wealthy bankers from Omaha, Nebraska, who had purchased 179,999 acres of pine land in Hardin County in the heart of the Big Thicket. The first leg, which ran from Sabine Pass to Beaumont, was completed in 1881. From Beaumont the road continued north into the Big Thicket region of Hardin County. By July 1881, the tracks reached the town of Kountze, which had just been established by the brothers. Over the next few years the road continued pushing north through the Big Thicket, servicing Woodville in Tyler County, and finally terminating in Rockland, a small community north of Woodville.[17]

In 1843, the Texas and New Orleans Railroad Company purchased the Sabine and East Texas Line. Over the next few years, the Texas and New Orleans railroad either purchased existing lines or built new tracks that connected Rockland with Dallas. By 1903, the Texas and New Orleans line extended across the entire north-south axis of the Big Thicket, opening markets for Big Thicket timber from the Gulf of Mexico to the budding urban center of Dallas.[18]

The construction of the Gulf, Beaumont, and Kansas City Railroad Company exposed the eastern flank of the Big Thicket to large-scale timber operations. Chartered in 1893, the line was the product of John Henry Kirby's fertile imagination. At the time, Kirby held thousands of acres of pine lands in the Big Thicket and other portions of East Texas. Since there were no available ways of transporting his timber to market, Kirby planned to build his own railroad into his own timber. Kirby obtained the necessary financial support from a group of wealthy Bostonians. The line began at Beaumont, and ran into Hardin County where Kirby established the town of Silsbee, named after one of his Boston associates.[19]

The Gulf, Beaumont and Kansas City tracks then veered into neighboring Jasper County and pushed north. By 1895, Kirby had established the town of Kirbyville along his line, and by 1896, the road had pushed further north to Roganville. In 1900, Kirby desperately needed capital to purchase more timberland. After consulting with his Boston advisors, he sold his line to the Santa Fe system. Under the terms of the sale, the Santa Fe Line agreed to extend the Gulf, Beaumont and Kansas City tracks further north to San Augustine. In addition, they agreed to build a line across the southern portion of the Big Thicket, which would connect the town of Cleveland, in northwest Liberty County with the Gulf, Beaumont and Kansas City line in Silsbee. This line, which was named the Texas, Louisiana and Eastern Railroad, was completed in 1902.[20]

Thus by the early 1900s, four major railroads traversed the eastern, western, southern and central portions of the Big Thicket. At this time, the Big Thicket was crisscrossed with over 200 miles of track. By the beginning of World War I, this total had risen to over 400 miles. Polk, Hardin, and Jasper counties were the sites of the heaviest railroad penetrations.[21]

The impact of the railroads on the development of the timber industry in the Big Thicket was tremendous. Towns destined to become important centers of timber production sprang up overnight. Silsbee, Kountze, Concord, and Votaw in Hardin County can trace their origin to the railroads. In Jasper County, the railroads gave birth to Kirbyville, Roganville, Call Junction and Evadale. Timber companies lured into the Big Thicket by the construction of railroads established the towns of Camden and Leggett in Polk County. In Tyler County, the Yellow Pine Lumber Company established Colmesneil while the Trinity and Sabine Lumber Company founded Chester.[22]

A number of smaller railroads, commonly called tram lines, radiated into the wilderness to tap the timber in the depths of the Big Thicket. Some of the tram lines were owned by private operators, but most were owned by the timber companies. These small lines were used to haul logs from the cutting site to the sawmill. By 1907, one of the major timber companies logging in the Big Thicket boasted over 170 miles of tram tracks. As soon as one area was logged out, the tram tracks were ripped up, and the same rails were laid into a new heavily timbered area. At first these tram lines were constructed with wooden rails. Oxen pulled the log-laden flatcars to the mill. Gradually, this method gave way to the steam engine and steel tracks. The workhorse of the tram system was the Shay locomotive. Weighing only 20,000 pounds, the Shay could speed along at a breathtaking ten miles per hour. Embers belching from the Shay's smokestack were a primary cause of forest fires during the early era of timber exploitation.[23]

Tram lines eventually gave way to trucks as logging roads were cut into the area. However, a different version of the tram line has been used in recent years. In the 1950s the Southern Pine Lumber Company purchased a 4,300-acre tract in Hardin County that was inaccessible to trucks. The land was simply too soggy to support the weight of fully loaded logging vehicles. The company solved the problem by building a tram line to the area. However, instead of using a locomotive, the company placed logging trucks on the tracks. Motor car wheels replaced the conventional truck tires. The trucks were further modified with a double transmission, which allowed them to travel both forward and backward at the same speed. The trucks traveled over the rails to the cutting site, and then backed their loads to the mill.[24]

Although the railroads were of primary importance in developing the Texas timber industry, other factors contributed to its rapid expansion. The great surge westward onto the treeless Great Plains in the 1870s and 1880s created a tremendous demand for lumber. At the same time, the traditional lumber sources in the East and along the Great Lakes region were rapidly declining. Texas, and more particularly the Big Thicket, contained billions of board feet of pine timber, which could satisfy this burgeoning cry for lumber. Experienced woodsmen from other states saw the opportunities in the untapped Texas wilderness. They poured into the Lone Star State, bringing with them two essential ingredients needed for massive development of the piney woods: experience and capital.[25]

Henry J. Lutcher and G. Bedell Moore were two such woodsmen drawn to Texas. Lutcher and Moore were partners in a lumber operation in western Pennsylvania. When their timber supply began to dwindle, Lutcher traveled to Texas to survey the potential of the piney woods. He was impressed, and by 1876, Lutcher and Moore had transferred operations to Orange, Texas, on the Sabine River. Here they built the first modern sawmill in Texas with a capacity of 80,000 to 100,000 board-feet per day. Most of Lutcher and Moore's acreage was in Louisiana, but at one time they owned over 87,000 acres just north of the Big Thicket. Joseph H. Kurth, a German immigrant who eventually possessed thousands of acres in East Texas, also arrived in Texas during this era. The family of Thomas L. L.

Temple who migrated from Virginia during the late nineteenth century in search of timber lands, still owned sizable plots in the Big Thicket when the Preserve was established in 1974.[26]

Other experienced timbermen poured in from Mississippi, Arkansas, Wisconsin, and Canada. Native Texans did not stand idly by and allow all of the forest to fall to the interlopers. Sons of the Lone Star State such as W. T. Carter, John Henry Kirby, and John Martin Thompson also amassed great timber holdings.[27]

These entrepreneurs followed the railroads through the piney woods, purchasing mammoth timber acreage at rock-bottom prices from the settlers in the region. The settlers' cry was, "We want farms not forests,"[28] and they were delighted to be paid by a logger who promised to spare them the back-breaking task of clearing the land. Before the native Texans realized the potential profit of their heavily timbered homesteads, they often sold the timber rights as cheaply as fifty cents per acre.[29]

In 1880, the Texas lumber industry was capitalized at only $1,660,952 and employed only 3,136 Texans. However, the combination of railroad construction, increased demand, adequate financial resources, and the influx of experienced lumbermen created an orgy of expansion in the timber industry. By 1890, capitalization had reached $10,674,707 and the work force had grown to 6,820. Production rose to 840,000,000 board-feet a year. With the massive increase in production, Texas steadily rose in the ranks of the timber-producing states. In 1870, Texas ranked twenty-third, but by 1890 it claimed seventeenth place. Texas reached its peak in 1907, yielding 2,230,000,000 board-feet of lumber, and ranking third among timber producing states.[30]

Loggers were originally drawn to Texas by the tremendous stands of longleaf and loblolly pines. Sandwiched between the shortleaf pine forest of northeast Texas, and the loblolly region on the south, the longleaf pine forest resembled an arrowhead thrusting its point from the Sabine River in the east to the Trinity River in the west. It encompassed nearly 5,000 square miles of southeast Texas. The loblolly region covered an additional six to seven thousand square miles. The Big Thicket counties contained millions of acres of both species. Newton, Jasper, Tyler, Polk, and the northeastern portion of Hardin County lay within the longleaf district, while the western area of Hardin County and the northern part of Liberty County were covered with great stands of loblolly.[31]

In addition to the two pine species, thousands of acres of various hardwoods grew along the waterways of the Big Thicket. At times, the loblolly pine joined the hardwoods along these alluvial strips. The association of the loblolly pine and hardwoods, with the accompanying vines and undergrowth, generally stretched 2 1/2 miles on either side of the streams. It was this type of forest that gave the Big Thicket its name.

The first assault of the timber magnates was directed against the longleaf region. The longleaf pine was the monarch of the southeast Texas woods. It sprang 100 to 120 feet into the sky, and measured three feet in diameter at its trunk. The wood was prized for its great strength. It supplied timbers for bridge construction and trusses for large buildings. Tram lines easily penetrated the parklike forest floor of the longleaf district. The higher elevation and drier soils of the longleaf forest also facilitated timber operations.[32]

As the supply of longleaf pine dwindled, timber operators began to attack the loblolly district. Here the loggers encountered more difficult problems than in the longleaf district. The wetter soils of the loblolly district made tram construction more difficult, thus adding to the cost of production. However, the major problem was the greater sapwood content of the loblolly. The increased sapwood made it more difficult to cut than its longleaf cousin. Also, loblolly logs could not be easily transported to the mill by water. The sapwood so increased the weight that loblolly logs frequently sank to the bottom of the rivers. Because of the high sap content, loblolly lumber had to be kiln dried before consumers would purchase it. This process further increased production costs. However, as the stumpage price of longleaf rose in the 1890s, more and more timber men turned to the loblolly forest which could be purchased at a cheaper rate. (The "stumpage price" refers to the amount per acre paid for standing timber.) Also, chemical treatment to preserve wood, which was introduced into Texas about 1899, acted as a further stimulant to the use of loblolly pine. The chemically treated loblolly made excellent crossties for the growing Texas railroad system.[33]

The hardwood forest in the Big Thicket eluded the timbermen operating in the region during the earlier twentieth century. Since hardwoods were located in nearly inaccessible areas, the cost of building tram lines to harvest these trees was prohibitive. However, the hardwoods did not escape entirely. Settlers who desired the alluvial bottom lands for farms indiscriminately destroyed acres of virgin hardwoods. Unfortunately, most of the lumber was not utilized; trees were simply left to rot in the fields. In later years, however, lumbermen eagerly sought the hardwood forests. Loggers found it increasingly profitable to harvest the stately beech and cypress trees that lined the waterways of the Big Thicket.[34]

A number of technical innovations also contributed to the pell-mell destruction of the Big Thicket during the first few decades of the twentieth century. The time-tested, single blade pole-axe gave way to the cross-cut saw, which allowed two workers to cut a hundred logs a day. Improved methods of hauling logs from the cutting site to the tram line also contributed to the demise of the forest. Prior to the 1890s, oxen and mules dragged the logs to the loading site. However, the larger firms replaced the animals with a mechanical device known as the steam skidder. It sat aboard a flat-car on the tram line at the loading area. The skidder had cables wrapped around a drum, much like a fishing line around a reel. When a tree was felled, horses pulled the heavy cables from the tram line to the fallen tree. "Tong men" attached the cables to the log and the skidder then reeled the log to the loading site. Skidding operations were devastating to the forest. Logs, skidding through the woods at high speed, flailed wildly through the air, crushing all seedlings and small trees in their path. The skidder was also a man-killer. Unwary woodsmen were crushed to death, or maimed for life by the logs hurtling through the forest.[35]

The cutting practices of the early loggers also contributed to the rapid destruction of the Big Thicket. Loggers cut the best trees, leaving only inferior ones to reseed the region. Furthermore, a large percentage of the tree was not utilized. Timbermen frequently left three-foot high stumps, and chopped off the top thirty feet of the tree. For economic reasons, most large firms cut trees only larger than fourteen inches in diameter. However, after a large operator moved out of a region, independent operators entered the area with portable mills, and attacked the remaining smaller trees.[36]

Tie-cutters operating in the loblolly region of the Big Thicket were notoriously wasteful. These men utilized trees only eleven to seventeen inches in diameter. Such a practice destroyed much of the young growth, and contributed to the demise of the wilderness. Tie-cutters usually hewed from two to five ties per tree. However, only twenty-six to thirty percent of the tree was utilized to produce the ties; the remainder was waste.[37] As one exasperated conservationist complained, "What escapes the big mill is caught by the small mill, and what the little mill does not get the tie cutter and rail splitter soon has chopped down."[38]

Several other factors contributed to the destruction of the wilderness. The waste products from logging and tie cutting operations were left on the forest floor making the area more susceptible to fires. When fire swept over the cut-over land, young seedlings struggling for survival were killed. What the fire missed, the hogs ate. Thousands of hogs ran wild in the piney woods, and longleaf seedlings were a porker's delight. One of these gluttons could eat over 300 seedlings in a single day. Also, the tax structure fostered a "cut out and get out" philosophy among the timber operators. The growing timber, as well as the land of the timber companies, was subject to taxation. Thus, the faster the growing timber was cut, the lower the taxes.[39]

Most of the early timber operators in the Big Thicket were not disturbed by the wasteful practices. They believed the timber supply to be inexhaustible. In 1890, Henry Lutcher, a pioneer timberman in Texas, proclaimed that the timber supply in the Gulf States was so vast that "If you were to take ships at 500 tons each, load them with the available longleaf pine timber and place them stern to stern beginning at Sabine Pass they would stretch around the world and there would still be 1600 miles to come out of Sabine Pass."[40] By 1911 the same convoy of ships would have stretched only one-third the distance around the globe.[41]

The pioneer timber operators felt no obligation to reforest their land, and they bitterly resented the verbal barbs of conservationists. One timber giant who felt the sting of conservationists' criticism, howled that no "chair warmer" could tell him how to run his business. Yet another multimillionaire timber baron bemoaned the fact that he could not afford to reforest his land.[42]

In addition to the destruction of the wilderness, the lumber industry also altered the social structure of the region. The large mill owners were feudal barons, and the workers were their subjects.[43] The reigning lord who claimed the Big Thicket as his fiefdom was John Henry Kirby, "The Prince of the Pines."[44] At one time Kirby owned or leased nearly all of the land included in the present Big Thicket National Preserve.[45] (See Map 3.)

Kirby was born on November 16, 1860, near Peachtree Village in Tyler County. Possessed with a keen intellect and driving ambition, Kirby acquired bits and pieces of formal education. In the rural East Texas environment, he was fortunate to attend school two months out of each year. Kirby's drive and ambition drew the attention of Judge S. Bronson Cooper of Woodville. Upon Cooper's encouragement, Kirby attended Southwestern University at Georgetown for one semester. In 1882, Cooper, who was a state senator, used his influence to secure a position for Kirby as Calendar Clerk of the Texas Senate. Kirby took advantage of his tenure in Austin to study law. In 1885, he was admitted to the bar, and established a practice in Woodville.[46]

In that same year, Kirby began his career in the timber business. Nathan Silsbee, head of a Boston law firm with business interests in Texas, hired Kirby as an agent for the newly formed Texas and Louisiana Land and Lumber Company. In this capacity, Kirby bought and sold prime East Texas pine lands for the company. Over the next few years, Kirby amassed a small fortune from his participation in the venture. In 1889, Kirby and his Boston associates chartered yet another timber enterprise named the Texas Pine Land Association. In addition to acquiring timber land, Kirby and his business colleagues planned to build a railroad from Beaumont into their holdings in East Texas. Construction on the road started in 1893, but in 1900, Kirby sold the line to the Santa Fe system. With the money from the sale, Kirby purchased over 500,000 acres of pine land, much of it in the Big Thicket.[47]

Prior to 1901, Kirby had been primarily interested in simply buying and selling timber. The discovery of oil at Spindletop in January 1901, altered his thinking. Kirby hatched a scheme that called for the organization of a lumber firm and an oil company, which would utilize the natural resources on the same land. Kirby traveled to the East Coast to obtain the massive financial backing needed for his plan. Through friends, Kirby was introduced to Patrick Calhoun, one of the premier corporation lawyers in

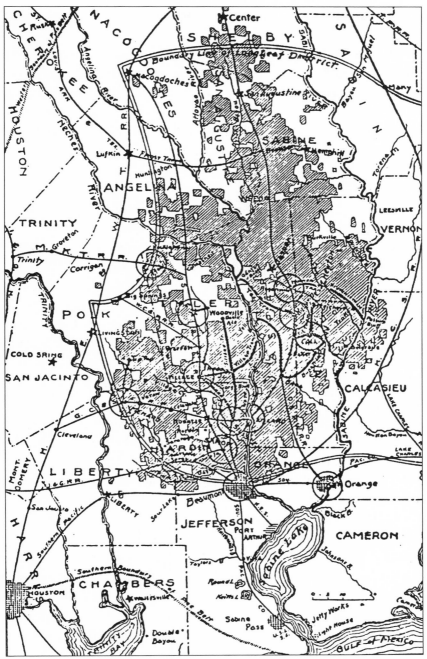

Timber Holdings of Kirby Lumber Company and
Houston Oil Company, 1902

America who had strong ties with several leading financial houses in New York and elsewhere. After much debate, the two men agreed upon a plan.[48]

Two firms, the Kirby Lumber Company and the Houston Oil Company, were formed to develop the resources of East Texas. The oil company was to acquire the pine lands that Kirby controlled, comprising approximately 900,000 acres. In addition, the oil company purchased fourteen sawmills scattered throughout the Big Thicket region. The oil company then reconveyed the mills to Kirby. For his part, Kirby purchased the timber rights to the 900,000 acres from the oil company. He then assigned the cutting contracts to the Kirby Lumber Company—the fourteen sawmills. Kirby agreed to pay for the timber rights from the lumber company's profits. In addition to the land leased from the Houston Oil Company, the Kirby Lumber Company purchased the timber rights to another 320,000 acres in the piney woods.[49] Armed with fourteen sawmills, and over 1,000,000 acres of timber, the Kirby Lumber Company began its assault on the Big Thicket.

Besides his mills and timber land, Kirby also controlled a labor force of approximately 5,000 men, over 100 miles of tram lines, and thirty locomotives. Mill towns such as Silsbee, Fuqua, Call, Kirbyville, and others were totally dependent on the Kirby Lumber Company for their prosperity and survival. They were company towns in the classic mold. Life in these towns was regulated by the piercing blast of the sawmill whistle. The whistle ordered men to work in the morning, told them when to eat lunch, and sent them trudging home at dusk.[50]

The Kirby Lumber Company operated commissary stores in its mill towns. Supplies for the stores were purchased by a central warehouse, and then distributed to the various stores. Prices at such company stores generally ran ten to twenty-five percent higher than at normal commercial stores. For example, a sack of milled whole wheat at one of Kirby's commissaries sold for $1.70 while selling for only $1.50 in a private store. Kirby's commissaries did a fantastic business. In just the second year of operation, the Kirby Lumber Company made a profit of $87,105 on commissary sales alone. Some years later, the manager of the commissary division of the company could boast of a profit of $96,000 for the first six months of the year.[51]

In many instances, the Kirby Lumber Company also owned the workers' houses. At Kirbyville, bachelors lived in a company boarding house, and paid between eighteen and twenty dollars a month for room and board. Married men with families rented small single family units for from three to ten dollars a month. At one point the private sector of Kirbyville tried to incorporate the city in order to obtain better sanitary conditions and adequate police and fire protection. The company opposed the movement, claiming it would lead to higher taxes, and the attempt failed.[52]

There were, however, some positive features about the company's operations. For example, the Kirby Lumber Company established a medical and accident insurance program for the workers. Also, the company maintained a resident doctor at each mill to treat the workers and their families. Monthly deductions were taken from the workers' wages to pay for the benefits. The medical fee ranged from $1.50 a month for a family, to $1.00 a month for a single worker. Accident insurance varied between fifty cents to a dollar a month depending on the worker's salary. The programs were progressive, but there were certain negative aspects. The deductions were compulsory, and all workers were forced to participate in the program. Additionally, claims paid to accident victims were not uniform. One worker who received a mashed finger at the Silsbee mill collected $4.35, while a worker with a similar injury at the Call mill received $15.00. The insurance company, however, honored most workers' claims. In one month, the Aetna Life Insurance Company paid $1,382.55 in claims to 129 Kirby workers. The payments ran from a high of $136.50 for a broken leg to a minimum of 85 cents for a bruised head and knee. One poor soul even collected $2.50 for sticking a nail in his nose.[53]

Workers for the Kirby Lumber Company were not overpaid. The mill foreman received little more than $100 a month, and he, along with the company doctor, was the highest paid employee at the mill town. Skilled workers such as a sawyer earned five dollars a day, while unskilled laborers working in the mill yard drew only $1.30 a day. In Kirbyville, prior to World War I, four-fifths of the workers received less than two dollars a day. In attempting to keep wages low, Kirby frequently exchanged his wage-scales with other timber operators. There was a "gentleman's agreement" that one firm would not pay more than a competing firm. This technique not only kept wages depressed, but also insured the companies a stable work force. Since wages were nearly the same at all mills, workers saw little profit in moving from mill to mill. In essence, the large timber owners socialized the wages of their workers.[54]

The most heinous feature of the Kirby Lumber Company' s operation was the method of paying the workers. Kirby did not pay his workers in cash, but rather with merchandise checks. These checks were accepted at face value by the company for rent payments and food purchases at the company commissary. However, the company would not cash the checks for hard money. If the worker elected to use his merchandise check in a private store, he was forced to accept a ten to twenty percent discount. Private merchants were forced to discount the checks at this rate because after accepting the check from the worker, they had to carry it to the Kirby Lumber Company, and redeem it in goods or merchandise that were ten to twenty percent higher at the company's store. In such a transaction, the private merchant broke even, and the commissary profited. Only the worker suffered.[55] Some unscrupulous men even speculated in merchandise checks. A worker in need of cash might sell his merchandise check at a thirty percent discount of the face value. The manager of the mill at Kirbyville admitted that such speculation was a common occurrence, but he was not sympathetic to the worker. He shrugged off the practice, exclaiming, "the people are ignorant."[56]

In emergency situations, a worker could receive his wages in the form of a time certificate. The time certificate operated much like a post-dated check. If the worker cashed the certificate before the maturity date, he was forced to accept a ten to twenty percent discount.[57] For example, a worker who accepted a twenty-dollar time certificate, which matured on the thirtieth day of a month, would receive only sixteen to eighteen dollars if he cashed the check even one day early. A federal investigator, working for the Congressional Commission on Industrial Relations, which was gathering information on working conditions in America, visited Kirbyville in October 1914. After exploring the conditions at Kirbyville, the agent in his report to the Commission proclaimed, "Both the time certificate and the merchandise check, especially the latter are the most terrible thing I ever have discovered in my work of investigation in our country. . . ."[58]

George Creel, the crusading journalist, read the agent's report, and in a burst of progressive outrage published a stinging indictment of the use of merchandise checks and time certificates in *Harper's Weekly*. "The splendid dollar, the friendly dime, even the humble penny," he protested, "seldom warm the hands of mill workers at Kirbyville. Disks cut out of pasteboard and stamped with the name of the company and the amount, are made to serve as a substitute for real money."[59] Even after this adverse publicity, Kirby continued to pay the mill workers in merchandise checks. He chose not to follow the example of the Lutcher and Moore Lumber Company, which paid its workers in cash every Saturday night.[60]

Although Kirby exploited his workers, he soothed them with liberal doses of paternalism. He frequently sponsored free barbecues at his mills on the Fourth of July, and on occasion passed out Bibles to his workers. However, he was at his best at Christmas. In preparation for the Christmas extravaganza, Kirby directed his mill foreman to compile a list of all children up to age seventeen. This was a mammoth task, and plans for the Christmas party began in August. The list of children was broken down by age, race, and sex. Children from ages one to six received six presents, while those from seven to ten received five. Four gifts were presented to the children in the eleven to sixteen age bracket. It was not uncommon for the total number of presents to exceed 25,000. Cost of the gifts ran as high as $25,000.[61] On Christmas Eve, the children in the mill towns would gather before the Kirby Christmas tree, and eagerly await their presents. Mill managers used this occasion to remind the workers and the children that Kirby was a benevolent employer, interested only in their welfare. Skits were sometimes used to enhance Kirby's image. At one Christmas party, a mill worker dressed as Santa Claus shouted the question, "Who's all right?" On cue, the local Boy Scout troop responded with the chant, "John Henry Kirby—HE'S ALL RIGHT—Rah Rah Rah, Rah Rah Rah, Rah Rah Rah—Mr. Kirby—Mr. Kirby Mr. Kirby."[62] For their present, workers received a free turkey and a five-dollar Christmas dinner card to purchase additional food at the company store.[63] Undoubtedly, Kirby's Christmas parties were genuine expressions of affection for the employees and their children. Yet no effort was spared to ensure that the workers understood that the gifts were due to Kirby's personal generosity and not as a reward for hard work.

One Christmas, in addition to the normal gifts, Kirby presented each mill with a radio.[64] On Christmas Day the workers gathered around the radio to hear Kirby's Christmas message. Speaking from a studio in Houston, Kirby, in his finest paternal tradition, reminded the workers of his deep personal concern for them. He proclaimed, "Our company, with whose operation you are connected and from whom you derive employment has at all times been faithful to every incident regarding your welfare . . . at no time have we faltered in our fraternity to you or in our desire to see you prosperous and happy."[65]

Eventually, the workers reacted against Kirby's paternal empire, and also against the domains of the other timber operators. Fearful of growing worker unrest, Kirby and the other major timber operators of the South organized the Southern Lumber Operator's Association in 1906, to combat unionization of their industry. The first inkling of dissent occurred during the depression of 1907. As a result of the financial crisis, demands for lumber dropped, and prices plunged downward. To offset their losses, the timber operators cut wages. Many timber workers in East Texas and Western Louisiana walked off their jobs in protest. The strike was short-lived. The workers returned after the operators promised to restore the wage cuts when lumber prices rose to their pre-depression level. Their first skirmish with the workers had been an easy victory for the Association.[66]

In 1910, the Association was once again aroused to action by the formation of the Brotherhood of Timber Workers whose intent was to unionize the woodsmen of Louisiana and East Texas. The first local was established in Carson, Louisiana, in December 1910. Its president, Arthur L. Emerson, had gained union experience while working in the timber camps of the Northeast. The union was pledged to non-violence, and stressed cooperation with management to achieve its goals.[67]

The union's demands were moderate. They hoped to obtain a two-dollar-a-day minimum wage for a ten-hour workday. Also, workers were to receive wages in cash every two weeks. Additionally, the union demanded an end to the discounting of wages, and revision of insurance and doctor's fees. The workers simply wanted to select their own doctor, and to be able to see the company's insurance policy. Finally, the union demanded that the lumber operators disarm and discharge all company gunmen, and rec-ognize the workers' rights of free speech, free press, and assembly.[68]

The mill owners reacted to these demands by branding the union an agent of anarchism and socialism. John Henry Kirby, who the more radical union members nicknamed the "Peon's Pal," led the attack of the South-ern Lumber Operators' Association. When Kirby had first organized his company in 1901, he seemed to be a moderate on the labor question. One of his first acts as head of the Kirby Lumber Company was to reduce hours without a decrease in wages. By 1910, this moderate image had faded. He became the most vociferous foe of unionism in East Texas. To Kirby, unions represented a force which would destroy the American way of life, and plunge the nation into a socialistic quagmire.[69]

Since Kirby was their most vocal opponent, the Brotherhood of Tim-ber Workers focused their recruiting drive against the Kirby mills in the Big Thicket. Kirby met these attacks head-on. Any Kirby employee sus-pected of being a union member was fired. In a letter to all mill managers, the Kirby Lumber Company spelled out its policy in no uncertain terms. "Above all things," it ordered, "move every union man off the job, if you have any. When in doubt, take the benefit of the doubt—move not only the union men but the agitators."[70]

The Kirby Company also hired detectives to follow union organizers in the region and to report on their operations. Weekly reports on union activities from each mill in the Kirby empire flooded into the home office at Houston. Lists of known union men were compiled and circulated to every mill and logging camp. Such a technique was designed to keep a union man who had been fired at one Kirby mill from obtaining a job at another of the company's operations.[71]

Since many workers kept their union membership secret, the Kirby Company hired spies to infiltrate the union to uncover the members. The spies were also used to test the loyalty of Kirby's workers. The infiltrator would flash his union card and ask a worker to join the union. If the worker accepted the offer, or if he seemed sympathetic to the union, his name was dutifully recorded and sent to the home office. Kirby's company eventu-ally resorted to force to stop unionization. At times, when an organizer for the Brotherhood came into the region, he was met at the train station by company men and warned to be on the next train out of town. On other occasions, workers suspected of belonging to the Brotherhood were forcibly searched to see if they were carrying a union card. In addition, Kirby utilized the "yellow dog" contract in which prospective workers pledged not to join the union.[72]

The techniques of Kirby and the Association were effective, and union membership dwindled. In desperate financial straits, the Brotherhood affiliated with the radical International Workers of the World in May 1912. The affiliation played into the hands of the Association who claimed such action proved the Brotherhood was a socialist organization intent on destroying the free enterprise system. The crushing blow to the union occurred in July 1912, at a labor rally in Graybow, Louisiana, where Arthur Emerson was addressing the workers near the Galloway Lumber Company. During the rally, shots were fired. Three union men and a Galloway employee were killed. Subsequently, Emerson and several other union men were indicted for the murder of the Galloway employee. Eventually, Emerson and the other men were acquitted, but the long trial had depleted the union treasury. The union ceased being effective, but it did not expire until 1916. Kirby and the Association reigned supreme.[73]

Although the union failed, the state government passed some legislation that alleviated the plight of the timber workers. In 1913, the legislature enacted the Texas Workman's Compensation Act which provided equitable payments for workers injured or killed on the job. Additionally, Governor James E. Ferguson pushed a bill through the legislature that outlawed the issuance of merchandise checks. Unfortunately, many operators defied the law and continued to issue the checks well into the 1930s.[74]

At the same time the lawmakers were passing legislation to improve the conditions of the workers, other reformers were leading a movement to save the forest from total destruction. W. Goodrich Jones was the leading figure, pushing and pleading for the conservation of Texas' forests. Jones had first become interested in forestry while attending school in Dresden, Germany, in the late 1870s. The beauty of the Black Forest and the accomplishments of the various German forestry schools greatly impressed young Jones. Jones eventually returned to the United States, graduated from Princeton, and entered the banking business. By 1888, he was president of a bank in Temple, Texas.[75]

In treeless Temple, Jones renewed his interest in forestry. Offended by the barren landscape, Jones led a campaign that called on the citizens of Temple to plant seedlings of all varieties to beautify the city. Within a few years he had helped push a bill through the Texas legislature establishing February 22 as Arbor Day. As a result of these and other conservation activities, Jones' reputation spread throughout the state.[76]

In 1898, Dr. B. E. Fernow, Chief of the U. S. Bureau of Forestry, asked Jones to conduct a survey of Texas' forests. Jones agreed, and he traveled through the piney woods in 1899. On the trip he was horrified by the wasteful practices of the timber operators. Jones estimated that at least forty percent of the tree was wasted by current lumbering techniques. The trip shocked Jones into action, and over the next several years he participated in several state conservation societies which urged the state legislature to take action to stop the plundering of the woods. His pleas were largely unheeded. By the first decade of the twentieth century the situation had become critical. U. S. foresters announced that Texas' forests would disappear in twenty years if timbermen refused to practice conservation.[77]

Out of desperation, Jones and a group of his conservationist friends gathered in Temple and formed the Texas Forestry Association in November 1914. The Association dedicated itself to the task of lobbying for the creation of a state department of forestry, and the development of a comprehensive program of forest conservation. Jones next appealed to the U. S. Forest Service for aid in the project. J. Girvin Peters of the State Cooperation Division of the U. S. Forest Service responded to Jones' plea. Peters traveled to Texas, and helped Jones draft the legislation needed to accomplish the Association's objectives. Jones and Peters then traversed the state trying to generate support for the measure.[78]

Some timber operators claimed to favor such legislation, but refused to campaign for the measure. The most enthusiastic support for the bill came from the education community. President William Bennett Bizzell of Texas A & M College, and Dean Edwin J. Kyle of the same institution, were joined by Professor J. T. Phillips of the University of Texas in support of the measure. These three men joined the lobbying effort to force the state legislature to act on the forestry problem.[79]

Finally, Representative Richard F. Burges of El Paso—hardly a wooded wonderland—introduced the bill in the legislature. After much delay, the bill, which established the Texas Forest Service, passed and was signed into law in the spring of 1915. Thus the fight to reforest Texas was largely the work of a banker, three educators, and one federal employee.[80]

The first year's budget of the Texas Forest Service was just $10,000. From this amount John H. Foster, the first State Forester, received a salary of $3,000. With the remaining funds, Foster initiated a fire prevention program. Six fire patrolmen protected 7,500,000 acres in East Texas. One of the patrolmen covered part of the Big Thicket from his headquarters at Livingston in Polk County.[81]

At first, many timber operators failed to support the efforts of the Texas Forest Service. They viewed the agency and its policies as an infringement on their rights to treat their land as they thought best. But as the timber supply in Texas continued to dwindle, the large mill owners began warmly to embrace the Forest Service's doctrines of sustained yield and multiple use of forest lands. By the 1920s, most operators finally realized that their businesses would vanish with the forest. Ernest L. Kurth, whose relative, Joseph Kurth, once had cursed chairwarming conservationists, began to reforest his cut-over land. Thomas L. L. Temple began to practice selective cutting techniques which spared the best seed trees on his land. As the years passed, the large timber owners became the most zealous supporters of scientific forestry.[82]

Unfortunately, the conservation movement did not begin early enough to save the longleaf pine region. It had been nearly totally destroyed by the beginning of the 1930s. Ironically, the timber company's destruction of the longleaf pine region helped to spread a Big Thicket forest. The aggressive loblolly pine and the hardwoods moved onto the cutover land of the longleaf district and created a forest with a tangled undergrowth.[83] Although much of the loblolly and hardwood forests were cutover, thanks to the efforts of Jones, Bizzell, Kyle, and the Texas Forest Service these new Big Thicket-type forests managed to reforest and survive.

Through the following decades and into the 1970s, timber operations continued to play a paramount role in the Big Thicket. When the Big Thicket National Preserve was created in 1974, over sixty percent of the land within its borders still belonged to timber firms.[84]

CHAPTER VI

Oil Exploration in the Big Thicket

In addition to timber, the Big Thicket also contained vast deposits of a natural resource that was to become synonymous with the name of Texas: oil. During the first decade of the twentieth century, thousands of wildcatters, roughnecks, and roustabouts poured into the Big Thicket searching for petroleum deposits. When oil was discovered, boom towns sprang up over night. The crude early drilling methods, combined with the neglect of the operators, spelled disaster for several acres of the Big Thicket wilderness. Oil spills killed trees and polluted waterways. The social institution of the Thicket was also strained by the influx of loose women and gamblers who followed the oil workers. Indeed, it was a tumultuous period, marked by a lack of concern for the wilderness. Men were determined to extract the precious fluid even if it meant destroying the wilderness. The mania of large-scale oil exploration in Texas dates from the discovery of oil at Spindletop, just a few miles south of Beaumont. On January 10, 1901, the Lucas gusher, which sat astride a salt dome, blew in, and inaugurated the modern era of oil exploration.[1] This was the first oil produced from this particular geological formation.

The salt domes were gigantic plugs of salt, at times measuring more than three miles in diameter. The domes had moved up from the bowels of the earth, thrusting themselves through thousands of feet of sediment. As the salt sprang upward, the surface land was often pushed into small mounds or hills. At times, the salt domes penetrated the surface, but usually they remained deep within the earth with only the surface mounds betraying their presence. The salt plugs were generally covered with a caprock of sand, sandy clay, or limestone. Within these various caprock structures, the oil explorers discovered the huge pools of oil that revolutionized the oil industry.[2]

After Spindletop, men sprinted over southeast Texas looking for the telltale mounds that promised unlimited riches to the lucky driller. They soon found the first salt dome within the Big Thicket at the sleepy resort village of Sour Lake in Hardin County. People had known of the existence of oil at Sour Lake long before Spindletop. Years before the white man settled in the region, Indians had drunk the sulfur-laced waters to cure a variety of disorders. The region around Sour Lake was first settled by Stephen Jackson, who received the area as part of his land grant from empresario Lorenzo de Zavala in 1835. As did the Indians before him, Jackson realized the curative effects of the waters.[3]

Actually, the settlement at Sour Lake was comprised of a series of small lakes. Escaping gas bubbled to the surface of the water, where it was joined by sulfur and small quantities of oil. Word of the curative waters spread through Texas, and Sour Lake became a resort haven. Sam Houston sought refuge and health at the resort, and Frederick Law Olmsted described the spa on his trip through Texas in 1856. Brochures from Sour Lake claimed that its seventeen varieties of water could cure eczema and all cutaneous afflictions. Men slapped Sour Lake mud on their bald heads and prayed for hair, while women, seeking to recapture faded beauty, spread the slimy concoction over their faces.[4]

Dr. B. F. Schumard, the State Geologist, officially proclaimed the presence of oil at Sour Lake in his 1858 report to the Texas legislature. Spurred on by the lure of oil, Peter Willis drilled a well at Sour Lake in 1866, and hit a small pocket of heavy oil. The discovery created little excitement, and large-scale exploration did not begin until nearly thirty years later.[5]

In 1895, W. A. Savage and his brother J. S. Savage, men with experience in some of the Eastern oil fields, began to drill for oil at Sour Lake. By the end of the year, the Savage brothers had three shallow wells in production; none were deeper than 230 feet. A few years later, the Gulf Coast Refinery Company, a small firm capitalized at only $25,000, began operating at Sour Lake. The refinery had a limited capacity of only 100 barrels a day. The company contacted the Savage brothers, and consummated a deal that called for the brothers to deliver fifty barrels of oil a day to the refinery. After negotiating the contract, the Gulf Coast Refinery Company laid a pipeline one-half mile long, connecting the Savage brothers' well to the storage tanks of the refinery. Unfortunately, the Savage brothers were unable to fulfill the contract, and the first oil refinery in Texas was forced to close in 1899. For the next few years, Sour Lake resumed its rather tranquil role as a health spa.[6]

In 1901, the tranquility was shattered by the discovery of new oil deposits. Encouraged by the success of Spindletop, the J. W. Guffey Company began drilling around the salt dome at Sour Lake.[7] By September 1901, the Guffey Company had struck oil that they claimed would rival Spindletop. The news of the Guffey find produced a flurry of excitement in oil-crazy Beaumont. The *Beaumont Enterprise* proclaimed, "Oil men, real estate men and speculators have begun to dig up their maps of the Sour Lake district and another favorable report from the Guffey well will inaugurate at least a small boom."[8] Just ten days later news reached Beaumont of another find at Sour Lake. This time the Oteri syndicate, headed by Santo Oteri of New Orleans, had brought in a small gusher.[9]

These discoveries were not able to lure producers from the Spindletop region. Nevertheless, favorable reports from Sour Lake continued to pour into Beaumont, and drillers kept a wary eye trained on the newspapers for accounts of new discoveries. In November 1901, the Gulf Western Oil Company encountered hot saltwater impregnated with sulfur at 800 feet. Encouraged by these signs, they moved the drilling rig to another location. The move proved profitable, for on March 7, 1902, they struck oil.[10]

Other promising reports filtered into Beaumont from Sour Lake. On July 11, 1902, at 8:00 A.M., the Guffey No. 2 well encountered exceedingly strong gas pressure at 800 feet. The drillers were unable to check the gas flow, and were forced to abandon the well. Just a few minutes later, the drilling pipe and bit were thrown from the hole by the escaping gas, and in the words of one observer, "danced around the derrick like popcorn in a skillet."[11] By 8:30 A.M. the roar of the gas was so deafening that it was impossible to converse within 200 yards of the well. People, hearing the roar from miles away, came to gape at the spectacle. The pressures in the well kept building, and by noon the entire derrick had crumbled. By this time a solid stream of gas and mud 12 1/2 inches in diameter was spewing from the well. When the well was finally brought under control, the gas had gouged a hole ten feet in diameter around the casing.[12]

All of these accounts excited the oil men in Beaumont, and they began drifting toward Sour Lake. In late 1902, Walter B. Sharp drilled two successful wells at Sour Lake, but he kept the discovery a secret. He knew that word of his success would bring a rise in land prices and a stampede of other drillers to the region. In January 1903, he struck a third gusher, which scattered oil over the nearby trees, but a heavy rainstorm washed away the oil and the secret was safe.[13]

The Texas Company, which had been formed during the halcyon days after Spindletop, also moved into Sour Lake and secured an option to purchase over 800 acres. The Texas Company evolved from the fertile imagination of Joseph S. Cullinan, an experienced oil man from Pennsylvania who had helped develop an earlier oil field at Corsicana, Texas. He drifted to Beaumont in time for the Spindletop phenomenon. Cullinan sensed the potential of the budding oil industry, and he joined with two influential Texans, ex-Governor James S. Hogg and Joseph W. Swayn, to form the Texas Company. At Sour Lake the Texas Company drilled two successful wells, but like Sharp they kept their discovery under wraps. The company then immediately began negotiating to purchase the option land. By keeping the discoveries secret, the Texas Company hoped to secure title to the land at a nominal price. However, news of the discovery leaked, and the Texas Company was forced to pay $900,000 for the 812-acre tract. The money to finance the venture was borrowed from John W. (Bet-a-Million) Gates, the barbed wire king of Texas.[14]

The success of the Gilber well No. 1, which blew in during May 1903, gushing from fifteen to twenty thousand barrels a day, signaled the beginning of the oil rush toward Sour Lake. The well produced $125,000 worth of petroleum in the first thirty days, and destroyed all doubts about the value of Sour Lake. By August 1903, the assault against the Big Thicket was in full swing. Two hundred and twenty wells dotted the land, and production was over 100,000 barrels a day.[15]

Early reports claimed that the productive area of the oil field measured one mile wide and three miles long, embracing between six and eight thousand acres. There were four main divisions of the field. The Texas Company's 812 acres was the largest tract; however, perhaps the most famous area was the Shoestring district. The district was divided into long, narrow strips measuring 27 by 1100 feet, which the drillers claimed resembled shoestrings. The West Davis tract, which resembled the shoestring district, was dotted with 150 wells. The last major division was the small Cannon tract. Prior to the oil rush, Pete Cannon, a peddler by trade, raised hogs and corn on his fourteen acres. By 1903, oil derricks had sprouted on his land.[16]

The boom at Sour Lake was short-lived. In the frenzy of 1903, over 8,700,000 barrels of oil poured from the wells. This level was not maintained. In 1904, production dropped to 6,442,237 barrels. Just one year later, only 3,362,153 barrels were pumped to the surface. The dismayed drillers began to drift away from Sour Lake. They did not have far to go, for just twelve miles away, oil fever had gripped the little community of Saratoga.[17]

Like Sour Lake, Saratoga had a long history of oil exploration before large-scale production began. Saratoga also possessed its own health springs where oil and gas seeped to the surface. John F. Cotton, an enterprising settler at Saratoga, had observed oil on his pigs that grazed in the region. Cotton easily found the oil by simply following his pigs into their grazing area. In 1865,Cotton joined in a partnership with Edward Von Hartin of Galveston to explore for oil on Cotton's land. According to the agreement, Von Hartin was to furnish all money, machinery, and labor. In addition, he agreed to supervise all the work and to sell whatever petroleum they discovered. In return for his labors, Von Hartin was to receive three-fourths of the profits. Von Hartin utilized the hand-powered spring-pole device to drill his well. He struck some heavy oil, but was forced to abandon the well because his crude drill was incapable of plunging deeper.[18]

Although this early attempt failed, other producers eventually moved into Saratoga. In 1896, the Savage brothers, who were also drilling at Sour

Lake, began operations in Saratoga. The brothers drilled a deeper hole at the exact site of the old Von Hartin well. At 250 feet they struck oil. Although the production of this well was very small, it vindicated the judgment of Cotton and Von Hartin.[19]

After Spindletop, a rash of drillers moved to Saratoga. By late fall,1901, Hooks Well No. I had tapped the salt dome and was producing 25–100 barrels a day. This discovery did not provoke much excitement. However, in March 1902, the Hooks Well No. 2 struck oil, and interest about Saratoga mounted. On May 1, 1903, the Teel No. 1 came in and cemented Saratoga's promise of oil in commercial quantities. By June, fourteen more wells were pumping oil at Saratoga. By the end of the year, the Saratoga field had yielded 150,000 barrels. While Sour Lake's production was declining, Saratoga's output rose. However, the boom at Saratoga was over by 1906. The field had reached its peak in 1905, producing 3,125,028 barrels of oil. Annual production at Saratoga leveled off to a steady but much lower level over the ensuing years.[20]

Unlike the other two boom towns in the Big Thicket, Batson did not have a long history of oil exploration. Located in Hardin County, just seven miles from Saratoga and twelve miles from Sour Lake, Batson was the last true boom town in the Big Thicket. Drillers were drawn to Batson by the presence of gas bubbles in water holes and shallow wells. Encouraged by these signs, the Libby Oil Company drilled a well over the Batson salt dome in 1901. The well reached a depth of 1,000 feet, but only slight traces of oil were encountered and the project was abandoned.[21]

A few years later, W. L. Douglas visited the region and collected some soil samples. Douglas traveled to Beaumont and hired a chemist to analyze the soil. The chemist reported that the soil contained paraffin: a good indicator of oil. Armed with the chemist's report, Douglas, S. W. Pipkin, and several other Beaumont businessmen formed the Paraffine Oil Company. None of the partners had any previous oil experience. By late October 1903, the Paraffine Oil Company began drilling its first well. On Halloween, they struck oil at 790 feet. Production was 600 barrels a day. Beginner's luck smiled on these inexperienced oil producers, for just six weeks later their No. 2 well struck oil at 1,000 feet, and was yielding 4,000 barrels a day. Their third well was an even greater success, producing over 10,000 barrels a day.[22]

Inspired by these successes, other producers from Beaumont, Sour Lake, and Saratoga swarmed into Batson. The original oil field covering approximately 400 acres was soon covered with derricks. Production soared. In January 1904, 440,000 barrels poured from the wells. February's production was a phenomenal 1,848,000 barrels. The peak monthly production at Batson occurred the next month. In March, 2,608,000 barrels of oil gushed from the field. The supply seemed endless, and drillers worked in a frenzy to complete new wells. By September 1904, over 440 wells had been drilled in an orgy of expansion. Most of the drillers were disappointed, for after the fantastic yield of March, production began a steady decline. By August 1904, production was only 585,900 barrels a month. Three months later, it had dipped to slightly over 300,000 barrels a month. Production remained steady, but the boom in Batson was over by 1908. Drillers left the Big Thicket in search of new salt domes that promised new gushers and new wealth.[23]

The three oil booms within the Big Thicket had been both a blessing and a curse. The discovery of oil offered the inhabitants of the region an alternative to working for the timber companies or plowing the soil. However, the chaotic development of the three fields resulted in both temporary and permanent damage to the environment. As oil producers rushed into the Big Thicket, trees were indiscriminately cleared from all possible drilling sites, and then used as building materials for derricks or as fuel for campfires. Frequently, gushers would flow for hours, saturating the land and flowing into nearby streams before the wells were brought under control. During the early days at Sour Lake, waste oil flowed as far as three miles from the production area. At one point this waste oil caught fire and began spreading toward the town. Fortunately, some enterprising men erected a barricade that stopped the fire short of the residential area.[24]

The oil seepage problem was largely due to the crude storing methods. Since the producers had not expected such a tremendous production of oil in the fields, they had failed to build adequate storage facilities. During the first few months of the boom, many of the drillers simply stored the oil in large wooden tanks. Others stored their oil in earthen pits. Such makeshift storage facilities were defective, and oil spilled onto the surrounding area, and eventually washed into the waterways. As a result, Pine Island Bayou and Little Pine Island Bayou, both of which flowed near the boom towns, were frequently polluted with oil. Stock animals along the waterway refused to drink the slimy fluid. On occasion, the oil in Pine Island Bayou would ignite, and spectators would be treated to the horrifying sight of burning water. Flames from the bayou spread onto the banks and razed several acres of timber.[25]

Saltwater, however, posed the greatest danger to the environment. Since these three oil fields were located over salt domes, huge amounts of saltwater were pumped to the surface along with the oil. The water was separated from the oil and allowed to flow freely over the ground and into the surrounding waterways. Naturally these man-made salt lakes strangled the vegetation and killed the trees. Rice farmers in the Sour Lake area, who depended on the waterways to irrigate their crops, finally secured an injunction, which prohibited producers from dumping huge quantities of saltwater into the streams.[26]

Eventually, both the problems of oil seepage and saltwater pollution were conquered. New steel storage tanks combined with an improved pipeline system greatly curtailed oil pollution. Also, new methods of saltwater disposal were invented. Producers began pumping the brine into specially built saltwater disposal pits. Here, the natural process of evaporation dissolved the water. Yet another method allowed the drillers to pump the saltwater back into the ground if such a practice would not pollute underground water supplies. Unfortunately, the damage to the wilderness was not totally repaired. In the 1970s, trees killed by saltwater around Sour Lake and Saratoga still stood as mute reminders of man's assault on the Big Thicket.[27]

At times it seemed as if the wilderness was fighting against this attack. On numerous occasions drillers struck gas pockets that sent gas rushing to the surface with such force that the entire derricks were destroyed. One of the most violent blowouts occurred at Saratoga. The Rio Bravo Company struck a pocket of highly pressurized gas at 500 feet. The gas burst to the surface with such velocity that the ground surrounding the derrick was cracked at a distance of 250 feet. Violent eruptions of mud were flung high into the air. Eventually, a crater approximately thirty-two feet deep and twenty feet wide appeared. The machinery and what was left of the derrick disappeared into the hole.[28]

The most spectacular episode, however, occurred at Sour Lake. George Anderson, a Texaco employee, first noticed a crack in the earth near a company storage tank at 7:15 A.M. At the time, the depression was about fifteen feet deep and 200 feet wide. By 8:30 A.M., the sink had plunged to fifty feet. Two sweet gum trees on the site of the depression were slowly sinking in an upright position. By noon, the trees were still standing, but they were totally below ground level. At this time, the sink had dropped to between sixty to seventy feet—its deepest level. Over the next few days the walls around the sink began collapsing and falling into the depression. Eventually, most of the sink was filled. When the ground finally stabilized, the sink was only thirty-seven and one-half feet deep, but possessed a circumference of 1400 to 1500 feet.[29]

The sink proved a disaster for several oil wells. Ten wells were adversely affected. Eight of the wells began pumping saltwater rather than oil. The production level of two other wells was dramatically curtailed. Prior to the sink, these two wells had been producing approximately 214 barrels per day. After the incident the wells yielded only ten barrels a day. The sink was probably caused by the removal of large amounts of solids from the ground during oil production. The solids, chiefly salt, had supported the ground. Once this support was removed by concentrated oil drilling, the earth simply collapsed.[30]

Such concentrated drilling had another far-reaching consequence. This practice led to the rapid depletion of the natural gas needed to force the oil to the surface. At times, wells were drilled within a few feet of one another. Lease holdings were small; some measured only 20 feet wide and 67.9 feet long. In the Shoestring district of Sour Lake, men boasted that they could walk on derrick platforms for over a mile without touching the ground. Conservation had not yet become an accepted doctrine. Fortunately, the leases at Saratoga were large, and there was no "pepper-box drilling" such as at Batson and Sour Lake.[31]

In addition to the adverse effects on the wilderness, the booms at Sour Lake, Saratoga, and Batson dramatically altered the economic and social

structure in these three communities. Land prices skyrocketed as speculators rushed to the region. Land that would have brought only fifteen dollars an acre before the boom sold for thirty thousand dollars. R. E. Brooks,
a resident of Austin, made a fortune overnight at Sour Lake. In one day he
pocketed $200,000 by buying and selling a tract of land. One boomer from
Georgia arrived at Sour Lake with $500, and six weeks later left with
$100,000. Land that was known to be barren of oil also sold for outlandish
prices. One businessman who wanted to build a livery stable at Sour Lake
during the boom bid $4,000 for a lot measuring 80 by 230 feet. Even grave
sites sold at a premium.[32] Although land prices were high, wages and other
prices were remarkably stable. Oil field workers generally drew ninety dollars a month for working a twelve-hour day. Room and board averaged
twenty-six dollars a month. Thirsty drillers paid only fifteen cents for a
shot of whiskey or a glass of beer. A haircut and shave cost only forty
cents, and workers purchased pants and shorts for fifty cents each.[33] Although living expenses were nominal, gamblers and painted ladies left many
drillers broke just a few hours after payday.

For their ninety dollars a month, oil field workers faced a variety of
dangers. The gas escaping from the Big Thicket wells was laced with poi-
sonous sulfur. The gas stung the eyes, choked the lungs, and frequently
brought death to the unsuspecting worker. One of the worst cases of poi-
son gas occurred at Batson. A new well highly impregnated with sulfur gas
blew in between 9:00 P.M. and 11 :00 P.M. Northerly winds carried the fumes
toward the sleeping workers in the residential area. Although some people
were killed, most were evacuated with nothing more serious than temporary blindness caused by the vapors. The animals of the city were less fortunate. One eyewitness proclaimed that Batson looked like a battlefield
with dead horses, dead chickens, and dead cats scattered about the town-
site.[34]

Gas, however, was not the only danger faced by the workers. At times,
explosions ripped through the storage areas, leaving only the charred remains of the drillers. Heads were crushed and hands were mashed as the
producers disregarded all safety procedures to extract the oil from the land.
One survivor of the Sour Lake boom vividly recaptured the terrible working conditions. He exclaimed,

How many men in the hurry, scurry, and irresponsible management in the field were taken out maimed, mashed, struck dead, will never be known. To get the oil out of the earth and get it converted into money was the sole thought of the acreage owners; and those engaged in other forms of business were moved by like motives. They halted at no obstacle. Employers paid good wages for what they had done, and slam, bang, clang they had to have results. Hence firemen with eyes so badly gassed they could hardly see the steam gauges worked around the boilers; hence well crews worked with old rattletrap outfits that were liable any minute to fly to pieces and knock them to kingdom come; hence men worked in the tops of derricks, hanging on with one hand, straining with the other to the limit of their muscles to adjust something gone wrong. After forty years of sobering absence, it still seems to me that there was more high-pressure work going on in Sour Lake than in any other place I have ever seen.[35]

Black workers were not allowed to share in the dangers or rewards of the oil field. The higher paying positions on the drilling platforms were viewed as white men's jobs. Consequently, black workers were primarily employed as teamsters to haul drilling pipe and other heavy machinery into the oil field. Black employees were not allowed to live within the city limits. They were forced to live in small all-black communities a few miles from the oil fields. The people in Saratoga went so far as prohibiting them from even visiting or shopping in the town.[36]

Living conditions in the boom towns were almost as dangerous as working conditions in the oil field. The small towns were totally unprepared for the tremendous influx of oil men. Prior to the discovery of oil, Sour Lake was a sleepy little community with only forty inhabitants. Almost overnight the population burgeoned to between fifteen and twenty thousand. Thousands more poured into the little hamlets of Saratoga and Batson during their boom periods. The environment suffered as result of these invasions.[37]

The tremendous influx of roustabouts and roughnecks with their heavy drilling equipment joined with the rainfall of the area to turn the roads and oil fields into sprawling quagmires. In Sour Lake one street had such a large mudhole that one local wag planted a "no-fishing" sign next to the morass. Since housing was unavailable, some men cut down the giant palmetto plants in the area and placed them over pole frames to form thatched huts.[38]

A stream of gamblers, thieves, pimps, and prostitutes followed the drillers into the boom towns searching for easy money. The Big Thicket became infested with a group of characters who could have graced the cover of a cheap paperback novel. One-Quarter Lawson and Monk Fife offered games of chance to the oil field workers. Women such as Six-Shooter Kate, the Swamp Angel, and Jew Annie offered the workers even more. Sour Lake could even boast of a prostitute with a heart of gold. Her name was Mooch Prank, and she was the worker's friend. Whenever a driller became sick or injured, Mooch circulated around the bar and collected money to aid the unfortunate worker. At times she even nursed the workers until they regained their health.[39]

At the peak of the boom, thirty-two saloons and one church operated in Sour Lake. At first, men were so wild in Sour Lake that the local officials made no attempt to enforce the law. As one eyewitness said, "All they done was to hold inquests and pick up dead bodies.[40]

The town was so wide-open that the people thought of the region as the "Free State of Hardin County."[41] Eventually, Sour Lake became so boisterous that some respectable citizens organized the Citizen's Law and Order League to break up the saloon halls and gambling dens. However, conditions in Sour Lake did not improve until the riffraff headed for Batson.[42]

Of all the boom towns in the Big Thicket, Batson was the roughest. One gambler remarked, "I do not say that everybody here in Batson is a son-of-a-bitch, but I do say that every son-of-a-bitch is here that could get here."[43] Another resident who had been in Deadwood, South Dakota, and at Cripple Creek, Colorado, during their boom days declared that he had never seen people as "low" as in Batson.[44] Yet another person proclaimed that Spindletop and Sour Lake had merely been the "training grounds in vice for Batson."[45]

Fannin Street, the main thoroughfare in Batson, was lined with saloons and bawdy houses. Lurid ladies of ill-repute frequently streaked nude through the downtown region much to the horror of the respectable citizens. One resident estimated that there were at least two hundred prostitutes in Batson at the peak of the boom. The saloons and cat houses ran twenty-fours a day. Business was so brisk that some establishments never bothered to hang the door on the hinges. Violence flourished in such an atmosphere. Murders, robberies, fist fights, and shoot-outs were common occurrences.[46]

Every Monday morning, deputies would stroll up Fannin Street and arrest all the prostitutes and saloon owners. The prisoners were then paraded before the Justice of the Peace who held court in the Crosby Hotel. While awaiting their turn before the bar, the women prisoners stood on the second floor balcony of the hotel and called to potential clients who had lined the street to watch the weekly performance. The official fined the girls $12.80, while the saloon keepers were forced to pay $25.00 for each gambling device in their establishment. After paying the fines, the prisoners were released and allowed to continue operations until the next "round-up." If a prostitute was unable to raise the money, the officials asked a man to pay her fine. The woman was then expected to work off the obligation to her benefactor. Persons arrested for serious crimes were chained to pine trees to await transportation to Kountze, the nearest town with a jail.[47]

The weekly fines and the degradation of being chained to a tree did not quell the rambunctious citizens of Batson. In desperation, the responsible people of the city organized a Good Government League, and called on the Texas Rangers for help. The Rangers, led by Captain Bill McDonald, responded to their pleas. McDonald immediately informed the riff-raff that the Rangers intended to restore order in Batson. In an address to the rowdies, McDonald threatened, "Men, the state of Texas sent us here to fight," then he added, "We like our job."[48] Unfortunately, the Rangers were not permanently stationed in Batson. Whenever they left, the town reverted to its decadent way, only to be tamed when the Rangers reappeared. The end of large-scale oil production between 1906 and 1908 signaled the demise of the houses on Fannin Street. The population of Batson sighed with relief as the gamblers and prostitutes rushed toward the new boom town of Humble outside the Big Thicket.[49]

Although the booms in the Big Thicket fields were over by 1908, oil production continued to be a vital part of the region's economy. New discoveries at Sour Lake in 1914 and at Saratoga in 1916 created brief flurries of excitement followed by disappointments as production once again declined. Over the ensuing years, new fields were developed in the Big Thicket. Sawmill towns such as Silsbee, Village Mills, Votow, and Buna produced oil as well as lumber. By the mid-1950s there were over 32,000 oil-producing acres within the Big Thicket counties. None of the new discoveries matched the boom towns in either debauchery or oil production. By the time President Ford signed the bill creating the Big Thicket National Preserve, over 231,371,600 barrels of oil had been pumped from the wells of Sour Lake, Saratoga, and Batson. Other oil production in the Big Thicket added well over 180,000,000 barrels to this total.[50]

In 1975, the amount of oil extracted from the Big Thicket since 1901 could have kept all the refineries of Texas operating at peak capacity for over one hundred days.[51] Oil pumps, with their monotonous up and down motion, still dot the landscape of the Big Thicket, and extract thousands of barrels of crude oil each day, but the great despoliation is over. Many of the scars left by the early oil explorations have been healed by the regenerative capacity of the Thicket; others, however, remain as a monument to the oil explorers' assault on the wilderness.

CHAPTER VII

The Drive for Preservation

In 1831, Stephen F. Austin proclaimed that his sole ambition was "The redemption of Texas from the wilderness."[1] In less than one hundred years, Austin's dream for the Lone Star State had been nearly fulfilled. During the last half of the nineteenth century and the first two decades of the twentieth century, hundreds of thousands of people poured into Texas. Railroads and highways crisscrossed the state. Bonanza timber operators, oil explorers, farmers, and cattlemen had whittled away sizable portions of the wilderness. By 1920, the Big Thicket was being depleted as were other wild regions of the state.

Some residents of the Big Thicket began to react against the wanton destruction. In 1927, R. E. Jackson, a railroad conductor whose route carried him through a portion of the Big Thicket, organized the East Texas Big Thicket Association at his home in Silsbee, Texas. The Association's motive was not the redemption of Texas, but rather the salvation of the wilderness. Their goal was simple. They merely wished to preserve for posterity a sizable portion of the Big Thicket in its natural state.[2] Jackson, a man of strong conviction, personally attempted to preserve a portion of the Thicket by leasing 18,000 acres of land in the southeast corner of Polk County along the Polk-Hardin County line. Because of the dense underbrush, this area was known as the "Tight-eye" country. Regarding this tract as a nucleus, Jackson and his followers agitated for both state and federal action to save at least 430,000 acres of the Big Thicket as a wildlife preserve. According to Jackson's plan, this acreage would cover nearly all of Polk County with a slight spill-over into neighboring San Jacinto County to the west. Jackson's proposal was enthusiastically endorsed by the Beaumont Chamber of Commerce, which believed such a project would bring more tourists into the Beaumont region. Ray Gill, an officer in the Chamber of Commerce, also served as secretary of the East Texas Big Thicket Association.[3]

In the early years, Jackson and his group were unable to generate enough widespread interest in the Big Thicket to gain the political support necessary to preserve the region. But gradually attitudes began to change. By the mid-1930s, the Association had won the support of several members of the Texas Academy of Science, who viewed the Thicket as an outdoor botanical laboratory.

More support was generated by Hal B. Parks and Victor L. Cory, who led a short botanical expedition into the Big Thicket in 1936. At the time, Cory and Parks were the two leading botanists in the state. Both men worked for the Texas Agricultural Experiment Station. Parks was the State Apiculturalist working out of the State Apicultural Laboratory in San Antonio. Cory served as the Range Botanist for the Sonora branch of the Experiment Station.[4] The East Texas Big Thicket Association subsequently published the findings of the expedition. The Cory and Parks report became the "Bible" of those wishing to preserve the region. It became the "most referred to" work about the Big Thicket.[5] In reality, the report was based on incomplete research, and was nothing more than a checklist of the plants, mammals, reptiles, fish, birds, and Mollusca that were supposed to inhabit the Big Thicket in the 1930s. However, since the Parks and Cory survey assumed such an auspicious place in the minds of those seeking to preserve the area, it deserves close analysis.

Parks and Cory first became involved with the East Texas Big Thicket Association while attending a field meet of the Texas Academy of Science at the dedication of the Palmetto State Park in Gonzales County in March 1936. The two botanists were visiting the park to obtain plant specimens and to act as lecture guides for those attending the dedication.[6]

At the field meet, supporters of the East Texas Big Thicket Association approached the men and asked them to conduct a botanical survey of the Thicket. Both Cory and Parks were non-committal, for they were extremely busy preparing a manuscript entitled "Catalogue of the Flora of Texas" for publication as Experiment Station Bulletin Number 550. Nevertheless, the members of the Association continued to badger the two botanists. Also, Dr. Don O. Baird, President of the Texas Academy of Science and a biology professor at Sam Houston State Teachers College at Huntsville, began to plead with Cory and Parks to conduct a survey of the Thicket. Gradually, Parks began to relent. He informed Baird that he would make the survey if Dr. Arthur B. Conner, the director of the Texas Agricultural Experiment Station, consented to the project.[7]

In July 1936, Baird and Parks met at a farmer's short course on the campus of Texas A & M College. Baird once again renewed his pleas, and Parks again referred him to Conner. The two parted company after Baird agreed to present the proposal to Conner. Parks remained on the campus for a few days following the completion of the short course.[8] During this time he talked with Dr. Walter F. Taylor, an employee of the United States Biological Survey stationed on the A & M campus, and a strong Big Thicket advocate. In their conversation, Taylor remarked that he was happy to hear that Parks and Cory were going to make a survey of the Big Thicket. Parks pleaded ignorance, claiming that the director had not informed him of any such project. Taylor answered Parks' protestation "with a smile from ear to ear."[9] Taylor indicated that he also would accompany the survey party. Returning to San Antonio, Parks could only surmise that the trip had been approved.

Official confirmation soon came. In early August 1936, Conner wrote Parks and Cory asking them to cooperate in the project. In addition, Conner sent the botanists a copy of a telegram he had received from R. E. Jackson. In the telegram, Jackson indicated that U.S. Senator Morris Sheppard of Texarkana, Texas, strongly urged that a biological survey of the Big Thicket should be completed immediately. At the time, Sheppard was supporting the East Texas Big Thicket Association's plans to create a national park in the region. With Sheppard's backing, Jackson officially requested that Parks and Cory be assigned to the survey. Cory, however, was not too enthusiastic about the project. He informed Conner that he wished to discuss the matter with Parks before consenting to participate.[10]

Eventually, Parks persuaded Cory to assist him, and the trip was scheduled for September 1936. At the appointed date, Cory and Parks met on the A&M campus, deposited their manuscript on Texas flora at the Experiment Station, and then proceeded to Huntsville. At Huntsville, the men were joined by Dr. Baird and by Dr. Samuel R. Warner, a botany professor at Sam Houston State Teachers College. On September 12, this little group reached Camp Jackson, a hunter's camp in the Big Thicket west of Kountze in Hardin County.[11]

The first day in the Thicket, Jackson and John Knight, a hunter for the U.S. Biological Survey, piloted Cory and Parks through a portion of the 18,000-acre lease. The party spent the morning of the second day exploring different localities within the Thicket. That afternoon, about 100 people from Beaumont and the surrounding area gathered at Camp Jackson for a barbecue to celebrate the survey. Cory and Parks gave talks relating to the plant life of the Thicket. A thunderstorm prematurely ended the proceedings, and the botanists drove into Beaumont to spend the night.[12]

On Monday morning, September 14, Parks and Cory addressed the Beaumont Chamber of Commerce on the plant life of the region. They spent the remainder of the day attending a meeting on the promotion of resources in southeast Texas and viewed a pasture demonstration in the southern part of Jefferson County.[13]

On Tuesday, the survey party again returned to the Big Thicket region just north of Silsbee. This time, P. A. Winkler, a landscape gardener and amateur botanist working on a study of the Trinity and Neches River bottoms, served as guide. On this second sojourn into the Thicket, Cory seemed more impressed with the spectacle of a burning oil well near Silsbee than with the flora of the Thicket. He remarked that the burning well was a magnificent sight, shooting a mass of flame, smoke, and mud over 100 feet into the air. After viewing the well, the party spent the rest of the day at Pine Knot, a private preserve of one of the Big Thicket backers. The next day Cory and Parks left the Big Thicket for a plant-collecting expedition along the Gulf Coast. The botanists had spent only 2 1/2 days of actual exploration in the Thicket. The remainder of their time had been devoted to speechmaking and other public relations activities.[14]

By the beginning of November 1936, Parks, who assumed total responsibility for the final report, was hard at work preparing a manuscript that described the findings of the expedition. In a letter to Cory, he outlined his general plan for the report. For some unknown reason he chose to define the Big Thicket based on its physiogeological factors rather than its botanical contents.

Pursuing this approach, Parks claimed that the Big Thicket was a natural life zone whose northern border was the last shoreline of the Pliocene Age. Its southern boundary was set as the shore line of the Gulf of Mexico during its transgression in the previous interglacial period. Parks set the western border as the bluff line of the "Ancestral Brazos River." Since the study dealt only with Texas, he established the eastern boundary of the Thicket at the Sabine River: the dividing line between the Lone Star State and Louisiana. Under this "physiogeology" definition, the Big Thicket encompassed 3,350,000 acres. Parks pointed out that there were regions of similar vegetation scattered throughout the northern United States. However, he maintained that the Big Thicket differed by being more extensive and by being less affected by lumbering operations. Later-day preservationists were to cling to the notion that the region stretched over 3,000,000 acres, yet they rejected the idea that the Big Thicket was unique simply because of its size.[15]

After completing this portion of his report, Parks compiled a series of six lists, which enumerated the mammals, birds, reptiles and amphibians, fish, Mollusca, and plants that were supposed to exist in the Big Thicket. All of these lists were based on excerpts from pre-existing checklists that had been published prior to the Big Thicket survey. Parks merely took these checklists and selected those organisms that he believed best described the flora and fauna within the Big Thicket region. After compiling these lists, he distributed them to people he considered to be biological experts. These experts were to make corrections and additions to the list.[16]

The largest list in the report dealt with the plant life of the Thicket. In compiling this list, Parks simply took his publication *Catalogue of the Flora of Texas* and extracted the names of those plants that grew in the timbered portion of southeast Texas. Next, he sent the list to Dr. S. R. Warner at Sam Houston State Teachers College for revision. Finally, in November 1936, Parks sent the plant list to Cory, soliciting his comments and corrections.[17] After omitting several plants, Cory returned the list to Parks complaining, "I suppose there are various others that should be omitted but my present knowledge of the vegetation of that area is too limited to know this as a fact."[18] Cory's remark merely served to underscore the superficiality of the entire report. It was at best nothing more than a speculative checklist of living organisms within an ill-defined region.

Over the next several weeks Parks continued to polish the manuscript. Finally, in late December 1936, he completed the report. Parks sent one copy to Dr. Walter Taylor. He retained only one copy for his personal file.[19] By this time Parks was enthusiastic about the report. In a letter to Cory, he exclaimed, "One thing is sure it is quite a complete and correct list of those organisms which occur within the limits of the original Big Thicket."[20] But he confided to a rather skeptical Cory that the report was "sufficiently flexible as to cover any demand made upon it."[21]

Eventually in 1937, the report was published under the title *The Fauna and Flora of the Big Thicket Area*. The Beaumont Chamber of Commerce and the Texas Academy of Science provided the funds to print the manuscript. The first edition of 2,000 copies were distributed in November 1937. A revised edition of 2,000 copies were published in 1938. From the date of its publication, the Parks and Cory survey was accepted as gospel by those pushing to preserve the Thicket.[22]

Actually, at least two scientific publications partially concerned with the Big Thicket region pre-dated the Parks and Cory study. Although neither publication contained as extensive a list of plants and animals as the Parks and Cory report, both studies offered alternative methods of identifying a Big Thicket-type environment from surrounding areas. Both explanations were superior to the "physio-geology" definition of Parks.

The first study, published as an article in the 1904 edition of the *Proceeding of the Iowa Academy of Science,* was entitled "An Ecological Study of the Sabine and Neches Valleys, Texas." James Gow, a U.S. Forest Service employee and author of the article, visited the Big Thicket region in the winter of 1902–3, and again the following year. Gow was in Texas as part of a United States Bureau of Forestry team, surveying the holdings of the Kirby Lumber Company. As a result of the survey, Gow traveled over Hardin, Jasper, Newton, Orange, Sabine, Angelina, and San Augustine counties. Gow was impressed with the wide variety of flora within the region, and he took the opportunity to record several observations on the ecology of the region.[23]

Gow identified six ecological systems that separated this region from the other forested areas of Texas. By utilizing an ecological approach, Gow predated those preservationists in the 1960s who attempted to define the Big Thicket on ecological rather than geological factors. Gow named his six systems pine flats, pine upland, high hammock, swamp, low hammock, and hardwood bottom. Each system contains its own unique association of plants and trees. Although this study was incomplete, it was the first attempt to describe the region based on ecological factors and not simply on myth or tradition.[24]

The second study, written by Professor Roland Harper, entitled "A Week in East Texas" appeared in the July 1920 edition of the *Bulletin of the Torrey Botanical Club*. On his abbreviated trip through Texas, Harper passed through Hardin and Polk counties in August 1918. He was in Texas to collect specimens of *Ilex vomitoria* (yaupon) for the United States Department of Agriculture. While searching for this plant, he also compiled extensive notes on the various botanical regions of East Texas. On his sojourn through the Big Thicket region, he was particularly impressed with the longleaf pine region in eastern Hardin County. In the longleaf forest he found shrubbery that generally prospers in damp spots growing in association with xerophytes.[25]

After viewing the longleaf region, Harper moved into the loblolly region just twelve miles southeast of Kountze. He referred to this region as the hammock belt, and claimed that it was probably the densest upland forest in Texas. He noted that the residents of the area referred to the hammock land as the Big Thicket.[26] After listing the primary trees, shrubs, vines, and herbs of the hammock land, Harper remarked that this region possessed more species of timber trees than any other "reasonably homogeneous area of the same size in Texas."[27] Although Harper did not attempt to define the Big Thicket, he believed that soil composition, not geological formation, was the determining factor in creating the hammock land plant community.[28]

In November 1937, Harper, now a botany professor at the University of Alabama, obtained a copy of *The Fauna and Flora of the Big Thicket Area.* After reading the report, Harper wrote to Cory questioning Parks' definition of the Big Thicket. Harper exclaimed that he was surprised to see that Parks had included the longleaf region in the definition of the Big Thicket. He remarked that he was under the impression that the term "Big Thicket" applied to only a portion of the hammock land. He finished the inquiry by stating that a longleaf pine forest should not be classified as a thicket.[29]

Cory dutifully responded to Harper's criticism. In his reply, Cory proclaimed, "So far as I am concerned my idea is in accordance with yours for I know I would not call a longleaf pine forest a thicket."[30] However, Cory informed Harper to contact Parks for a full explanation of the definition of the region. Unfortunately, there is no evidence to indicate if Parks ever answered Harper's criticism.[31]

Although Parks and Cory's report was superficial, it served as a rallying point for the East Texas Big Thicket Association. As a result of the survey, articles describing the scenic beauty of the Big Thicket began to appear in various Texas newspapers. If nothing else, the report secured some much needed publicity for the preservation movement. After the publication of the report, the Association continued to gain the support of the scientific community. At the June 1937 meeting of the Texas Academy of Science, R. E. Jackson addressed the group on the importance of preserving the Thicket for scientific experimentation and study. Others, such as Dr. Don O. Baird, president of the Academy, echoed Jackson's sentiment. Virtually every speaker who addressed the session commented that the Big Thicket should be preserved because of its value to the botanist and biologist.[32]

Armed with the Cory and Parks' survey, and the growing support of the scientific community, the East Texas Big Thicket Association, with the aid of Senator Sheppard, now began to agitate for the federal government to consider the Big Thicket as a potential site for a national park. Finally, in January 1938, Herbert Maier, a regional director of the Park Service, notified the Association that he planned to inspect the Big Thicket in the near future to determine if it should be included in the National Park System. Buoyed by this news, the Association and the Beaumont Chamber of Commerce began recruiting guides to carry Maier into the depths of the Thicket.[33]

However, a series of unforeseen events frustrated the early preservationist movement. The discovery of large deposits of oil in Polk County in 1936, and again in 1942, upset the plans of the Association to set aside the entire county as a wilderness preserve. Suddenly, men were more interested in drilling for oil than in saving wildlife. Also, the outbreak of World War II brought on an unprecedented demand for lumber products. Timber production began increasing in 1940. By 1942, total wood production in Texas, stimulated by heavy war orders, increased by twenty percent over the previous year. Washington authorities placed twenty-two items made from wood on the war's critical list. Wood was being used in building battleships, training aircraft, and barracks. Nearly every new cargo ship required 500,000 board-feet of timber. Faced with the wartime need for wood products, the drive to remove the Big Thicket from timber production faded into the background.[34]

Additionally, just a few years prior to the Park Service survey, the federal government had expended nearly $3,000,000 to establish over 1,700,000 acres of national forest in Texas. The national forest land was divided into four separate units called Sam Houston National Forest, Davy Crocket National Forest, Angelina National Forest, and Sabine National Forest. The four units formed an arc over the northern and northwestern boundaries of the Big Thicket. As a result of this large acquisition, it was doubtful that the federal government would have been willing to assume an additional 435,000 acres so close to the newly established national forest.[35]

Faced with these reverses, the drive to save the Big Thicket lost its momentum. Jackson, however, continued to campaign for the preservation of the region. His efforts were not entirely in vain. In the early 1950s, a Houston group, known as the Outdoor Nature Club, purchased a 450-acre tract in San Jacinto County and named it the Little Thicket Nature Sanctuary. The club, which also called itself the Little Thicket Association, intended to preserve the tract's original ecological balance. This group also transplanted endangered species of trees, plants, and shrubs to their Houston homes.[36] As the drive to save the Thicket faded, newspapers carried such stories as "Do you Remember the Big Thicket?"[37] The East Texas Big Thicket Association continued to exist as a paper organization until it finally expired in the late 1950s.[38]

Although the East Texas Big Thicket Association ceased to be an effective organization, other groups kept the Big Thicket before the public. In 1955, Bill Daniel, a wealthy rancher from Liberty County and a former Governor of Guam, organized an annual Big Thicket Trek leading from his Plantation Ranch to Beaumont. The trek, which traveled throughout the Thicket, was simply a trail ride to celebrate the opening of the annual rodeo in Beaumont. Although the treks were not designed to preserve the Big Thicket, they did serve to remind the public of the region. However, Bill Daniel was to play a more important role in the preservation of the Thicket than merely leading a group of contemporary cowboys through the region once a year.[39]

In 1957, Bill's brother Price Daniel was inaugurated as governor of Texas. After his brother became governor, Bill, an avid Big Thicket hunter, urged his brother to establish a state park in the region. Price, however, was not a woodsman, and at first he paid little attention to his brother's plea. He was soon to change his mind. In 1960, enroute to a governor's conference, Daniel spent several days vacationing in Yellowstone National Park. Here, he was overwhelmed by the number of tourists flocking to the park. After viewing Yellowstone, he became determined to create a similar tourist-attracting park to bolster the economy of the Big Thicket region.[40]

Daniel did not immediately publicize this plan after he returned to Texas. First, he personally toured the Big Thicket searching for potential park sites in September 1961. His wife and Speaker of the House Sam Rayburn accompanied the governor on this trip. Lancelot Rosier, a lifelong resident of the region and the foremost authority on the flora of the Big Thicket, served as a guide for this little party.[41] Rosier's entire life revolved around the preservation of the Thicket. He had even accompanied Cory and Parks on their survey in 1936. Although Rosier possessed little formal education, he was a voracious reader of botanical publications.

Through sheer hard work he mastered the scientific nomenclature of hundreds of plants in the region. His expertise was so well-known that trained botanists researching in the Thicket sought his advice. A shy, unassuming man, he was ill-equipped to lead a movement to preserve the Thicket; yet his love of the region served to motivate other more capable leaders. His major contribution was providing an almost spiritual inspiration for the preservationist movement. On this tour, Rosier showed the governor several sites that would have been suitable for a park. Daniel later returned for a few other exploratory trips in the region.[42]

Since the timber industry owned a majority of the land in the Big Thicket, Daniel knew that he would need their support to establish a state park in the region. Consequently, before making his plan public, Daniel summoned representatives of the largest timber firms in the state to a meeting at the Rice Hotel in Houston in late 1961. About thirty representatives answered the Governor's call. At the meeting Daniel presented his program, and asked for timber industry support.[43]

The governor's plan called for the state to purchase 15,000 to 20,000 acres in fee from the timber firms. This acreage would contain the park headquarters and also serve as the primary tourist attraction. Also, he told the representatives that he wished to lease an additional 200,000 to 300,000 acres as a wildlife preserve. Within this lease the state would regulate hunting, fishing, and timber cutting—similar to the arrangements in a national forest. In addition, Daniel told the group that certain areas of the proposed park would be set aside as total wilderness areas with no access roads or nature trails.[44]

In order to make his plan more palatable, Daniel, a strong states-righter, informed the meeting that if the state failed to act, the federal government might eventually seize a large portion of the Big Thicket, declare it a wilderness area, and halt all lumbering activities. At least, he argued, the state plan would keep most of the land in active timber production. This was not an empty threat. In 1961, the Park Service's "West Gulf Coastal Plain Type Study" had identified the Big Thicket as an area that should be studied for possible inclusion in the National Park System. Although a few firms were noncommittal, Daniel left the meeting believing that a majority of the timber people would support his program.[45]

On February 22, 1962, Daniel unveiled his program to the public. In a press release he claimed that a Big Thicket State Park and Game Preserve would be a major boost to the sagging Texas tourist industry. Daniel maintained that with the restoration of such native game as bear, bobcat, and mink, the region would rival Yellowstone Park. The governor again sounded the warning that if the state failed to act then the federal government would probably intervene in the region. In concluding his remarks, Daniel called on all interested parties to meet in Beaumont in March 1962, to initiate plans for the park.[46]

Daniel's endorsement of a Big Thicket park was ill-timed, for he was also campaigning for an unprecedented fourth term as governor. Some of his political opponents used this announcement to accuse Daniel of playing politics with the state park system. According to the opposition, Daniel was simply using the Big Thicket State Park concept as a ploy to gain more votes. Archer Fullingim, the liberal editor of the *Kountze News*, was one of Daniel's most vocal critics.[47] After reading about the proposed park, Fullingim proclaimed, "I can smell P. Daniel politics in the air."[48] Fullingim further claimed that the park would adversely affect the economy of Hardin County by taking timber land out of production. He feared such a move would lead to high unemployment in the region. "The thicket is our meal ticket," he exclaimed.[49] Also, rumors began to circulate claiming that Daniel planned to set aside over 400,000 acres for the park, a move that some counties felt would cripple their tax base.[50]

Shunting aside these attacks, Daniel proceeded to place his plan before the State Parks Board: the governmental agency that recommends the establishment of new state parks. At the board meeting, the cries of "politics" filled the air. Board member Ed Kilman, editor emeritus of the *Houston Post* editorial page, led the attack. Kilman proclaimed, "This is obviously a political thing, no sensible person would deny that."[51] Brad Smith, a Daniel aide who presented the plan to the board, argued that he was unaware that the Big Thicket park was a campaign issue. Kilman snapped, "Then you haven't had your eyes open."[52]

Kilman based his attack on the timing of Daniel's announced support of the park. According to Kilman, the Big Thicket had "been there for years, and it will last until after the May 5 primary."[53] Finally, the Parks Board vice-chairman, Reese Martin, moved that the board take no action on the Big Thicket plan, and the motion was adopted.[54] Daniel was both surprised and dismayed by Kilman's attack, for he had re-appointed Kilman to the State Parks Board in 1957. As Daniel stated, "Kilman stuck the knife."[55]

Although the State Parks Board failed to endorse his plan, Daniel held high hopes of gaining popular support at the Beaumont meeting. The meeting was held on March 29, 1962, at the Ridgeway Motor Hotel. Over 300 people representing twenty-two counties and civic organizations attended the confab. In his opening remarks, Daniel stressed that the meeting was to be only a planning session and lead to both the establishment of a Big Thicket Association and a survey concerning the feasibility of a park in the Big Thicket. Once again, Daniel reiterated the danger of federal action if the state failed to act. He declared, "No development of public roads, no residences, no mechanical equipment, no economic uses such as grazing, timber management, and oil development would be permitted under this federal plan."[56] After the meeting, Daniel led the representatives on a 160-mile trip through the Big Thicket, pointing out prospective sites for inclusion in the park. Daniel left the meeting feeling confident of success. He claimed over ninety-six percent of those attending the conference approved of the park.[57]

Daniel drew his chief support from elements who would have profited from the establishment of the park. Various chambers of commerce, the Texas Tourist Council, and the Texas Restaurant Association enthusiastically endorsed the park. They were, of course, excited about the prospective economic benefit of a large state park. Additionally, the Alabama-Coushatta Indians strongly supported the project. They believed that a park would probably bring a large increase to their tourist-based tribal treasury.[58]

Daniel's plans for a park were dashed by the results of the May 5 Democratic gubernatorial primary. Daniel finished a dismal third. John Connally, a rancher from Floresville, Texas, captured the nomination in a second primary later that year. The election results were a bitter blow to Daniel, and over the next few months he did not pursue the park project. However, by the fall of 1962, his spirits had revived, and he renewed his efforts to establish a state park in the Big Thicket.[59]

On October 31, 1962, Daniel sent letters to thirty-one Texans asking them to serve on a Big Thicket Study Commission designed to formulate an objective survey of the region and to select sites for the park. However, this time Daniel ensured that the timing of his renewed effort would not raise the cry of "politics." He cautioned the committee members to keep their appointment a secret. He stated that he would announce the formation of the committee after the November general election. The committee was composed of a mixture of civic leaders, politicians, oil men, and timber company officials.[60]

Daniel also outlined the criteria that the committee was to follow in studying the park problem. First, he maintained that "Any land included in the park would be limited to gift and leases which would not detract from the state's financial responsibility to parks already established."[61] He informed the appointees that the size and location of the park must contribute to the economy of the area, and also protect timber, mineral, grazing, and hunting rights. Finally, Daniel directed the committee to meet with him at the Alabama-Coushatta Indian Reservation near Livingston, Texas, on November 19, 1962, to formalize the arrangements.[62]

Daniel knew that the establishment of a state park still hinged on the support of the large timber firms. For this reason, he announced at the gathering that Dempsie Henley would head the committee. At the time, Henley was a real estate broker in Liberty, Texas. Because of his occupation, Henley enjoyed a business relationship with several of the timber firms in the region. Daniel reasoned that Henley would be able to use his contacts to gain timber industry approval of the project. Once again, Daniel reiterated that a leasing system with the timber firms would be the best hope for the park. Daniel asked Henley and the other committee members to prepare a "general approach" report before January 1, 1963. Daniel established this short deadline because he wished to include the report in his final recommendations to the legislature.[63]

Shortly after the meeting at the Indian reservation, Henley called the committee to its first working session in Beaumont. At the gathering, Henley announced that the major concern of the committee was to secure the support of the timber industry. Unfortunately, attendance at this first meeting and subsequent meetings was light. As a result, the park never received the support of the timber companies. Consequently, the final report did not reach Price Daniel before he left the Governor's Mansion in January 1963. Nevertheless, armed with a preliminary report from Henley, Daniel in his final message to the legislature, urged the creation of a Big Thicket Park Authority. This agency would be allowed to accept leases and gifts of land and also be empowered to purchase land and develop the park by issuing revenue bonds. If properly established, Daniel believed the park could be self-financed.[64]

Coupled with the apathetic attitude of the committee and the prospective loss of strong gubernatorial support, Henley realized that the prospects of securing a park were dim. Faced with this dilemma he decided to try to generate popular support for the project, hoping that an aroused public would force the politicians to create the park. To initiate his plan, Henley called on all those who supported the park to attend a barbecue dinner at Liberty, Texas. Four hundred and fifty people showed up to voice their approval of the project. Both Governor Daniel and his brother Bill attended the celebration, and enthusiastically endorsed the project. At the meeting, Bill Daniel suggested that the Big Thicket Park should be composed of several small scattered portions. Daniel believed that, by utilizing this technique, representative samples of the entire region would be included in the park. The idea was unique, and Henley decided to pursue this approach. Daniel's suggestion later became known as the "String of Pearls" concept.[65]

Although the celebration gained publicity for the project, it did not remove the undercurrent of opposition to the park. One of the primary arguments against the park centered around the possible loss of tax revenue. The critics contended that the park would remove a large tract of timber land from the tax rolls. Some county officials were afraid that such a move might wreak havoc with the finances of the county school systems, which received a large share of their revenue from the taxes paid by the timber firms. Also, some people were frightened that they would lose their homes if their land were inside the proposed boundaries of the park. Others feared that a park would restrict their hunting and fishing rights. Faced with this opposition, and the uncertain support of the new governor, John

Connally, the Big Thicket supporters realized that they needed a permanent citizens' organization to focus publicity on the Big Thicket Park issue.[66]

Eventually, a group of concerned citizens met in Saratoga, Texas, on October 4, 1964, and formed the Big Thicket Historical Association. Lance Rosier was named temporary president. In addition to preserving a portion of the wilderness, the group hoped to establish a museum displaying natural history exhibits of the Big Thicket region. One week later, Henley was invited to address the Association. In early November 1964, he became the permanent president of the organization. The Association also selected a full slate of officers, and petitioned the state for a charter. The appropriate articles of incorporation were filed with the office of the Secretary of State, and the charter was granted. The official name of the organization was the Big Thicket Association.[67]

To celebrate the formal establishment of the Association, the group decided to hold its first annual "Get Together" in Saratoga on January 9, 1965. The Association hoped the celebration would entice new members, gain publicity, and earn some money for the Association's treasury. They had hoped to attract about 600 people, and they were amazed and delighted that nearly 1,600 people attended the gathering to support the park. The large turnout was even more amazing since a norther hit Saratoga in midmorning dumping sleet and rain on the event. The first annual "Get Together" was a success. The membership list jumped to 358 and the treasury was enriched by over $668.[68]

As a result of this display of support, Henley's confidence grew. Since he was finally nearing completion of the Big Thicket Study Committee report, he wrote Governor Connally asking for an opportunity to present his findings and recommendations. An appointment was made with the governor for March 24, 1965. Before making his report to Connally, Henley presented a rough draft to ex-Governor Daniel and solicited his comments. Next, he wrote the members of the Study Committee and established a meeting to review the findings before printing them in final form. Following their apathetic pattern, only a few members of the committee attended the meeting. Finally, Henley presented his report to the Big Thicket Association and gained its endorsement for his recommendations.[69]

On March 24, Henley and over 250 Big Thicket supporters journeyed to Austin to present the report to Connally. The Big Thicket report called for six separate components totaling 52,200 acres. The first component was a 2,000-acre addition to the Alabama-Coushatta Indian Reservation. The second section of the park was simply a 200-acre camping area adjacent to the reservation. A third section designated 10,000 acres near the small community of Fuqua as a Big Thicket State Forest. This region was to be honeycombed with nature trails, riding paths, and foot trails. Primitive overnight camping would be allowed in the forest area.[70]

The report also recommended the establishment of a wildlife and wilderness area of at least 15,000 acres around the Sour Lake-Saratoga region. The plan called for the area to be restocked with bear, panther, moose, buffalo, and English boar. Hunting and access by automobile would be restricted in this area. Henley further proposed an additional 25,000-acre buffer zone around the wildlife area. This land would be leased from the timber firms. Selective logging, under the close scrutiny of the state, would be allowed in the buffer zone. Timber firms were to receive a reasonable tax adjustment in return for the land lease. A park headquarters, located at Saratoga, rounded out the park plan. These areas were to be connected by scenic easements. In summation, Henley called on the executive branch to introduce immediately a park bill into the legislature.[71]

Connally thanked Henley for the report, but remained noncommittal about the proposed park. One month after the presentation he wrote to Henley restating his interest in a Big Thicket State Park. However, he voiced doubt if the legislature would be able to act on a park bill in its current session. Instead of agreeing to introduce a bill, Connally suggested the establishment of a Legislative Study Committee to investigate the possibilities of a park. The governor claimed such a committee would generate needed public support for the park plan.[72]

Henley and the other members of the Big Thicket Association were disappointed by the governor's reaction. Nevertheless, the Association continued to publicize the need for a park. The group decided to hold a second Big Thicket "Get Together" in June 1965, to manufacture more support for its program. The celebration was a smashing success and drew over 4,500 people.[73] Even with this outpouring of public support, the state government did not act. The Association, for all its efforts, had failed to generate enough political support to push a Big Thicket Park bill through the Texas Legislature. Nor had the Association been able to gain the approval of the large timber firms for a park. As Henley stated, "We were just more or less witnessing among ourselves."[74]

The Association finally realized that additional pressure would have to be applied to jar the state from its apathetic position. In order to apply this pressure, Henley invited Senator Ralph Yarborough to tour the Big Thicket in October 1965. At the time, Yarborough and Connally were bitter political enemies, fighting for the control of the state Democratic Party. Yarborough led the liberal-labor element of the party, while Connally represented the conservative-business oriented segment of the Democrats. Henley hoped to make the Big Thicket an issue of contention between the two men, and thus force either state or federal action on the park plan. Yarborough accepted the invitation, and on October 8, 1965, the senator began a much publicized tour of the Big Thicket.[75]

The Yarborough Years

Senator Ralph Yarborough had heard tales about the Big Thicket during his childhood days in Henderson County just north of the Big Thicket region. As a youth, Yarborough listened to his father spin yarns about his hunting exploits in the Thicket. The Big Thicket became an almost legendary land to the impressionable boy. Fired by these stories, young Yarborough envisioned the Thicket as the "Bali Hai land."[1]

However, as his youth passed, the vision of the Big Thicket faded as other pursuits captured his interest. At age eighteen, Yarborough left Texas and journeyed to Europe on a cattleboat. One year later he returned home, entered college, and eventually graduated from the University of Texas Law School. An appointment as assistant attorney general by Governor James Allred whetted Yarborough's political appetite, and in 1938, he ran for attorney general. During this campaign, Yarborough renewed his acquaintance with the Big Thicket. As he drove along the unpaved roads of the region, he was awed by the beauty and solitude of the woods. It was during this campaign that the Big Thicket "physically impressed itself" on his conscience.[2]

During the canvass, Yarborough had what can only be described as a "wilderness experience." After a hard day of campaigning, Yarborough was driving between Houston and Beaumont on SH87, which skirts the Gulf

Coast. As midnight approached, the exhausting pace of the day began to weigh on the candidate. He stopped the car for a few minutes of rest and strolled along the beach. There were no other cars churning down the road nor airplanes droning overhead. Only the sounds of the waves were audible. In this surrounding Yarborough had "a peculiar feeling of the immensity of the universe,"[3] and he felt particularly close to nature. Refreshed after thirty minutes of reflection, Yarborough continued his journey. Although he was defeated in the campaign, the thirty minutes on a deserted beach had a tremendous impact on him; for during his years in public office he constantly struggled to preserve various portions of the Texas wilderness.[4]

Yarborough ran for governor in 1952, 1954, and 1956. Although he was defeated in all three contests, each campaign carried him through the Thicket, and each time he was disturbed by the expanding timber operations in the region. Eventually, in 1957, Yarborough was elected to the United States Senate. He was finally in a position to help save a portion of the Big Thicket. However, more pressing conservation issues demanded his attention. Several corporations were trying to purchase Padre Island near Corpus Christi. This consortium, known as the "Seven Corporations," hoped to develop Padre Island along the pattern of Miami Beach, Florida. Yarborough was disgusted by the plan, and in 1958, he introduced a bill to establish a Padre Island National Seashore which stipulated that the beach would remain in its virgin state. After years of wrangling, Yarborough won the contest, and the Padre Island National Seashore was established in 1962.[5]

During the intervening years, Yarborough had not forgotten the Big Thicket. In 1958, Mary Lasswell, a Texas writer, published a book entitled, *I'll Take Texas*. The book contained a series of stories about the various Texas regions. One chapter was devoted to the Big Thicket. As Yarborough read the book his interest in the Thicket revived.[6]

Yarborough, however, had to postpone the initiation of federal action on the Big Thicket for a number of reasons. Governor Price Daniel was trying to establish a state park in the Thicket region. Yarborough believed that Congress would not act to create a national park while the state was attempting to establish a park in the same area. Additionally, Yarborough had become involved in a struggle to form the Guadalupe Mountain National Park near El Paso. He believed that it would be impolitic to be pushing for two national parks in Texas at the same time.[7]

Yarborough, nevertheless, maintained a watchful eye on the Thicket. In November 1963, he attended the dedication of a "Big Thicket scenic area" in Sam Houston National Forest. The scenic area covered only 1,130 acres in northwest San Jacinto County. Apparently, this small tract was set aside on the recommendation of the United States Forest Service, and not as the result of any agitation by those hoping to preserve the Thicket. With the exception of a few picnic tables and some footpaths, the region was left in its wilderness state. Speaking at the dedication, Yarborough proclaimed that the scenic area "is a beginning, but only a beginning"[8] toward preserving the Big Thicket. Earlier in the year, Yarborough had asked Secretary of Interior Stewart Udall to investigate the death of over 300 herons in a rookery within the Big Thicket. The birds were apparently killed by pesticide dropped from an aircraft. Although it was never determined if the incident was accidental or by design, the episode strengthened the senator's desire to preserve the region.[9]

When the Big Thicket Association invited Yarborough to tour the region in October 1965, the major obstacles to his participation in a Big Thicket movement had been removed. The state was no longer pushing for a park, and his Guadalupe Mountain National Park bill seemed headed for approval. The fact that John Connally was governor of Texas probably served to sweeten Yarborough's involvement in the project.[10]

On October 8, 1965, Dempsie Henley and a small delegation of well-wishers greeted Yarborough as he stepped from the Air Force jet that had flown him from Washington to Ellington Air Force Base near Houston. The party then flew by helicopter to Liberty for a reception for the senator. Price Daniel, Yarborough's past political nemesis, was at the reception to welcome the senator to the Big Thicket. After the ceremony, Yarborough, Daniel, and a few others headed for Henley's ranch to spend the night. On the trip to the ranch, Yarborough and Daniel shook hands, and agreed to set aside past political differences in order to work for the creation of a national park.[11]

The next morning the party began the tour. Yarborough had invited several prominent environmentalists to join the survey. Dr. Clarence Cottam, the director of the Welder Wildlife Institute, Dr. Donovan Correll of the Texas Research Institute, Bill Bowen, superintendent of the Padre Island National Seashore, and Jim Bowmer, president of the Explorer's Club of Texas, all joined the senator for the tour.[12] After a forty-mile trip through the depths of the Thicket and a brief helicopter ride over other portions of the region, Yarborough proclaimed, "I will go back and urge faster action by federal agencies after what I have seen today."[13] Arrangements had already been made for a National Park survey team to explore the region in November 1965, in order to determine the Thicket's suitability for inclusion in the National Park System.[14]

Yarborough's visit and his announced intention of creating a national park in the region shocked the timber firms from their apathetic position. Less than two weeks after the senator's visit, the major timber firms began to plan a meeting on the Big Thicket issue. As one timber company official proclaimed, it was time for the timber firms to decide "What our move should be and when."[15] On November 9, 1965, representatives of the Kirby Lumber Corporation, Carter Brothers Lumber Company, and Eastex Incorporated met in Houston to discuss the project. Partially as a result of this meeting, Vice-President O. R. "Ollie" Crawford of Eastex, journeyed to Austin to confer with Governor Connally and Weldon Watson, the executive director of the Texas Parks and Wildlife Department. After the meeting, Crawford wrote the other large timber firms and claimed that both Connally and Watson desired that the state act before the federal government became too deeply involved. Also, Crawford informed his colleagues that Watson planned to tour the Big Thicket in January, and wanted to meet with the large landowners to discuss a course of action.[16]

On January 11, 1966, Watson met with the timber firms at the Eastex guest house in Silsbee. Nearly every major timber firm in East Texas was represented at the meeting. Lud King of Champion International, Otis Lock of Southland, Tom Carter of Carter Brothers, Ollie Crawford of Eastex, and John Wood of Kirby Lumber Corporation all attended the conference. As host, Crawford opened the meeting by proclaiming that the Big Thicket had evolved into a controversy between Connally and Yarborough, and he expected the controversy to widen. Closing his remarks, Crawford called on the timber firms to work with the state, for in his view a state park would be more compatible with the aspirations of the major land-owners.[17]

Watson then addressed the gathering. He stated that the Parks and Wildlife Department had not yet formulated a master plan for the Thicket. However, he presented a skeletal outline of a program to the timber repre-sentatives. He announced that land for the park would probably be pro-cured by lease instead of being purchased in fee. He envisioned that the whole area would cover approximately 20,000 acres. Within this acreage, Watson proposed the establishment of a wildlife region and three smaller areas to be developed for nature observations. These three areas would contain restrooms, nature trails, and camping facilities. Watson assured the firms that they would retain freedom of action to remove timber from the proposed park with the possible exception of small areas within each of the three nature observation units. He concluded the presentation by remarking that only indigenous animals would be introduced into the wild-life area.[18]

After listening to his report, the timber officials caucused and agreed on a course of action. They informed Watson that the state should de-velop a specific plan, indicating the location of the park. During the de-velopment of the plan, representatives of the major timber firms would be invited to Austin to review the findings and offer criticism. After review-ing the state's plan, the firms would meet to accept or reject any portion or all of the plan. If the plan was acceptable, there would be a final meeting of all affected landowners, large and small, to again review the plan.[19]

The timber representatives, however, were not in total accord. They could not agree on the location of the Big Thicket. Ollie Crawford was the most adamant. He believed that the Big Thicket was located solely along the Pine Island Bayou watershed in western and southern Hardin County. Other representatives disagreed with Crawford's concept, and argued that the Big Thicket covered a much larger area. They could not, however, offer an alternative definition to satisfy Crawford. Since Crawford believed that the Big Thicket was located in one central area, he basically favored a single unit park. However, in order to present a united front, Crawford eventually agreed to support the other timber firms' contention that a Big Thicket park should be composed of several small dispersed units.[20]

After the meeting, Watson returned to Austin to begin working on a master plan. On February 9, 1966, he summoned the timber representatives to Austin and presented his proposals. The state program called for a single-unit park of 20,000 acres. Of this amount, the state wished to acquire 5,000 acres in fee. This tract would be the main tourist attraction, and also would include the residences and headquarters of the park staff. The remaining 15,000 acres were to be under a multiple-use lease system that would permit timber harvesting by the owners.[21]

Watson maintained that one large single tract had certain advantages over the string of pearls concept advocated by Henley and the Big Thicket Association. Watson claimed a single-unit park would be more economical to administer, a fact which he believed would make it easier to obtain the necessary appropriations from the legislature. He also proclaimed that this plan would satisfy the public's demand for a park. Watson next presented two sites as alternative locations for the park. The first area was the "Hathaway" site located five miles west of Sour Lake in Hardin County. The second proposal was the "Bragg" region seven miles east of Votaw.[22]

The timber firms were not satisfied with the plan. They disliked the one-unit concept. Most favored the string of pearls idea because it distributed the proposed land loss among several firms. Under the state's proposal, nearly all of the land would come from Eastex or Kirby holdings. The timber representatives also complained that the extent of fee ownership was too great. Additionally, the firms voiced doubts that this plan would satisfy the demands of the public. They believed that the city-dwelling nature lovers would prefer a number of smaller parks located near their residences. However, the firms' greatest criticism centered around the fear that the state might remove the 15,000-acre lease land from multiple-use timber management once the park was established. They concluded that the state plan was less appealing than action by the federal government.[23]

Also, the timber executives were offended by Watson's manner. He intimated that the Parks and Wildlife Department would not consider alternative plans for a state park. Watson also insinuated that Governor Connally approved of the Parks and Wildlife Department's proposal. Some members of the timber firms secretly believed that Crawford had persuaded the governor to pursue the one-unit concept. Discouraged by the plan, timber representatives left Austin uncertain of their next move. Finally they agreed to meet in Houston on March 22 to further discuss the project.[24]

Prior to the Houston meeting, some of the timber firms officials had an opportunity to talk briefly with Governor Connally. On March 18, 1966, Connally visited the Alabama-Coushatta Indian Reservation, and several timber firms had representatives at the meeting. In fact, Connally arrived in Woodville, just a few miles from the reservation, aboard an Eastex airplane piloted by Crawford. Connally was visiting the reservation at the request of Dempsie Henley, whom the governor had recently appointed Chairman of the Texas Commission for Indian Affairs.[25]

On the way from the airport to the reservation both Henley and Crawford talked Big Thicket business with the governor. During the conversation, Henley convinced Connally of the soundness of the string of pearls concept. Connally proclaimed, however, that he favored a much smaller park than the original 52,000-acre proposal submitted by Henley in 1963. In the course of the discussion, Crawford informed the governor that the timber firms were meeting in Houston in a few days to consider the problem. The governor requested that the firms present him with any suggestions that the meeting might generate.[26]

After the March 22 gathering, Crawford wrote the governor and outlined the timber firms' proposal. According to Crawford, the timber firms decided to back Henley's proposal for a series of small parks. By utilizing this concept, Crawford maintained that no taxing jurisdiction would be damaged. As a result of the meeting, Henley and the timber firms began consulting to determine the size and locations of the park.[27]

While Henley and the timber firms were trying to hammer out an agreement, the Big Thicket had another important visitor. In April 1966, Supreme Court Justice William O. Douglas tramped through the region. Douglas was in Texas gathering material for a forthcoming book to be entitled *Farewell to Texas: A Vanishing Wilderness*. The book was designed to be a series of stories about the wilderness areas of Texas. Since Douglas hoped to write a chapter on the Big Thicket, he decided to tour the region firsthand. As he had with Yarborough, Dempsie Henley served as guide and host. Douglas' visit once again focused statewide attention on the Big Thicket. A bevy of newspaper reporters and television stations covered the Justice's tour of the East Texas wilderness.[28]

On the tour, Douglas viewed a famous Big Thicket tree known as the county-line magnolia. The tree was so-named because it stood on the intersection of Hardin, Polk, and Liberty counties. The tree was estimated to be nearly 1,000 years old. Unfortunately, a month before the Justice's visit, Henley discovered that an unidentified vandal had poisoned the tree. Douglas was only able to view the dead remains of the once-majestic magnolia. The group also saw several other magnolia logs lying rotting on the ground. The sight of such waste enraged Douglas, and in his book he lambasted the Texas timber industry.[29]

He shrieked that the lumber men of Texas were "Robber Barons" who pillaged the land for profit. He compared the timber owners to the biblical character of Ahab, King of Samaria, who destroyed Naboth's vineyard. He ended his polemic by charging that the federal government must act to save the region because the "state government is solidly controlled by the Establishment."[30] The book had Douglas' desired effect. One timber company official remarked that the book prompted the Department of the Interior to move into the Big Thicket like "gangbusters" searching for park sites.[31]

Shortly after Douglas' visit, Henley completed his negotiations with the timber firms and drafted his park plan. At the suggestion of Ben Barnes, Speaker of the Texas House of Representatives, Henley wrote for an appointment to present his program to the Parks and Wildlife Commission, the agency that had supplanted the old State Parks Board. The commission scheduled a hearing on Henley's proposal for May 31, 1966. In his presentation to the commission, Henley intimated that his revised plan had the backing of the timber industry. In fact, he maintained that if the state legislature passed a Big Thicket bill, several timber firms would probably donate a sizeable acreage for the park.[32]

Henley's new plan was a drastically reduced version of his March 1963 report to Governor Connally. He retained the string of pearls concept, but reduced the acreage from 52,000 acres to between 10,000 and 15,000 acres. The first pearl was a 5,000-acre tract near Fuqua, a ghost town in northern

Hardin County. The remaining acreage was to be composed of several smaller pearls varying in size from twenty to 1,000 acres. The so-called string would stretch from the Fuqua site northward toward the Alabama-Coushatta Reservation. After questioning Henley on the cost of the park, the Parks and Wildlife Commission unanimously agreed to recommend the establishment of a Big Thicket State Park to the legislature.[33]

The legislature never acted on the Parks and Wildlife Commission's recommendations. Part of the inaction was probably due to the personnel changes in Austin. On June 21, 1966, Weldon Watson resigned as executive director of the Parks and Wildlife Department. He was replaced by Joseph R. Singleton on September 14, 1966. Governor Connally's attitude toward the project was yet another possible reason for a lack of action. Former Governor Price Daniel speculated that Connally simply never really caught the spirit for saving the Big Thicket. Daniel maintained that if Connally had felt strongly about the issue, he would have pushed a Big Thicket bill through the Texas legislature regardless of the opposition. Also, since the federal government had expressed an interest in setting aside a portion of the Big Thicket, the state adopted a "wait and see" attitude before committing state funds for the project.[34]

The state did not have long to wait. On October 20, 1966, in the waning months of the 89th Congress, Senator Ralph Yarborough introduced Senate Bill S3929 entitled "A Bill to Establish the Big Thicket National Park in Texas." There had been over a year's lag between Yarborough's visit to the Thicket and the introduction of his bill. The delay had been unavoidable, for during that year Congress had been considering Yarborough's Guadalupe Mountain National Park bill. However, on October 15, 1966, President Lyndon Johnson had signed the Guadalupe Mountain bill into law, and Yarborough was freed to act.[35]

Immediately after the passage of the Guadalupe Mountain bill, Senator Alan Bible, the chairman of the Senate subcommittee on Parks and Recreation, who had held hearings on both the Padre Island and Guadalupe Mountain proposals, remarked to Yarborough, "Senator that's two national parks for Texas. I hope I never hear from you about another national park as long as you are in the Senate."[36] To this Yarborough replied, "Senator, I'm not going to bother you 'til next week."[37] Yarborough did not even wait a full week. Just five days after his conversation with Bible, he introduced his Big Thicket proposal.

From past experience, Yarborough realized that it might be years before his bill passed the Congress and became law. First, the bill would be referred to the Senate Committee on Interior and Insular Affairs, headed by Senator Henry Jackson. Jackson would then give the proposal to the Interior Committee's subcommittee on Parks and Recreation chaired by Senator Bible. Bible, at his pleasure, would call for hearings on the measure. After the hearings, Bible would ask for the Park Service's and the Office of Management and Budget's recommendations on Yarborough's bill. After receiving these recommendations, Bible's subcommittee would then issue either a favorable or unfavorable report on the bill. Once the bill was reported out of committee, the entire Senate would vote on the measure. If the bill passed the Senate, it faced the same rigorous procedures in the House of Representatives.[38]

Yarborough's bill called for a national park not in excess of 75,000 acres to be located within Hardin, Liberty, San Jacinto, Polk, and Tyler counties. The senator purposely refrained from enumerating the exact location of the park, for he knew that the Big Thicket was still an ill-defined region. Since there was no consensus definition, he felt that any attempt to specify the exact location of the park would open his bill to more criticism.[39] In presenting his proposal, the senator remarked that the 75,000 acres was an arbitrary figure, which "may well be adjusted one way or the other during considerations of detailed proposals."[40]

Yarborough further stipulated

> The proposal I introduce today is not a detailed proposal ready for immediate enactment; it is rather an attempt to focus attention on the need until we have available the best recommendations from all those who have taken an interest in conservation of the Big Thicket. Particularly needed are the recommendations of the National Park Service resulting from its on-site inspection in November, 1965. Perhaps introduction of this bill will help convince that agency of the urgency of having a concrete plan for preservation of this unique biological area.[41]

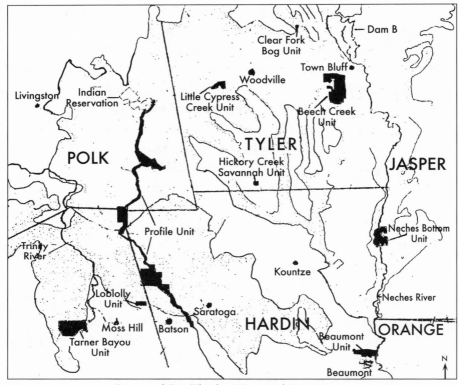

Proposed Big Thicket National Monument

Yarborough's speech in the Senate fired the National Park Service to act. The November 1965, survey had done nothing more than analyze the significance and suitability of the Big Thicket for inclusion in the National Park system. Consequently after the senator's remarks, a new Park Service survey team journeyed to the Big Thicket to gather the information needed to develop specific recommendations on the size and location of the proposed park. Since the survey team was unfamiliar with the Big Thicket, several members of the Big Thicket Association acted as guides for the party. Dempsie Henley, Lance Rosier, Dr. Donovan Correll, and Arman Yramategui, president of the Texas Conservation Council, all offered their services. However, the survey team received the most aid from Professor Claude McLeod, a biology professor at Sam Houston State College.[42]

McLeod had been studying the Big Thicket for years. When the professor had first begun teaching at the college, he was intrigued by stories about the Big Thicket, yet he was puzzled that no one was able to define the region. Consequently, he decided to research the area. His investigations were concentrated on two crucial points: what is the Big Thicket, and where is it located? By the time the National Park survey team arrived in November 1966, McLeod had completed his research, and had prepared a manuscript for publication. The survey team quickly borrowed McLeod's definition and description of the Big Thicket and used them as the basis of their entire report.[43]

McLeod maintained that the Big Thicket could be delineated from adjacent woodlands by the species composition of the vegetational structure of the region. According to McLeod, the Thicket represented a loblolly pine-hardwood forest with a particular type of understory shrubs and trees. Using this definition as a guide, McLeod had mapped the region of southeast Texas that fell into this category. (See Map 1.) McLeod's Big Thicket covered over 2,000,000 acres and spilled across nine counties. He further defined the region by dividing it into an upper thicket and a lower thicket. In the upper thicket, the loblolly pine, white oak, beech, and magnolia were co-dominant trees. In the lower thicket, the beech was absent. Here it was replaced by the swamp chestnut and laurel oak.[44]

Using McLeod's manuscript, the party surveyed the region for several days searching for possible park sites. Due to the inroads of logging activities, farming, and subdivisions, the survey team was unable to locate even a 5,000-acre tract that was roadless or unaltered. For this reason, they decided to adopt the "string of pearls" concept instead of selecting one large site. Like the preservationists, the park team concluded that this would be the best way to preserve representative samples of the wide variety of flora in the region. Also, they maintained that the dispersal concept would spread the economic benefits of a national park among several counties. After concluding the survey, the Park Service recommended the establishment of nine units totaling 35,500 acres. Due to man's inroads, the Thicket did not contain a large enough block of wilderness area to meet the standards for a national park. However, the Thicket did qualify for inclusion in the Park System as the Big Thicket National Monument.[45] (See Map 4.)

The principal unit selected by the survey team, named the Big Thicket Profile Unit, encompassed 18,180 acres. The Profile Unit was a long narrow strip starting from the Alabama-Coushatta Reservation on the north and terminating just southwest of the old oil boom town of Batson—a distance of forty miles. The Profile Unit passed through Polk, Liberty, and Hardin counties. Since this unit traversed both the upper and lower thickets, the survey team felt it offered a "profile" of the "greatest range of topography and vegetative variations in the Big Thicket forest."[46] The team also recommended that the Park Service construct a parkway down the middle of the unit that would allow the visitors to drive the entire length of the "profile" completely surrounded by forest.[47]

The minimum width of the narrow profile unit was set at 1,000 feet. However, at three points along the ribbon-like route the unit was to be expanded beyond the 1,000-foot minimum to encompass significant flora specimens and ecosystems. The first bulge in the Profile Unit—designated the Big Sandy Creek area—was established seven miles south of the Indian reservation. The Big Sandy Creek area contained examples of several Big Thicket subsystems ranging from dry-upland communities to bogs, baygalls, and flood-plain forest. The survey team felt the Big Sandy area provided an excellent area for nature trails and picnic facilities.[48]

The second enlargement in the Profile Unit, called the Tight-Eye section, was located along the boundary of Hardin, Polk, and Liberty counties near the ghost town of Fuqua. The Tight-Eye section was true Thicket country. The dense underbrush made the region almost impenetrable. The survey team felt this section was unsurpassed for its wilderness qualities. The team, in their enthusiasm for the Tight-Eye section, proclaimed that it was the ideal location for the administrative headquarters.[49]

The Pine Island Bayou section represented the final enlargement in the Profile Unit. Located just north of Batson, the Pine Island Bayou area contained a number of hardwood associations, and splendid specimens of baygalls and streambank vegetation. This section was slated to contain a wildlife exhibit shelter as well as picnic facilities and nature trails.[50]

Beech Creek Unit, covering 6,100 acres in eastern Tyler County about thirteen miles east of Woodville, was the second largest unit in the proposed monument. The unit was situated on well drained land and supported stands of the beech-magnolia-white oak-loblolly pine association that characterized the upper thicket. From outward appearances, the Beech Creek Unit contained a grove of virgin forest that had somehow escaped the timber firms. The survey team was excited by the grove, for it represented a sample of the type of forest that would evolve in the Big Thicket once the region was removed from timber production. Since much of the unit was in a virgin state, the survey team recommended only minimal development of nature trails.[51]

The Neches Bottom Unit of 3,040 acres was the third pearl. This acreage, located along the Neches River in Jasper County, just eight miles west of Buna, contained a representative segment of a pure hardwood forest. The team was particularly impressed with the giant specimens of bald cypress and water tupelo. However, they warned that the region was in danger because of timber firm activities. The team recommended that access to this unit should be limited to boats only. They stipulated, however, that the government should build a dock in the unit to serve as a launch-site for visitors wishing to tour the unit.[52]

Tanner Bayou, the fourth pearl, covered 4,800 acres just twelve miles north of Liberty. The Tanner Bayou unit, which represented the westernmost extension of the proposed monument, was the only unit west of the Trinity River. Because of its isolation and near inaccessibility, the unit had escaped timber operations. It was considered the best example of floodplain forest within the region. Also, the team felt it was worthy of preservation because it served as a bird rookery. Large colonies of herons, egrets, ibises, and roseate spoonbills nested in Tanner Bayou's bottomland. Except for a nature trail, the unit was to remain in an undeveloped state.[53]

The fifth pearl, known as the Beaumont Unit, was a wedge of land at the confluence of Pine Island Bayou and the Neches River in southeast Hardin County. Located just north of Beaumont, the region encompassed 1,700 acres of virgin hardwood. Since the area was completely surrounded by water, it had managed to escape timber operations. As this was a true virgin wilderness, the park team recommended that the area remain totally undeveloped. They did, however, call for the construction of a bridge that would allow visitors to cross from the mainland to the unit.[54]

The remaining four units were all much smaller. None was larger than 860 acres. Scattered throughout the Big Thicket, each of these smaller units represented a specific type of flora association. Little Cypress Creek, an 860-acre tract in western Tyler County five miles west of Woodville, contained excellent samples of upper thicket vegetation. The 550-acre Loblolly Unit, just five miles northeast of Moss Hill in Liberty County, represented one of the last remaining stands of virgin loblolly pines in the state. The Hickory Creek Savannah unit, five miles south of Warren in Tyler County, covered only 220 acres. It represented the longleaf pine-grassland association that bordered the Big Thicket on the east.[55]

The smallest pearl was the Clear Fork Bog Unit. It covered only fifty acres just seven miles east of Colmesneil in Tyler County. The team justified the selection of this unit because of its scientific value. The bog was primarily a sphagnum-swamp tupelo association but it also contained many species of orchids and the only species of wild lilies in Texas. This unit was to be closed to the public. Only scientists guided by qualified personnel would be allowed to inspect the bog. The estimated price for land acquisition and development of the entire monument was estimated to be $21,135,000.[56]

Since the survey team realized that cost would be a factor in the decision to establish a Big Thicket National Monument, they offered two alternatives to the 35,500-acre total. The first alternative removed the Clear Fork Bog, Loblolly, Little Cypress Creek and Beaumont Units from the proposed Monument. Under this plan, the acreage dropped to 32,140 acres, and the cost was reduced to $19,740,000. The second option consisted of only the 18,180-acre Profile Unit. According to the team, this was the "irreducible minimum national monument." The estimated cost was $15,450,000. Of this amount, seven million was earmarked for the construction of the forty-mile parkway.[57]

While waiting for the Park Service's report, Yarborough had reintroduced a Big Thicket Park bill into the 90th Congress on January 11, 1967.[58] The new bill, number S 4, was identical to his earlier measure. This move was necessitated by a Senate rule that charged that bills not passed in one Congress must be reintroduced in the next Congress if they are to remain under consideration. When the report was made public in May 1967, Yarborough was dismayed at the recommendations.[59] "Monuments are for dead things," he declared.[60] The senator proclaimed that the acreage figures must be increased if the Thicket was to survive. Yarborough's demand for more land was echoed in the House of Representatives. On June 27, 1967, Congressman James C. Wright of Ft. Worth introduced bill HR 11188 to establish a Big Thicket National Park similar to Yarborough's proposal.[61]

The Park Service's proposal also dismayed the lumber industry. It suddenly became apparent that the timber firms had made a classic tactical blunder in refusing to accept the various proposals for a state park. Because of their own obstinacy, they were now faced with the prospects of losing a minimum of 35,500 acres, and perhaps much more, if Yarborough's bill was enacted. The state, however, offered the timber firms one final plan, which might have forestalled federal action in the Big Thicket.

On August 21, 1967, Joe R. Singleton, the executive director of the Texas Parks and Wildlife Department and members of his staff met with representatives of Eastex Incorporated, Champion International, Temple Industries, International Paper Company, and the Kirby Lumber Corporation at Jasper, Texas. Singleton announced that he controlled $450,000 of special "number nine" funds for wildlife betterment. The funds had been earmarked two years previous for acquiring land to establish a wildlife management area. Singleton then presented the companies with his proposal. He desired to acquire, in fee, 10,000 acres in the Big Thicket from the timber firms. Additionally, Singleton's plan called for the acquisition of another 100,000–150,000 acres by a leasing system. Singleton warned the firms that he had to spend the money before September 1, 1967, or it would revert to the general wildlife fund.[62]

Some of the representatives believed that this plan might act as a deterrent to a Big Thicket National Park. Others, however, disagreed. Most of the representatives maintained that a wildlife area would not satisfy the growing demands of the public for a park in the Thicket. Also, the firms told Singleton that they still favored a "string of pearls" concept over a single unit area. They simply believed the state's proposal would not block federal action in the region; however, as a courtesy to Singleton, the firms agreed to reserve final judgment until the state informed them of the sites selected for the proposed wildlife area.[63]

Since time was a crucial factor, Singleton immediately set his staff to work. On August 23, Eugene A. Walker, one of Singleton's subordinates, wrote to R. M. "Mike" Buckley, president of Eastex, and described two alternate sites that had been selected for the wildlife area. The first tract was five miles east of Sour Lake, and the second was seven miles east of Votaw. Most of the land in both tracts belonged to Eastex and the Kirby Lumber Corporation. Walker reminded Buckley that the timber firms only had until September 1 to accept the offer. However, the deadline passed without any actions by the firms, and the state's last major proposal died. The firms, by their action, had committed themselves to accept federal action in the Thicket. They hoped, however, to keep the federal park as small as possible.[64]

Since Yarborough continued to press for a larger park, the National Park Service representative returned to the Big Thicket in October 1967, to conduct yet another survey more in line with Yarborough's recommendations. In return, the senator agreed to withhold further action on his bill until the new report was completed. Additionally, pressure was mounting on Congressman John Dowdy of Athens, whose district covered nearly all of the Big Thicket, to take some action on the issue. Dowdy's position was critical, for according to congressional courtesy, the House of Representatives would not vote to create a national park in a congressman's district without his approval. Dowdy, a supporter of the timber industry, refused to commit himself to a large park. Instead, he said he would make his recommendations only after reviewing the results of the National Park Service's new survey.[65]

While awaiting the results of the new survey, the timber firms moved to gain some much needed favorable publicity. In late 1967, the major firms, acting through the Texas Forestry Association, announced a cutting moratorium within the 35,500-acre proposed monument. In addition, the Texas Forestry Association contacted all of its members who held land in the units, and asked them to suspend logging operations in the monument sites. Secretary of Interior Udall publicly praised the Association for its actions. He particularly singled out W. T. Carter and Brothers, Eastex Incorporated, Kirby Lumber Corporation, Temple Industries, and International Paper Company for their cooperation. However, not even the largest land owners intended to observe the moratorium for years. Arthur Temple, president of Temple Industries, suggested to several of the other firms that they should announce that the moratorium would last for only one year. He believed that such a threat might force the government to take faster action on the issue. As events unfolded, it became apparent that the moratorium was another blunder by the timber firms.[66]

By agreeing to suspend operations in the 35,500-acre region, the timber firms had given de jure recognition that the monument was a unique region, which should be preserved. By their own action, they had established the 35,500-acre site as the minimum area to be preserved. Also, they could not renege on the much-heralded moratorium without facing an outpouring of adverse publicity. Members of the Big Thicket Association vigilantly patrolled the region, and any cutting in the proposed units, whether by accident or design was eagerly reported to the news media. As one exasperated timber official proclaimed, "The best thing we could have done would have been to oppose it totally."[67] Such opposition would have put the timber firms in a much stronger bargaining position. Instead of bargaining from 35,500 acres, they would have been able to bargain from zero.

As the months dragged past, both timber firms and preservationists anxiously awaited the report from the Park Service. On one occasion the hopes of the preservationists rose rapidly as the result of a press conference held by Secretary Udall on July 2, 1968. When asked if a Big Thicket National Park or National Monument would be established within the near future, Udall remarked that he agreed that a park should be established, but the major problem centered around the size of the project. He then announced, "Senator Yarborough is making an appeal for a large park, and naturally, instinctively this is what I favor."[68] The preservationists proclaimed that the secretary's remarks constituted an endorsement of the 75,000-acre park. Actually, this was not an official Department of the Interior endorsement of Yarborough's bill, but merely the secretary's own inclinations. Nevertheless, the senator proclaimed that Udall's endorsement was "the greatest boost we've had."[69]

Eventually, Yarborough grew weary of waiting on the Park Service to unveil their new recommendations. On August 13, 1968, the senator met with National Park Service Director George Hartzog to discuss the issue. At the meeting, Hartzog suggested the establishment of a Big Thicket National Recreational Area, which might eventually receive national park status. As the name implied, recreation not preservation was the thrust of the new program. Hartzog intimated that the Park Service would issue a negative report on Yarborough's proposal unless the senator would support the new recreational concept. The director further stated that he would send Park Service personnel back to the Thicket for a fourth time in order to develop the concept. He pledged, however, that the new proposal would be ready in September. Faced with this dilemma, Yarborough agreed to hear the plan for a recreational area.[70]

On September 20, 1968, Hartzog, using an aerial map of the Thicket, personally briefed the senator on the plan. The new Park Service proposal retained the string of pearls concept. However, the total acreage was larger than the original scheme. Under the new plan, the Park Service was to acquire 43,000 acres in fee and another 32,000 acres in easements. Also, the plan called for an "environmental conservation zone," which would loop around the entire string of pearls and much of the adjacent land. The Park Service would regulate timber cutting as well as oil and gas exploration in the conservation zone. In all, the "environmental conservation zone" encompassed approximately 1,335,000 acres. Yarborough tacitly approved of the concept, but asked that the Park Service's report not condemn a national park.[71]

Just a month after the meeting, the Advisory Board on National Parks, Historical Sites, Buildings and Monuments recommended the enactment of this plan to Secretary Udall. However, the plan now called for reduced acreages in the recreation area. The final proposal called for the government to acquire only 36,000 acres in fee and 12,000 acres in easements, but the environmental conservation zone had increased to approximately 1,400,000 acres. This new plan was not immediately made public.[72]

The Park Service decided to present the formal proposal to a meeting of timber firm representatives, preservationists, and politicians scheduled for December 14, 1968, at Silsbee, Texas. However, news of the new proposal leaked, and two days before the meeting, the Texas Forestry Association formally announced their support for a 35,500-acre National Monument. In addition, the Association established their own Big Thicket Preservation Committee to lobby for their proposal.[73]

As the time approached for the meeting in Silsbee, Yarborough could look back on the accomplishments of the past two years with some satisfaction. The senator's involvement in the preservation movement had been instrumental in convincing the Park Service to take some action on the Big Thicket question. Also, Yarborough's strong support for a 75,000-acre national park had forced the Texas Forestry Association to endorse a 35,500-acre national monument as an alternative to his plan. The Texas Forestry Association support of a national monument was a milestone for the Big Thicket movement. It marked the first time the timber industry publicly agreed that a portion of the Thicket was worthy of preservation. With the Texas Forestry Association's endorsement of a national monument, it was clear that a portion of the Big Thicket would be preserved. However, the size and location of the park was still in dispute. Unfortunately, these differences were not settled at Silsbee; in fact, the meeting drove Yarborough and the timber industry even further apart.

CHAPTER IX

Urbanites and Intellectuals

Following the general Big Thicket convocation in Silsbee in December 1968, the Big Thicket preservation movement experienced a transformation. The talk and controversy began to resolve into clear legislative proposals. By 1970, it had become eminently clear that federal Big Thicket legislation would occur. When, how much, and where, were questions that would remain unresolved. Preservationists and timber interests had distinct versions of what the Big Thicket Preserve should be, but the important thing was both sides agreed that a preserve should be established. Senator Ralph Yarborough almost secured legislation for a Big Thicket Preserve, but the vagaries of politics left the issue still in the lap of Congress by the close of Yarborough's term.

The meeting in Silsbee had been called by Edward C. "Ned" Fritz, chairman of the Texas Committee on Natural Resources and a seasoned environmentalist. He had summoned all interested conservation and preservation groups to send representatives to the meeting to decide which areas of the Big Thicket should be saved. Fritz, a Dallas attorney, had been involved in the Big Thicket movement for two years, and he vigorously disagreed with the manner in which Dempsie Henley was running the Big Thicket Association. He believed that Henley had become a tool of the timber industry and should be replaced by a more dynamic preservationist, namely, himself.[1]

Nearly 150 people were present at the Silsbee meeting, including Ralph Yarborough, Congressman Bob Eckhardt of Houston, representatives of the Texas Forestry Association, and delegates from several preservation societies. Henley and a group from the Big Thicket Association were also in attendance. At the gathering, Ernest Borgman, superintendent of the Padre Island National Seashore, presented the Park Service's proposal. The plan failed to please either the timber firms or the preservationists. Yarborough labeled the proposal "timid" and pledged to introduce a new Big Thicket bill calling for a 100,000-acre park. His pledge was enthusiastically endorsed by most of the preservationists. A Texas Forestry Association spokesman announced that his organization would continue to support the 35,500-acre national monument. Henley, who felt that "outsiders" such as Fritz were attempting to take control of the Big Thicket Association, said that he supported the Park Service's new position.[2]

The Silsbee meeting was a major turning point for the preservationist movement. Since Henley, as president of the Big Thicket Association, refused to endorse a 100,000-acre park, Fritz formed the Big Thicket Co-ordinating Committee to work for Yarborough's new plan. The Co-ordinating Committee was composed of two or more delegates from the various environmental groups that supported the senator's position. Orrin Bonney of the Lone Star Chapter of the Sierra Club was selected as president of the committee. For the next few years, the Co-ordinating Committee became the most vocal organization pushing for a large Big Thicket National Park. Also, the meeting split the Big Thicket Association. Some members supported Fritz, while a loyal cadre of local people backed Henley. A third element of moderates did not support Fritz, but felt that Henley should be replaced in order to infuse fresh leadership into the movement.[3]

The moderates prevailed. They amended the Big Thicket Association's constitution to read that any person could serve as president for only two years. Since Henley had headed the organization since 1964, he was now ineligible for reelection. At the next election, Charles Wilbanks, a member of the moderate element and a professor at Lamar State University at Beaumont, became the new leader of the Association. Henley, embittered by this treatment, withdrew to his real estate practice in Liberty.[4]

Perhaps the best explanation of Dempsie Henley's removal from the Big Thicket movement is not that Henley had become an obstructionist, but that the preservation movement had moved into new dimensions. Henley, in fact, had been instrumental in bringing the Big Thicket issue to a critical stage of development. His participation on Price Daniel's study commission, the tours with Yarborough and Douglas, and his many speeches on the need to save the Thicket had been major factors in gaining support for the park. Like many leaders, Henley came to believe that his views represented the will of the Association, and he shut his ears to other, more liberal, proposals. This tunnel vision made him vulnerable to criticism that he had been "bought" by the timber firms. In short, his obstinacy made him expendable.

Henley's defeat also reflected the changing composition of the Big Thicket Association. From its inception in 1964, most of the Association's support had come from local people. However, by 1968, a new, more vigorous element was pushing to take over the organization. The timber firms recognized this power struggle and viewed it with some apprehension. As one timber official wrote, "urbanites and intellectuals" were wrestling control of the Association from the local supporters.[5]

Professors and attorneys from the Houston, Beaumont, and Dallas areas comprised the nucleus of the new leadership in the preservationist movement. This group, however, received strong support from some of the local residents who had been members of the Association since its inception. The ideology of the new group was also more sophisticated than that of the old guard. The older thicketeers had been primarily interested in saving the Thicket in order to preserve their vanishing woodland heritage. The new element possessed the same instincts, but they also tended to view the struggle as a microcosm of the larger question of man's destruction of his environment. Convinced of the righteousness of their cause, the new leadership directed their attacks against a new timber technology that called for the establishment of large-scale slash pine plantations to feed the growing appetite of the Texas pulpwood industry.[6]

The concept of pine plantations was not new. The first slash pine plantation was established in 1926, at the State Forest near Kirbyville in Newton County. It was simply a small experimental plantation to determine if the slash pine was adaptable to the Texas environment. The experiment was a success. The slash pine proved to be a fast-growing specie suitable to reforest some of the cutover portion of southeast Texas. However, the slash pine assumed a much more important role with the establishment of the Southland Paper Mill at Lufkin in 1940. The mill was designed to produce newsprint paper out of pine trees, and the slash pine became the primary timber in the papermaking process. Yarborough maintained that the destruction of the Thicket dated from the opening of the mill at Lufkin.[7]

The venture proved successful, and other firms began establishing pulp and paper mills in the state. By 1969, there were eight pulp mills in East Texas. These eight mills consumed approximately the same volume of wood as the 132 sawmills in East Texas. To meet the demands of the pulp and paper mills, the timber industry began to plant more and more pine plantations in the Big Thicket.[8]

To establish a pine plantation, the timber firms first clearcut all marketable timber from the chosen site. Next, the remaining small trees and shrubs are bulldozed into hedge rows and burned. Heavy machinery then prepares the site for planting. The object of site preparation is to suppress hardwood trees that might compete with the more profitable pines. After the pine plantations begin to grow, they are sometimes treated with herbicides and pesticides designed to suppress hardwoods and insects. Eventually, when the pines reach the desired height, the trees are harvested and the whole process is repeated.[9]

The preservationists railed against this technology. They argued that pine plantations were aesthetic warts, presenting nothing but row after monotonous row of pine trees to the viewers. Pine plantations were irreversible, they said, altering the entire ecology of the Thicket. The use of herbicides and pesticides, the preservationists believed, polluted the land, destroyed fragile ecological systems, and putrified the waterways. However, their primary concern was the seemingly wanton eradication of the hardwoods. Since the hardwoods were an integral link in the ecological integrity of the Thicket, their destruction significantly altered the uniqueness of the Big Thicket region. Many preservationists believed that the timber firms were purposely destroying the hardwoods so that the Thicket would not be a suitable area for a national park. In an attempt to gain the support of the hunting clubs in the region, the environmentalists pointed out that hardwoods furnished mast for the wildlife. Once the hardwoods disappeared, they warned the hunters, so would the game animals. Finally, they labeled the pine plantations "biological deserts" that failed to provide food or shelter to wildlife.[10]

The timber firms responded to these attacks by announcing that pine plantations were simply another method of timber management to utilize fully the forest products of Texas. The plantation system, they maintained, represented just one of the several multiple uses of the forest. They also disputed the charge of "biological desert." A pine plantation, the timber firms argued, would support some wildlife, and also provide shelter for small game such as rabbits and quail. The industry explained that the use of pine plantations was not a plot to destroy the Thicket, but rather a movement of simple economics. Pine plantations simply offered the cheapest method of producing pulpwood for the mills.[11]

Both sides mustered strong arguments to bolster their positions. However, there has not been sufficient scientific research to support the claims of either group. Since large-scale pine plantations are a fairly recent phenomenon, it is impossible to ascertain if they are an economic blessing for the timber industry, or a permanent despoiler of the environment, as the preservationists argue.

Buoyed by the strong support of the new urban-intellectual element, Yarborough returned to Washington from the Silsbee meeting brimming with confidence. The senator contacted the White House and tried to gain President Lyndon Johnson's support for the Thicket. Over the past years, Yarborough had talked to Johnson about the Big Thicket a number of times, but the president had never committed himself to the project.[12] On this occasion, Yarborough asked the president to include in his final State of the Union Message the six-word phrase, "approve a Big Thicket National Park."[13] Yarborough believed that such a statement "will electrify conservationists all over Texas."[14] The president replied that his State of the Union Message was already being printed, and thus he was unable to grant the senator's request. However, Johnson promised that he would say something in support of the Big Thicket at a later date.[15]

Undaunted by the president's reply, Yarborough, on January 15, 1969, reintroduced S. 4, a bill calling for a Big Thicket National Park of not less than 100,000 acres. Like his previous bills, this new measure did not specify the exact location of the park; this was left to the discretion of the Park Service. The increased acreage was added to include environmental corridors along the streams between the units. Since the waterways were the life blood of the Thicket, the preservationists argued that the rivers, streams, and creeks in the region must also be preserved if the widely dispersed units were to survive. In essence, these water corridors were the string that held the pearls together. Although Yarborough's bill was non-specific, the environmentalists had a firm idea of the land and stream corridors they wished to preserve. Like the other measures, the bill was referred to the Committee on Interior and Insular Affairs to await a hearing.[16]

While Yarborough was pleading with the Sub-Committee Chairman on Parks and Recreation, Senator Alan Bible, to hold a hearing, both the Texas Forestry Association and the preservationists mounted a publicity campaign to gain support for their respective proposals. The Forestry Association centered its campaign around the adverse economic impact of a 100,000-acre park. In speeches to clubs, chambers of commerce, and sportsmen's clubs, timber spokesmen proclaimed that the removal of such a large acreage would harm the tax structure of the region and might even lead to higher unemployment. The forest, they maintained, must be managed on a multiple-use principle if timber production was to keep stride with the growing demand for wood products.[17] In order to spread their views, the Texas Forestry Association published a brochure entitled *Stewards of the Land*. It was a beautifully illustrated pamphlet with full color photographs of towering pines, glistening lakes, blooming flowers, and flourishing wildlife. The brochure showed that the once depleted forest of Texas had been regrown under the stewardship of the timber industry. The booklet ended by urging the public to support the 35,500-acre park. It never mentioned that other proposals were being considered. The brochure made many vital points, but the impact of its arguments may have been weakened by a statement at the end of the text. Just below the last paragraph, in small but readily discernible print, was the notation, "This brochure has been produced on paper manufactured from the trees of East Texas."[18]

The Big Thicket Association and the Big Thicket Co-ordinating Committee also presented their views to the public. They argued that a national park would help, rather than hinder the economy of the region. According to their calculations, nearly 2,000,000 people would visit the Thicket each year, bringing an influx of tourist dollars that would more than offset the loss of timber revenues. Additionally, they announced that a park would provide much-needed recreational opportunities for people from the growing metropolitan areas of Houston and Dallas. Publications espousing the Big Thicket as the "Biological Crossroads of North America" began appearing in such wildlife magazines as *Living Wilderness* and the *Sierra Club Bulletin*. Through their connection with the news media, the preservationists were able to secure favorable articles in such newspapers as the *Chicago Tribune* and even the *Wall Street Journal*.[19]

Also, the preservationists appealed to "Texas Nationalism" by pointing out that most of the timber firms were owned by non-Texas companies with corporate headquarters based in the North. Eastex Incorporated was a subsidiary of Time, Incorporated, and Kirby Lumber Corporation was controlled by Santa Fe Industries of Chicago. Additionally, Champion-International and International Paper were controlled from New York. How, the preservationists argued, could such distant firms be entrusted to save the Big Thicket?[20]

Although the preservationists centered their attack on the highly visible timber firms, they also criticized real estate developers for destroying the Thicket. New weekend estates began to spring up in the Big Thicket region as the residents of Houston and Beaumont sought a few days' relief from the pressures of urban life. These subdivisions were more devastating to the ecology than pine plantations. The roads and houses in these estates were permanent. Even the regenerative capacity of the Thicket could not grow trees in the concrete.[21]

While the two sides were fighting for public opinion, Yarborough was pushing for a hearing on his bill. There was, however, one major obstacle to his plan: Congressman John Dowdy. Dowdy refused to support the senator's bill. In fact, on October 16, 1969, he introduced his own Big Thicket bill. The congressman's plan, which represented the proposal of the Texas Forestry Association, called for a 35,500-acre Big Thicket National Monument. As long as Dowdy refused to support Yarborough's measure, there was little chance of passing a bill for more than the minimum acreage. Just five months later, this obstacle was removed. In March 1970, Dowdy was indicted by a federal grand jury on charges he had taken a $25,000 bribe to interfere with a Justice Department investigation of a Maryland home improvement firm. The indictment neutralized Dowdy's opposition. Apparently the custom of congressional courtesy did not extend to indicted felons.[22]

With Dowdy out of the way, Yarborough began to exert strong pressure on Chairman Alan Bible to hold a hearing on the bill. Since Yarborough had already established two national parks in Texas, Bible was reluctant to hold hearings. However, Senator Henry Jackson, chairman of the Senate Committee on Interior and Insular Affairs and a good friend of Yarborough's, "put the heat on Bible"[23] to hold a hearing. In April 1970, Bible announced that his subcommittee would hold a field hearing on June 12, at Beaumont.[24]

Once the hearing date was established, Yarborough turned his full attention to the upcoming elections in Texas. Lloyd Bentsen, a wealthy Houston insurance company executive, was challenging Yarborough for his Senate seat in the May 2 Democratic primary. In a well-organized and well-financed campaign, the challenger defeated Yarborough for the nomination. George Bush, a Houston-based congressman, captured the GOP senatorial nomination. Prior to the primary, neither Bentsen nor Bush had ever visited the Big Thicket, but after the election both candidates expressed support for the park. A few weeks after the election, Bush toured the region, and delivered a pro-preservationist speech at the Indian reservation. Dismayed by his defeat, Yarborough nevertheless prepared for the Beaumont meeting, and declared that he would fight for his bill until he left office.[25]

On June 12, 1970, at 8:00 A.M. Bible called the hearing to order at the U. S. district courthouse in Beaumont. Bible was the only member of the subcommittee who made the trip; however, some committee staff personnel were present. Also, at the insistence of Bible, George Hartzog, the director of the National Park Service, attended the hearing to listen to the various recommendations of the witnesses. As a matter of senatorial courtesy, Bible invited Yarborough to sit with him during the hearing. After making some brief introductory remarks, Bible began to take testimony.[26]

Yarborough was the first witness. After tracing the history of his Big Thicket bills, the Senator focused his comments on the economic impact of the Big Thicket Park in East Texas. He dismissed the arguments that the park would hurt the economic base of the Thicket counties. To the contrary, Yarborough cited a National Park Service-sponsored report which indicated that national parks added $6.4 billion to the economy of the nation. Also, he quoted from a study of the economic impact of Mt. Rainier and Olympic National Parks in Washington State. Studies found that tourists to these two parks added $36.2 million to the wealth of the state. Thus, the senator argued that the park would boost the economy rather than harm it.[27] Summing up his arguments Yarborough said, "I am not an enemy of the lumber interests. I have helped them over many years in my thirteen years in the Senate, but they have been shortsighted in fighting this park. It is pulpwood against the people and the things people have, and right and justice, I think, Mr. Chairman, demand that the people win."[28]

Congressman Bob Eckhardt then testified for the park. He first commented on the needs of his urban constituency to have a place to escape from the noise and pollution of Houston. However, most of his comments were an oblique attack on the timber industry. "I wonder," he mused, "if there aren't well planned programs to destroy the hardwoods—hickory, pecan, and beech—and supplant them with fast-growing pines for money-hungry lumber barons resembling those which a noted conservationist, Gifford Pinchot, fought so many years ago."[29] Many preservationists were not as gentle in their criticism. In his testimony, Orrin Bonney, president of the Big Thicket Co-ordinating Committee, flatly accused timber firms of cutting down the Thicket so it would not be worth preserving as a national park. Even Dempsie Henley, who had recovered from his wounded pride, endorsed Yarborough's bill.[30]

Eventually, the timber firms presented their views. Oliver Crawford of Eastex, who was serving as president of the Texas Forestry Association, outlined the timber industry's position. In his testimony, Crawford bore down on the economic impact of forestry in Texas. The timber industry, he maintained, provided 161,850 jobs, and each pulpwood truck added

$25,000 annually to the community in which it operated.[31] In defending the 35,500-acre proposal, Crawford informed Bible that "It has been through the management of its present owners that . . . the Big Thicket is what it is today. We have regrown what was destroyed in years past."[32] After concluding his testimony, Crawford was sharply questioned by Yarborough.

The senator was primarily concerned with the propaganda effort of the timber firms. The senator asked Crawford if the Reves-Dykes agency, a public relations firm in Houston, was campaigning across Texas in an attempt to persuade clubs and organizations to endorse the Texas Forestry Association's proposal. Crawford replied that Reves-Dykes was helping set forth the timber industry's program, but he denied that they were waging a propaganda war to kill the Big Thicket National Park. Arthur Temple of Temple Industries and James Webster of the Kirby Lumber Corporation offered testimony supporting Crawford's position. Also, Paul Kramer, the director of the Texas Forest Service, testified and proclaimed that his primary concern was the shrinking timber acreage in Texas. While he did not endorse either the timber firms' proposal or Yarborough's bill, he did state that the future demand for timber products could not be met if large blocks of land continued to be removed from production.[33]

On the surface, the hearings were a triumph for the preservationists. Of the thirty-nine witnesses, thirty favored a national park of 100,000-acres or larger. But more importantly, Yarborough's proposal secured strong support from the scientific community. Six men who held Ph.D.'s in botany or biology testified to the unique character of the Big Thicket, and all agreed that at least 100,000 acres should be preserved. Bible was particularly impressed by the testimony of Dr. Clare A. Gunn, a faculty member of the Recreation and Parks Department at Texas A&M University.[34]

Dr. Gunn proposed that the Big Thicket should be classified as a National Recreational Area. He called on the timber industry and oil firms to establish educational centers in the region. He believed the timber educational center should demonstrate modern silvicultural practices to the tourist, while the oil industry exhibit should explain the mining, processing, and distribution system of petroleum. Gunn reasoned that by utilizing this technique, both industries would be able to explain their impact on the environment to the public. Also, Gunn's proposal specified that certain areas should be set aside for pure preservation. He envisioned a cable lift which would carry tourists over the more fragile ecological areas. In this manner tourists could still see rare plants, but would not trample them. Camping facilities and nature trails rounded out the Recreational Area.[35]

Finally, Gunn struck at the bickering between the preservationists and the timber firms. He believed that if the environment were to be saved, a cooperative effort among preservationists, industry, and government would have to replace the "obsolete public versus private polarized dichotomy"[36] of the past. In short, Gunn's plan called for a cultural, ecological, and recreational program, which would serve to enhance man's understanding of his relationship to the natural environment.

After listening to Gunn's program, Bible exclaimed that it was one of the finest presentations he had heard. He recommended that Director Hartzog pay close attention to this proposal when the National Park Service began to draft its recommendations. However, the witness who most impressed Bible was former Governor Price Daniel. Bible and Daniel had been friends for years. They had first met when they both served as attorney generals of their respective states. Later, they cemented their friendship while serving together in the United States Senate. Daniel only testified for a few minutes, but since Bible knew that Daniel was a strong states-righter, he was tremendously impressed by his old friend's support of Yarborough's bill.[37]

As the hearing drew to a close, Bible attempted to summarize the future of the bill. He stated that the controversy over the Big Thicket really amounted to a dispute over acreage. Also, he stipulated that cost would be a major factor in determining the Interior Committee's action on the bill. Finally, he proclaimed that he would ask the Park Service for an evaluation of the various proposals and also for their recommendations for the region. Once he received the Park Service's report, Bible pledged to move as fast as possible to resolve the issue. The hearing adjourned at 3:00 P.M. Bible, Hartzog, Yarborough, and a few others then toured the Big Thicket by helicopter.[38]

Just four days after the hearing, the Big Thicket was again injected into a political campaign when George Bush introduced a Big Thicket bill into the House of Representatives. Since Lloyd Bentsen, Bush's opponent in the November general election, had endorsed Yarborough's bill, the Houston Congressman apparently felt compelled to introduce his own bill to build his image as an environmentalist. Bush's measure called for a Big Thicket National Park of not more than 150,000 acres. In addition to the standard "string of pearls," the bill also called for the preservation of a large area along the Neches River, and a system of connecting corridors between the units. Bush also hinted that the Nixon administration, which was anxious for his election, would back his proposal.[39]

On the same day that Bush introduced his bill, Congressman Bob Eckhardt of Houston announced that he planned to submit a 185,000-acre Big Thicket National Park bill. Eckhardt had been a strong supporter of the Thicket for several years. However, since the Thicket lay within Dowdy's district, the custom of congressional courtesy had prevented him from pushing his own proposal. With Dowdy's indictment, Eckhardt felt justified in disregarding custom, and he decided to campaign actively for his own Thicket bill. Like Bush's bill, Eckhardt's proposal called for a "string of pearls" connected by water corridors.[40]

Over the next few months, the Big Thicket became one of the primary issues in the senatorial contest. The Thicket controversy received ample press coverage because there were few other issues that divided the two candidates. Both men seemed to support the Thicket in the hopes of gaining the vote of Texas environmentalists. However, the preservationists viewed both men with wary eyes. Bush had become actively involved in the movement only after receiving the Republican nomination. Bentsen's support of Yarborough's bill was also suspect, for he had enjoyed the support of several of the wealthy timbermen during his primary campaign against the senator. The preservationists pointed out that Bentsen had never even visited the region.[41]

In the closing weeks of the campaign, Bush began pushing his proposal even harder. On October 14, just a few weeks before the election, he announced that the Department of Interior had accepted his proposal for the Big Thicket. To further Bush's chances, the Nixon administration dispatched Secretary of Interior Walter Hickle to Texas to campaign for the Houston congressman. On his soiree through Texas, Hickle visited the Big Thicket. After touring the region, Hickle, at a press conference in Houston, announced that he wholeheartedly endorsed the plan to set aside between 100,000 and 150,000 acres of the Thicket. However, he stipulated that the region should be classified as a recreational area instead of a national park. Hickle's endorsement of the bill had little effect, for Bentsen won the Senate seat in the November election. After Bush's defeat, the Interior Department's support for a 150,000-acre park rapidly dissipated.[42]

When Congress reconvened following the general elections, Yarborough began frantically pushing for action on his Big Thicket bill. His term expired on January 2, 1971, and he desperately wanted to pass his proposal before he left office. Once again he called on Senator Bible to take some action on the measure. Responding to his plea, Bible set a new hearing for November 24 to review the recommendations of the Park Service. Only two witnesses were scheduled for the hearing: Yarborough and a representative of the Parks Department. The senator testified first, and simply reviewed his efforts to save the Thicket. After his testimony, Yarborough rose to leave the hearings to attend another function. Bible halted the senator, and read a letter containing the Park Service's recommendations. The letter, written by Assistant Secretary of the Interior James Smith, stunned and angered Yarborough. Smith had recommended that action on the bill be deferred until the Park Service completed a new survey of the Big Thicket.[43]

With this news Yarborough exploded. He exclaimed, "They have already made two reports. . . . Now they have retreated from both of them, they have retreated into nothing, into destitude, I believe. Might as well disband the Park Service if that is all they can do, study for 4 years and then fall flat in the middle."[44] He concluded his harangue by wistfully commenting, "We will have only the tree stumps and the memories left."[45] Bible agreed with the senator and announced there was no need for another study. Bible then spoke with Assistant Secretary of Fish, Wildlife, and Parks Leslie L. Glasgow, who was representing the Park Service at the hearing. After mildly chiding Glasgow for the Park Service's delay on the issue, Bible informed Glasgow that he wanted a specific Park Service proposal on his desk by December 4. Glasgow agreed.[46]

However, fate intervened. Just one day after the hearing, President Nixon fired Interior Secretary Hickle. In the "house-cleaning" following Hickle's demise, Glasgow was dismissed. As a consequence of the turmoil at the Interior Department, the National Park Service's report failed to reach Bible by the deadline. For a short period it appeared as if Bible was not going to issue a subcommittee report on Yarborough's bill without the Park Service's recommendations. Once again, Senator Henry Jackson intervened. Jackson informed Bible that if the subcommittee refused to report on Yarborough's bill, then the full Senate Committee on Interior and Insular Affairs would take the bill away from Bible's subcommittee, and report it directly to the Senate. A disgruntled Bible agreed to issue the subcommittee's report.[47]

As Bible was preparing the report, he received a letter from Ollie Crawford of Eastex offering a compromise. Crawford suggested that the best solution would be a single-unit park of 81,500 acres. This was a significant concession over the 35,500-acre proposal he endorsed at the Beaumont hearing. The park would consist of a 63,000-acre tract in the Sour Lake, Saratoga, Kountze region: an area referred to as the Saratoga Triangle. Additionally, the park would include the 18,180-acre Profile Unit. Crawford had not cleared the plan with the Texas Forestry Association or the other major timber firms. Apparently, it was his own handiwork. Crawford's proposal reflected his firm belief that the Big Thicket was located only along the Pine Island Bayou watershed. Crawford had not suddenly become a preservationist. His firm had substantial holdings along the Neches River that would have been lost if Yarborough's bill became law. In fact, after proposing his plan, Crawford added, "I would like to suggest that any further talk regarding the Neches River or its flood plain be dropped."[48] Crawford also sent copies of the letter to John Tower, the conservative Republican senator from Texas, and to Congressman Dowdy.[49]

Crawford's attempt at compromise was too late. On December 8, 1970, Bible issued the subcommittee recommendations. The report favored Yarborough's bill with one exception. The original bill had called for a park of not less than 100,000 acres. Bible changed the bill to read that the park should not exceed 100,000 acres. On December 16, 1970, the bill as amended passed the Senate, and the measure was sent to the House of

Representatives where it was referred to the House Committee on Interior and Insular Affairs.[50] Unfortunately, there was not enough time remaining in the 91st Congress for the House Interior Committee to hold hearings on the bill. Congressman Wayne Aspinell, chairman of the House Interior Committee, was on a tour of Southeast Asia, and the committee clerk announced that "the only things that we will meet on is something of a great emergency."[51] Apparently the Big Thicket did not meet this criterion, for Yarborough's Big Thicket bill died in the House Committee when the 91st Congress expired on January 2, 1971. When the new Congress convened on January 21, Yarborough was not there; Lloyd Bentsen had replaced the most ardent backer of the Big Thicket.[52]

A bear hunt, early 1900s. (Source: Big Thicket National Preserve files.)

Longleaf pine stumps, circa 1920s. (Source: Commercial booklet, nd. In possession of D. D. Shine.)

Dearborn, site of the McShane Lumber company mill, 1903–18, north of Saratoga, was named for the mill superintendent. The mill had a capacity of 150,000 board feet per day, and the peak population was 800 in 1905. (Source: Big Thicket Association files)

R.E. Jackson, 1880–1957. A visionary leader now recognized as "Father of the Big Thicket," Jackson led the movement to establish a national park of 435,000 acres.
(Source: *New Encyclopedia of Texas*, Texas Development Co., nd. Courtesy of Thomas, Richard, and George Hardy.)

Justice Douglas and Dempsie Henley on Thicket tour. Upper left corner, Laurence Walker; center Barbara Correll, Armand Yramategui, Justice William O. Douglas; Dempsie Henley by tree; others unidentified. (Source: Big Thicket Association files.)

Dempsie Henley, Texas Indian Commissioner, at Alabama-Coushatta event, 1966. On the platform at the left: Justice William O. Douglas; at the right: Chief Fulton Battise, Emmett Battise(?) and Walt Broemer. (Source: Big Thicket Association files.)

Representative Bob Eckhardt. (Source: Big Thicket Association files. Courtesy of office of Rep. Bob Eckhardt.)

Rep. Emmett Lack, Gov. Price Daniel, and Dempsie Henley (Source: Big Thicket Association files. Courtesy Tom Bean.)

Archer Fullingim, Editor, *Kountze News* at the Senate hearings, February 1974. (Source: Big Thicket Association files. Courtesy of office of Congressman Charles Wilson.)

Senator Ralph W. Yarborough, center; Lorraine Bonney, right, at the Senate hearings, February 1974. (Source: Big Thicket Association files. Courtesy of office of Congressman Charles Wilson.)

James Webster, Vice-President, Corporate Relations, Kirby Lumber Company, at the Senate hearings, February 1974. (Source: Big Thicket Association files. Courtesy of office of Congressman Charles Wilson.)

Edward C. "Ned" Fritz, Chair, Texas Committee on Natural Resources, at the Senate hearings, February 1974. (Source: Big Thicket Association files. Courtesy of office of Congressman Charles Wilson.)

Geraldine Watson at Senate hearings, February 1974 (Source: Big Thicket Association files. Courtesy of office of Congressman Charles Wilson.)

Arthur Temple honored by BTA at luncheon, 1976. Temple speaks, flanked by Darrell Mack (then editor of *Enterprise*) and Howard Peacock (BTA president). (Source: Big Thicket Association files.)

The Preserve's first Superintendent Thomas E. Lubbert, whose planning and research initiatives led to the Preserve's designation as a UNESCO Man and the Biosphere Reserve. (Source: Big Thicket Association Files. Courtesy Maxine Johnston.)

Professor Claude McLeod with Howard Peacock attending Addition Act meeting. (Courtesy of Maxine Johnston.)

Congressman Charles Wilson discusses Addition Act and fields questions. (Courtesy of Maxine Johnston.)

Lance Rosier with Spanish liveoak planted by grand-father's slaves in 1861. (Courtesy of Roy Hamric.)

Pete Gunter giving keynote address at dedication of Visitor Center, 2001.
(Courtesy of Maxine Johnston.)

CHAPTER X

Consensus and Compromise

Despite the confusion of plans and motives, and the apparent lack of success by environmentalists or legislators to create a Big Thicket Park, by 1970 there had been a decision. A portion of the Big Thicket would be preserved. Who would initiate it, when, and in what shape, form, or size had not been established. Over the next few years, a multitude of proposals, numerous compromises, countless hours of public hearings, and an untold quantity of print, film, and conversation finally resolved into the passage of an act of Congress to establish the Big Thicket National Preserve.

The struggle to pass the bill represented an example of the controversy between preservationists and business interests over the use of the nation's dwindling natural resources. For in the Big Thicket controversy, as is true with many modern environmental issues, the champions of preservation were the urban groups removed from the wilderness environments. Furthermore, the Big Thicket issue illustrated the gulf between preservationists and conservationists. Timber interests, depicted as villains by the preservationists in the Big Thicket struggle, were in fact ardent conservationists dedicated to the concept of multiple-use forestry. The preservationists, however, sought to preserve the wilderness not because it was good business, or even exclusively to preserve the natural environment, but because it sustained America's contact with its rich heritage of the past and thereby nurtured the unique American spirit. It was in support of this idealistic and elusive appeal that the great diversity of interests involved in the Big Thicket struggle finally rallied.

When the 92nd Congress convened in January 1971, the new Texas senator, Lloyd Bentsen, moved to establish his credentials as an environmentalist. On January 25, Bentsen introduced his first legislative proposal as a senator, a bill calling for a 100,000-acre Big Thicket National Park. The measure was identical to Ralph Yarborough's bill, which had passed the Senate in the last days of the 91st Congress.[1] Not to be overshadowed by his Democratic colleague, Texas' Republican senator, John Tower, joined the Big Thicket bandwagon. On January 27, Tower addressed the Senate and boasted, "I rise to offer a new approach to the establishment of a Big Thicket National Park."[2]

Tower maintained that past Big Thicket bills had ignored the recreational needs of Texas. He claimed his "new approach" would rectify this oversight. Tower's plan rejected the string of pearls concept as being too difficult to administer. Instead he proposed a single-unit park. Tower's "new approach" was actually similar to the plan set forth by Oliver Crawford, vice-president of Eastex, in a letter to Senator Alan Bible in December 1970. The single unit included the Saratoga Triangle and the Profile Unit: a total of 81,472 acres. The only "new approach" in Tower's plan called for the establishment of several recreational areas totaling 18,528 acres. These areas were to be located near the numerous lakes of the region and in the national forests.[3]

Although both Texas senators claimed to champion the Thicket project, the real battle to save the Big Thicket was fought in the House of Representatives. During the next four years, 1971–1974, sixteen separate Big Thicket bills were introduced in the House of Representatives. Congressman Jack Pickle of Austin led the procession. On February 4, he submitted a companion bill to Bentsen's proposal. On the same day, Bob Eckhardt, the preservationists' congressional champion, introduced the most detailed Big Thicket bill ever presented in Congress.[4]

Eckhardt's proposal called for a mammoth 191,000-acre national park. Unlike earlier measures, his bill specified the locations of the various units and listed the acreage of each. The proposal consisted of nine separate

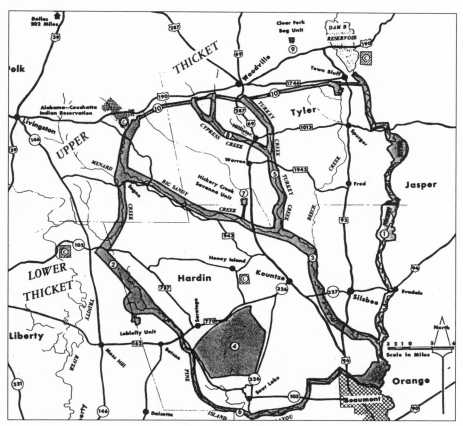

Congressman Bob Eckhardt's "Wheel of Green"

units connected by a series of water corridors and nature trails. Virtually every major stream in the area—Pine Island Bayou, Menard, Big Sandy, Cypress, Turkey and Village Creeks, plus a forty-mile strip of the Neches River—was included in the water corridors.[5]

Eckhardt had formulated this plan only after consulting with the preservationists to determine which areas should be included in the park. The preservationists proclaimed that Eckhardt's bill accomplished two primary objectives. First, it encompassed all but one of the ecosystems that the Big Thicket Association was striving to preserve. Secondly, the preservationists maintained that most of the land in the bill, with the exception of the 40,000-acre Saratoga Triangle (which later became known as the Lance Rosier Unit), was located on swampy bottomland that was too wet for profitable timber operations. Hence, the environmentalists argued that the timber firms would lose little productive timber land under this proposal. Former Senator Ralph Yarborough added his enthusiastic support to the plan. It was, he claimed, the best Big Thicket bill ever introduced in Congress.[6]

The proposed park's configuration, which resembled an ill-shaped circle, was nicknamed the "wheel of green." (See Map 5.) In addition to encircling the park units, the wheel also encompassed a large area that was not included as part of the park. The timber firms viewed the proposal with some apprehension. Since the so-called "wheel of green" could be entered only by passing through federal property, timber men feared that once such a bill became law, the federal government might deny them access rights to the timber within the "wheel." If this happened, over 1,000,000 acres would be removed from timber production. The apprehension of the timber interests was not unfounded, as the thought had also occurred to at least some preservationists.[7]

Undaunted by the preservationists' enthusiastic endorsement of Eckhardt's proposal, Congressmen Jack Brooks of Beaumont, Earle Cabell of Dallas, and Wright Patman of Texarkana all introduced their own Big Thicket plans. Both Brooks and Patman called for a national park, but Cabell proposed a 35,000-acre national monument.[8]

While the congressmen and senators were each trying to gain the Department of Interior's support for their own pet plan, the Big Thicket

Association was searching for a new president. In the summer of 1971, Charles Wilbanks, who had succeeded Dempsie Henley as president of the Association, was about to complete his second term in office. Wilbank's administration had been marked by a number of accomplishments. Under his direction, the Association won a $10,000 award from the American Heritage Society for outstanding work in conservation. The money was used to improve both the museum and Association headquarters at Saratoga. The award also provided funds for the public relations campaign. During Wilbank's tenure, the Association had also staged an Annual Big Thicket Nature Pilgrimage. The Pilgrimage, which consisted of nature walks and a slide presentation, attracted 2,000 visitors and gained more publicity for the movement. The Association had also paid the final installment on the mortgage of the headquarters property, and produced two publications entitled *Handbook for Members* and *Big Thicket Bibliography* during Wilbank's administration. Additionally, the Association had begun to publish a quarterly *Big Thicket Bulletin* to keep its widely dispersed membership up-to-date on social gatherings and the status of the various Big Thicket bills.[9]

Although Wilbanks improved the administrative procedures and financial status of the Association, some preservationists felt that he had not been forceful enough in dealing with the timber industry. A rather quiet man, Wilbanks had been the opposite of the flamboyant Henley. As one preservationist stated, "Wilbanks was a field sparrow to Dempsie Henley's flamingo."[10] To achieve a more aggressive stance against the timber firms, the Association elected Pete A. Y. Gunter as their new leader.[11]

Gunter, a native of Houston, had enjoyed numerous hunting trips into the Big Thicket region as a boy. In the early 1960s, Gunter left Texas to study at Yale. While at college he read Mary Lasswell's *I'll Take Texas*, and this aroused his desire to save a portion of the Thicket. After graduating from Yale with a Ph.D. in Philosophy, Gunter taught at Auburn University in Alabama, and then at the University of Tennessee at Knoxville. In 1969, he returned to his home state and became chairman of the Philosophy Department at North Texas State University at Denton, now the University of North Texas. In addition to his academic duties, Gunter submerged himself in the movement to preserve the Thicket. He epitomized the "urbanites and intellectuals" whom the timber companies feared had taken control of the Big Thicket Association.[12]

Gunter believed that the Association was floundering, and after his election in 1971, he established two primary objectives to re-energize the movement. His first goal was to gain more publicity for the Big Thicket. To accomplish this end, Gunter began "raising hell"[13] about the abuses of the timber firms. He began speaking to ladies' clubs, garden clubs, fraternal associations, and chambers of commerce. In each speech, he flailed at the timber firms for destroying the Thicket. He told his audiences that "These guys (the timber owners) are carpetbagging. They are northern companies, they're destroying our wilderness, a unique Texas area."[14] By using such inflammatory rhetoric, Gunter hoped to "irritate people into irritating their congressmen"[15] to vote for a Big Thicket National Park. During his two years in office Gunter spoke to over thirty organizations across the state. Other preservationists also presented their views to similar gatherings. The speeches to small groups had an impact. Postcards from garden clubs, chambers of commerce, and even sixth-grade schoolchildren flooded into the Texas delegation urging them to act on the Big Thicket.[16]

While realizing that speeches might generate support in specific localities, Gunter knew that the Thicket needed statewide and even nationwide publicity to force Congress to act. To accomplish this objective, Gunter launched a media campaign. He appeared on numerous radio talk shows and television programs. In 1971 alone, twelve radio shows in urban areas either interviewed Gunter or carried stories about the Big Thicket. During the same period, he appeared on fourteen television programs in Houston, San Antonio, Ft. Worth, and Dallas. The high point of the television campaign came in 1972. On January 29, 1972, the NBC evening news carried a story on the Thicket, and on June 12, 1972, Gunter appeared on the NBC *Today Show* to plead for preservation of the Big Thicket.[17]

Gunter also wrote numerous articles for newspapers and wilderness magazines extolling the virtues of the Thicket and denigrating the timber companies. Articles submitted by Gunter and other preservationists began appearing more frequently in nature publications such as *American Forest* and *Audubon*. Gunter personally authored over twenty articles on the

Thicket. He capped his publication record with *The Big Thicket: A Challenge for Conservation*, a full-length book released in 1972.[18] Gunter, an aspiring folk singer, even recorded a song entitled "The Last Big Thicket Blues." The song's doleful lyrics asked, "What are you gonna do with your quiet hours, when there's nothing left but plastic flowers?"[19] The ferocity of Gunter's attack stung the timber industry. As one exasperated timber official proclaimed, "He whipsawed us to death."[20]

Although Gunter's herculean efforts gained reams of publicity, his antics created a reservoir of ill-feelings between the timber firms and the preservationists. His tirades hardened the timber firms' position and prevented any meaningful negotiations between the Texas Forest Association and the Big Thicket Association. Some timber officials simply believed that Gunter could not be trusted, and they made no attempts to compromise with him.[21] The timber industry firmly believed that they had been a positive force in saving the Texas forests from total annihilation. Indeed, the timber firms had been among the first conservation groups in the state, and they bitterly resented being called villains, rapists, and butchers of the wilderness. The timber firms could muster impressive arguments to prove that they were concerned with saving the forest. With the aid of the Texas Forest Service, the timber industry had initiated a vigorous program of fire control which saved thousands of acres a year. Additionally, the large firms had largely repaired the damage to the forest caused by the bonanza timber operations of the 1890–1920 period. Each major company had been involved in timber research and a massive reforestation effort to ensure that the Texas forests would survive.[22]

The timber firms tried to initiate their own media campaign to blunt Gunter's charges. However, most of their publications appeared in forestry magazines, and reached a limited audience that already shared their views. The "underdog syndrome" also hindered the efforts of the timber firms in gaining support for their program. To the general public it probably appeared that the multimillion-dollar timber corporations, which owned millions of acres of Texas forest, were persecuting a small, brave band of environmentalists who were trying to save the land from total despoliation. Timing was yet another factor that worked against the timber firms. The United States had entered the "Age of Ecology," and people were more suspicious of firms engaged in extracting natural resources from the earth. The timber firms, however, were also victims of their own folly. By refusing to accept any of the state's proposals for a park, and by their total opposition to a national park, the timber officials made it easy for the preservationists to paint them as the "bad guys" in the Big Thicket scenario. By refusing to compromise with the state government or the Big Thicket Association in the early 1960s, the timber firms had forced the preservationists to seek federal aid to preserve the region at a time when a viable state Big Thicket conservation program could have been achieved.[23]

Gunter's second major goal was to gather accurate information on cutting operations within the boundaries of Eckhardt's proposed national park. Consequently, the Big Thicket Association hired a helicopter to fly a professional photographer over the area to take pictures of newly bulldozed areas. Gunter used the pictures as part of his media campaign. Also, the Association instituted a "timber watch." Members living in the Big Thicket region patrolled the backroads looking for new timber operations within the "wheel of green." If they sighted new cutting areas, they recorded the name of the company and the location of the operation, and sent the information to the news media. As a result, timber firms were constantly faced with adverse publicity whenever they moved into a new region slated for inclusion in Eckhardt's proposed park.[24]

In achieving these two goals, the preservationists followed one ironclad rule: never say anything bad about Arthur Temple, president of Temple Industries. Of the major timber owners, Temple was the most moderate. Although he did not support a large national park, the preservationists felt that Temple was trustworthy. He had agreed to hold bulldozing to a minimum and he believed that portions of the Big Thicket should be set aside for preservation. By praising Temple, the preservationists hoped that he would exercise a moderating influence on the other major timber owners.[25]

While Gunter and the timber industry were flailing at one another, Eckhardt attempted to gain the Park Service's support for his 191,000-acre park. The Park Service, however, refused to endorse the bill. Their experts simply did not believe that the Thicket met the criteria for a national park. Instead, the Park Service advocated a Big Thicket Cultural Park.

Using this totally new concept, the Park Service proposed to honor the forces that had had an impact on the development of the culture of the region, namely timber operations, oil exploration, and farming. Under this plan, the timber firms would be able to continue timber operations in the park under the regulation of the Park Service. Fishing, hunting, and oil and gas exploration were also sanctioned under the plan.[26] Park officials realized that the main problem with this approach was "how to sell" the project to the preservationists since they were "at loggerheads with the cultural entities (logging, oil, and farming industry) that"[27] the Park Service planned to commemorate. One Park Service official predicted, "we can expect that conservationists are not going to fall all over themselves in endorsing our proposal."[28] He was right. The proposal was rejected by the preservationists.

Eckhardt was also having difficulties in gaining congressional support for his plan. A staff member of Senator Bible's subcommittee informed Eckhardt that the Senate would not act on any new Big Thicket legislation until the House of Representatives passed a bill. Additionally, Texas members of the House of Representatives refused to rally behind Eckhardt's bill. However, certain members of the Texas delegation intimated that they would support a 100,000-acre park if Eckhardt would revise his bill to meet this standard. Faced with these alternatives, Eckhardt began to re-draft his measure. To meet the 100,000-acre limit Eckhardt reduced the size of the stream corridors, and completely deleted the 60,000-acre Saratoga Triangle. He hoped that the Interior Department would later acquire the triangle as a wildlife preserve. After revamping the plan, Eckhardt sent the new proposal to the Big Thicket Co-ordinating Committee for its approval.[29]

Many members of the Co-ordinating Committee were shocked at the new measure. The delegates from the Big Thicket Association were particularly disturbed that the Saratoga Triangle had been removed from the bill. Since it was the heart of the traditional Big Thicket, the Association delegates demanded that the triangle be reinstated in the bill. Finally, Keith Osmore, Eckhardt's legislative assistant, met with the Co-ordinating Committee in October 1971, to hammer out a proposal that would satisfy the preservationists and also meet the 100,000-acre figure.

The Co-ordinating Committee almost dissolved in disputes over the compromise. Each wilderness group on the committee had its own special area that it hoped to preserve. Consequently, each organization fought to retain its pet region in the bill. Eventually, after four tumultuous sessions, the committee drew up a new 100,000-acre plan to present to Eckhardt.[30]

After Eckhardt received the Co-ordinating Committee's plan, he incorporated their recommendations in his new proposal. Like his earlier plan, the new measure contained specific locations and designated acreage for each unit. Before he introduced the measure in the House, Eckhardt attempted to unite the Texas delegation behind his proposal. On November 15, 1971, he wrote Senator Bentsen asking him to call a meeting of all House authors of Big Thicket bills. Eckhardt hoped such a meeting would result in a compromise measure that would be introduced in both houses of Congress to assure rapid action on the Thicket.[31]

On November 30, Bentsen responded to Eckhardt's letter. The Senator stated that he was not in favor of such a meeting. Bentsen argued that he favored presenting a Big Thicket bill in general form rather than specifying certain locations. The Senator felt his plan would arouse less opposition from the timber firms. Undeterred by Bentsen's attitude, Eckhardt talked to members of the Texas delegation at their weekly luncheon on December 1, 1971. He spent considerable time with Representative Jack Brooks of Beaumont who was contemplating introducing a companion bill to Bentsen's proposal. Eckhardt left the luncheon believing that the delegates had agreed to meet with him and draft a single bill that they could all support.[32]

Apparently, all the delegates had not agreed on a joint measure, for the next day, December 2, Brooks introduced a companion bill to Bentsen's Senate bill. Eckhardt was shocked and angered. He immediately contacted Brooks and expressed his displeasure. Brooks defended his action, stating that he believed a Big Thicket bill containing no specifically designated areas stood a better chance of passing the House. Brooks also informed Eckhardt that several other members of the Texas delegation had signed the bill as cosponsors. He then invited Eckhardt to cosponsor the measure. A disgruntled Eckhardt agreed to cosponsor the plan, but only because he felt a consensus bill was needed to ensure passage. Eckhardt believed that other Texas congressmen had cosponsored the bill because they mistakenly assumed that he and Brooks had jointly agreed to the provisions.[33] Bentsen hailed the measure as "a major Congressional breakthrough in our efforts to save this magnificent ecological resource."[34] To Eckhardt, it appeared that Brooks and Bentsen had worked in tandem to frustrate his plan.

Nevertheless, Eckhardt pressed forward, and on December 15, 1971, submitted his own 100,000-acre park bill, containing designated acreages, to the House. Two other Texans, James Wright and John Young, cosponsored the measure.[35] After introducing his bill, Eckhardt, in an unusual move, began publicly to criticize Brooks' proposal. In a news release, Eckhardt described Brooks' bill as "an invitation to a lumber interest hornswoggle."[36] He charged that if a Big Thicket bill did not contain specific locations for the units, the timber industry would have a voice in selecting the sites for the park. If this occurred, Eckhardt warned that the park would be composed of "burned over or cut-over swamps and marshes of little value except for frog-gigging."[37]

While Eckhardt and Brooks were trading verbal blasts, Senator John Tower was revamping his own Big Thicket bill. On January 21, 1972, Tower announced that he was inclined to support a park of 100,000 acres that would preserve the ecology of the Thicket, provide recreational opportunities, and yet not harm the timber industry. A Tower aide proclaimed the senator was planning to introduce this bill in the hopes of gaining both the timber industry and preservationist support for the measure. Actually, Tower's revived interest in the Big Thicket was due to the political situation in Texas. Former Senator Ralph Yarborough was hoping to win the Democratic primary and then challenge Tower for the Senate seat in the November general election.[38]

To solidify his position, Tower met with Assistant Secretary of the Interior Nathaniel Reed. Since the elections were approaching, Reed indicated that "the time appeared right for some kind of park area in the Big Thicket." Reed thought that if Tower's Big Thicket proposal became law it would improve the environmental image of the Republican Senator, and help him defeat Yarborough. Reed's ardor for the park cooled after Yarborough was defeated in the May Democratic primary by Barefoot Sanders.[39]

While Tower was re-drafting his Big Thicket bill, Eckhardt and Brooks exerted pressure on the House Interior and Insular Affairs Committee to hold hearings on their bills. Finally, on May 4, the Interior Committee's subcommittee on Parks and Recreations announced it would hold field hearings on Brooks and Eckhardt's bills in Beaumont on June 10, 1972.[40] At 9:00 A.M. on the appointed day, subcommittee Chairman Roy Taylor of North Carolina called the hearing to order. In addition to Taylor, Interior Committee Chairman Wayne Aspinall of Colorado attended the hearing. Congressman Abraham Kazen of Texas, who was a member of the subcommittee, was also on hand to hear the testimony.[41]

Much of the testimony was a repeat of the Senate hearing held in Beaumont in July 1970. Of the forty-six witnesses who testified, eighteen supported the timber industry's national monument proposal while thirty-six favored a 100,000-acre national park. At the hearing, one new group offered testimony on a facet of the proposed park that had been previously overlooked. The group, called the Save Our Homes and Land Committee, consisted largely of individuals who owned homes within the proposed park areas described in Eckhardt's bill. They believed that if the bill became law, they would be forced to sell their property to the government, and would be ejected from their homes, a prospect that they viewed as intolerable.[42]

Homeowners in the Big Thicket region had voiced little opposition during the long debates over the Thicket between 1966 to 1972. However, in February 1972, a letter from the National Park Service spurred several homeowners to organize the Save Our Homes and Land Committee. The letter stated, "Property you now occupy is located within the boundaries of an area under study for inclusion in the National Parks System."[43] The letter concluded by asking the property owners to submit a form to the Park Service outlining the ownership of the land and the estimated value. Unfortunately, several residents misunderstood the letter. Many believed it was an offer to buy their property, and they felt the government was going to seize their homes at any moment. As a result of the homeowners' uproar, the Park Service dispatched a second letter in April apologizing for the misunderstanding, but the damage had been done.[44] The homeowners along Village Creek and Turkey Creek organized and opposed the inclusion of these areas in any park bill. The Big Thicket Association tried to assuage the homeowners' fears. Pete Gunter announced that the Association favored a provision in any Big Thicket bill that would guarantee residents the right to live in the park for the rest of their lives. This information, however, failed to reassure homeowners.[45]

Three witnesses from the Save Our Homes and Land Committee testified against the bill. Congressmen Roy Taylor and Wayne Aspinall became very interested in this new problem. The witnesses claimed that between 200 to 400 families would be displaced if Eckhardt's bill became law. Homeowners claimed that the park would be used only by a few preservationists, and not by the general public. They argued that their homes were more important than the desires of a handful of environmentalists to traipse through the wilderness. Although the congressman remarked that some arrangement could be made to allow the people to live in the park as long as they desired, the homeowners continued to fight against the Eckhardt bill.[46]

At the hearing, Big Thicket Park proponents received additional scientific support. Dr. Paul Feeney and Dr. Thomas Eisner, both biologists at Cornell University, supported Eckhardt's bill. The professors, who were entranced by the Big Thicket's biological richness, had formed the Ad Hoc Committee to Save the Big Thicket, an organization of nearly 1,000 members, most of whom were professional biologists. Feeney and Eisner testified that they had researched in Europe, Africa, Asia, and South America, and concluded that the Big Thicket's biological diversity was unrivaled anywhere else in the "temperate region of the Northern Hemisphere."[47] The impact of their testimony was lessened, however, when both admitted that they had researched in the Thicket for only three weeks.[48]

When the hearing concluded, neither Taylor nor Aspinall voiced their personal feeling concerning the establishment of the park. However, Aspinall announced that the Interior Committee would hold additional hearings on the problem in Washington. He stated that the Washington hearing would be scheduled only after the Interior Committee had received the Park Service's recommendations on the Brooks and Eckhardt bills. The hearing adjourned at 4:00 P.M.[49]

The entire summer passed without the Park Service providing its recommendations to the Interior Committee. Finally, in September, Eckhardt, weary at the delay, began pressing both the House Interior Committee and the Park Service to act on his bill. A staff member of the Interior Committee informed the congressman that the committee could not hold formal hearings until the National Park Service provided its recommendations. The National Park Service, on the other hand, maintained that they could not furnish a firm recommendation to the Interior Committee until members of the Texas delegation reached agreement on exactly what areas were to be included in the park. To complete this bureaucratic shuffle, Eckhardt learned that the Senate absolutely refused to act on the Big Thicket until the House of Representatives passed a bill.[50] The whole legislative process seemed to have ground to a halt. This absurd situation prompted one preservationist to complain, "The Buck Stops Nowhere."[51] Clearly, before any bill could pass the House of Representatives, the Texas delegation would have to agree on the size and location of the park. Such agreement was never reached, and the 92nd Congress expired without further action on the bill.

When the 93rd Congress convened in January 1973, a new avalanche of Big Thicket bills poured from the Texas delegation. Bentsen reintroduced his bill in the Senate, while Congressman Dale Milford of Grand Prairie, a newcomer to the Big Thicket struggle, submitted a 100,000-acre park bill in the House. Also, on March 21, 1973, Bob Eckhardt reintroduced his 100,000-acre proposal, but he had changed the designation from a national park to a national biological reserve. Since the Park Service had never supported the concept of a Big Thicket National Park, Eckhardt hoped the redefinition of his plan as a national biological reserve would win Park Service endorsement. Biological reserves are valued more for their scientific significance, while parks are created for a variety of reasons such as recreation and sightseeing. Also, because development costs were lower for a biological reserve, Eckhardt hoped that this feature would attract more support.[52]

Passage of any Big Thicket bill, however, remained doubtful until freshman Congressman Charles Wilson of Lufkin, Texas, introduced his own Big Thicket proposal on June 13, 1973. Wilson had replaced the discredited John Dowdy as the representative from the Second Congressional District. Since the Big Thicket was almost entirely within his district, Wilson became the key man in the fight to preserve the Thicket. Wilson was not an avid supporter of the Big Thicket; however, he was anxious to reach a compromise solution so he could devote his energies to other issues. During his campaign for Dowdy's seat, Wilson had supported the concept of a park, but he refused to endorse any of the proposed legislation. "Timber Charlie," as some preservationists called Wilson, had worked for Temple Industries prior to his election to Congress. Consequently, many Big Thicket backers were suspicious of the new congressman. Much to their relief, Wilson was moderate in his approach to the Thicket problem. He announced that after he had carefully studied the problem, he would introduce legislation to preserve from 69,000 to 100,000 acres of the Big Thicket.[53]

Before presenting his proposal to Congress, Wilson conferred with several groups. In January 1973, he met with representatives of Kirby Lumber Company, Southwest Pine Lumber Company (a subsidiary of Eastex), and Temple Industries. At the meetings most of the firms privately agreed that they could accept a 100,000-acre park. However, they publicly continued to push for a 35,500-acre national monument. On February 2, Wilson met with Park Service officials, and tried to gain their support for a 100,000-acre Big Thicket National Park and Preserve. Although the Park Service agreed to prepare a map displaying the congressman's proposal, the officials refused to endorse any proposal for a 100,000-acre park. At the time, the Park Service was contemplating recommending the establishment of a 70,000- to 75,000-acre biological reserve to the Interior Committee.[54]

On March 6, Wilson returned to the Park Service headquarters, and announced that he had formulated a new plan. The new proposal called for a 75,000-acre national biological reserve. Apparently Wilson had reduced the acreage because of criticism of homeowners in the Thicket, and in the hope of gaining Park Service support. Wilson, however, was adamant on one point—any Big Thicket proposal was to include a corridor along the Neches River. Wilson believed that the Neches River offered the only true recreational area within the Thicket. Because he felt that most of the reserve would be of interest to only a few environmentalists, he was determined to include the Neches corridor as a recreational region for the general public.[55]

While Wilson was drafting his bill, the National Park Service was conducting internal meetings to finalize their recommendations to the House Interior Committee. On May 22, Nathaniel Reed, assistant secretary of Fish and Wildlife and Parks, briefed Secretary of Interior Roger Morton on the Big Thicket issue. Reed presented two alternative plans to Morton, both calling for a 70,000-acre biological reserve. The first proposal contained seven units but no corridor along the Neches River. The second alternative called for the same units plus an 800-foot wide corridor on the Neches. Inasmuch as Wilson had been insistent on including the Neches corridor in any Big Thicket bill, Morton agreed to the second alternative. Also at the briefing, Andrew Sansom, a special assistant to the secretary, announced that he would be meeting with the major timber firms in Houston on May 31, to explain the program and also to seek their support. In the week between the briefing and the meeting in Houston, the Park Service decided to add an additional 5,000 acres to their recommendation, bringing it in harmony with Wilson's proposal.[56]

On May 31, Sansom and Homer Rouse, another Park Service official, journeyed to Houston and presented the plan to the timber firms. Arthur Temple and his vice president, Kenneth Nelson, were present, as were Mike Buckley, president of Eastex, and Thomas Orth, president of Kirby Lumber Corporation. At the conference, Sansom and Rouse informed the industry leaders that the 75,000-acre figure was "cast in concrete"[57] and would not be changed. Sansom did promise that the Park Service would try to keep the companies' productive pine plantations from being included within the reserve boundaries. The meeting closed on a general note of agreement that the industry would support the 75,000-acre plan.[58]

On June 13, Wilson unveiled his 75,000-acre proposal to the House of Representatives. Wilson had good reason to be confident that his bill would become law. He had the tacit support of the Park Service, which was going to recommend a 75,000-acre biological reserve, and the timber industry had agreed to support the measure. Additionally, because of the custom of congressional courtesy, Wilson felt assured that his colleagues in the House would not pass a bill creating a park in his district without his approval. Wilson realized that the preservationists still supported Eckhardt's proposal, but he knew that once the preservationists found that they could not pass a bill without his support, they would be forced to rally behind his 75,000-acre measure.[59]

Wilson's bill was a masterpiece of compromise, designed to appeal to every interest group affected by the Big Thicket plan. To appease the preservationists, Wilson specified the locations of eight units and two stream corridors. The units were called Big Sandy, Turkey Creek, Hickory Creek Savannah, Beech Creek, Neches Bottom and Jack Gore Baygall, Beaumont, Lance Rosier, and Loblolly. The proposed corridors ran along the Neches River, from Dam B to Beaumont, and along Little Pine Island Bayou connecting the Beaumont and Lance Rosier Units. The projected units encompassed most of the ecosystems that the preservationists hoped to save.[60]

Wilson's bill also stipulated that property owners whose homes fell within the boundaries of the reserve, could retain the right of occupancy until their death or the death of their spouse, whichever occurred last. Wilson hoped this provision would assure the homeowners that the federal government did not intend indiscriminately to cast them out of their homes. Additionally, the bill provided that if a homeowner sold his house to the government, he could lease it back from the Secretary of the Interior for up to a twenty-year period. However, if the owner chose this option, the purchase price of the home would drop five percent for each year of the lease. Wilson purposely excluded the Village Creek area from his bill in order to appease the Save Our Home and Lands Committee.[61]

Wilson attempted to gain sportsmen's support for his measure by allowing regulated hunting and fishing in certain areas of the reserve. To still the protests of county governments and school districts over the projected loss of tax revenue, Wilson's bill stipulated that the federal government would pay the full amount of property taxes lost as a result of the establishment of the reserve. Payment of such revenue was to continue for twenty years. Wilson reasoned that this provision would allow the county governments and school districts ample time to find new sources of tax revenue for their programs.[62]

Just two weeks after Wilson introduced his plan, the subcommittee on Parks and Recreations announced that hearings on the Big Thicket would be held in Washington on July 16 and 17.[63] Once the hearing dates were established, Wilson began lining up prospective witnesses who would support his proposal. He phoned an official of Kirby Lumber Corporation, and suggested that the timber industry should procure witnesses from labor unions, the academic and business communities, as well as individuals from hunting clubs, and homeowners' associations, to testify for his measure. Wilson cautioned that such witnesses should be responsible people who "feel that 35,000 [acres] is enough to set aside and over 75,000 is too much to set aside."[64]

Wilson's hope for fast passage of his bill was quickly dashed. Just four days before the hearing was scheduled to convene, Alan Steelman, a freshman Republican Congressman from Ft. Worth, introduced a Big Thicket measure calling for a 100,000-acre National Biological Reserve. Wilson had reason to be concerned. Since Steelman was a member of the House Interior Committee, and also a member of the subcommittee on Parks and Recreation, he was in a position to damage Wilson's bill. Steelman's bill was cosponsored by eleven members of the House Interior Committee. Clearly the Republican intended to have a major voice in formulating any Big Thicket legislation.[65] Steelman's measure resembled Bob Eckhardt's proposal but with one major difference. The Republican congressman's bill contained a proposal for "legislative taking" of the reserve's land. Normally, land in a national park or reserve is acquired over a number of years. Title to the land remains with the owner until the land is purchased by the government. During the interim between the passage of the bill and purchase of the land, the owner is free to use his land in any manner he desires. However, under the concept of "legislative taking," title to the land is immediately transferred to the government. Payment to property owners is deferred until Congress appropriates the money. Steelman believed that "legislative taking" was necessary in order to keep timber owners from cutting large tracts of timber during the period between passage of the bill and actual purchase of the land.[66]

The fatal blow to Wilson's hopes for quick passage of his bill came from the Department of the Interior. On July 14, just two days before the hearings were to open, Roy Taylor, chairman of the Parks and Recreation Subcommittee, received a letter from the Interior Department stating that they recommended a biological reserve of only 68,000 acres. The new figure was reached by deleting 7,000 acres of stream corridors, including the corridor along the Neches River. The Interior Department had been forced to renege on their 75,000-acre proposal because the Office of Management and Budget objected to the cost of the reserve. By removing the corridors, the purchase price of the reserve dropped from $60 million to $47 million.[67]

When the hearing opened on July 16, every politician who had introduced a Big Thicket bill in the 93rd Congress offered testimony. Steelman, Wilson, and Eckhardt all testified for their respective measures. Senators Bentsen and Tower both indicated that they favored a 100,000-acre biological reserve; but neither man endorsed any House bill. Congressman Dale Milford, who had presented his own Thicket legislation, deferred to Eckhardt's bill. Representative Jack Brooks, on the other hand, testified for Wilson's measure.[68]

Since the proposed biological reserve was almost entirely within Wilson's district, the subcommittee was particularly attentive during his testimony. Speaking against a 100,000-acre biological reserve, Wilson maintained that by supporting a 75,000-acre area he was already endorsing twice as large a preserve as most of his constituency desired. Wilson was adamant on two points. First, he announced that he firmly supported the Neches River corridor that the Interior Department had deleted. He reiterated his belief that the preserve units would only attract a select group of individuals interested in plants and insects. The Neches River corridor, he maintained, would appeal to a wider variety of people, including hunters, fishermen, and camping enthusiasts. Wilson also strongly condemned any measure that included the controversial Village Creek Unit.[69] To underscore his opposition to Village Creek, Wilson commented, "there is more hostility to that inclusion than anything else in the bill."[70] Wilson ended his testimony by asking the subcommittee members to "put yourself in my place, pretend this is in your district and vote accordingly."[71]

Although Wilson opposed the Village Creek Unit, the preservationists were equally determined to include the area in the reserve. Since Wilson's bill only included six of the eight different ecosystems the preservationists were trying to save, they maintained that without Village Creek Unit, which contained one of the two excluded ecosystems, the reserve would be incomplete. One preservationist emotionally described Village Creek as "the jewel of the Big Thicket."[72] Wilson's measure also excluded the prairie ecosystem. However, the preservationists were not disturbed about this oversight because they were negotiating with private landowners to purchase a representative sample of the prairie plant community. Wilson was unimpressed by these arguments, and he refused to change his bill.

After the politicians testified, Taylor called on the Department of Interior to present recommendations. Assistant Secretary Nathaniel Reed attempted to defend the Interior Department's decision to reduce the acreage from 75,000 to 68,000 acres. As Reed took the witness stand and saw the disgruntled faces of the politicians and preservationists, he remarked, "I feel a little bit like those Christians entering the arena in Rome for the first time."[73] In his testimony, Reed affirmed that the Interior Department had dropped the corridor concept primarily because of the cost. He also tried to justify the decision by declaring that the corridors would be used for recreation and not for biological preservation, the primary function of a biological reserve. Reed maintained that inasmuch as the corridors would be used for recreation, the state of Texas should purchase the land along the streams for its citizens. However, under sharp questioning from Congressmen Steelman and Kazen, Reed admitted that the only reason the Interior Department had reduced the acreage was OMB's refusal to endorse more than 68,000 acres.[74]

After grilling Reed, the subcommittee accepted timber industry testimony. James R. Shepley, president of Time Incorporated, testified that his subsidiary, Eastex, supported Wilson's 75,000-acre proposal. Shepley also agreed that Eastex would extend its cutting moratorium to include the areas in Wilson's bill.[75] Apparently, Time Incorporated was beginning to feel the pressure of the environmentalists. Arthur Temple echoed Shepley's sentiment, and claimed that his firm would also extend the moratorium to the 75,000-acre limit. Temple, however, chided the preservationists for calling the timber owners Robber Barons, a label he vehemently denied. He added that it was time to stop the name-calling and to "join hands and be friends."[76] James Webster of Kirby Lumber

Corporation, who was president of the Texas Forestry Association, also endorsed Wilson's proposal and announced that he would try to get all members of the association voluntarily to observe a moratorium.[77]

Before the hearing adjourned, Chairman Taylor informed the audience that the subcommittee would shortly meet on the matter, and try to resolve the differences among all of the bills. However, just a few days after the hearings, Taylor announced that serious consideration of a Big Thicket bill would be delayed until after the August congressional recess. The House Interior Committee was in no hurry to draw up a compromise bill. Taylor and the other members were faced with the distasteful task of trying to reconcile Wilson's firm position with the opposition of Eckhardt, Milford, and Steelman. Fortunately, the subcommittee was spared this chore.[78]

In the late summer of 1973, Pete Gunter joined Bob Eckhardt's staff in Washington for a few weeks. Gunter had just completed a two-year period as president of the Big Thicket Association. Because of his outstanding work, Gunter had been elected president of the Big Thicket Co-ordinating Committee. By the time Gunter joined Eckhardt's staff, he had decided it was necessary to compromise. Gunter shifted from his original hardline position because he felt that the inflationary spiral of the economy in 1973 had shifted attention away from environmental issues. He now believed that if a Big Thicket bill failed to pass in the 93rd Congress, the entire project would die. To forestall such an occurrence, Gunter persuaded Eckhardt and Wilson to negotiate their differences.[79]

On October 4, 1973, Eckhardt and Wilson held a joint news conference and announced that they had reached a compromise. The Wilson-Eckhardt plan called for an 84,000-acre biological reserve consisting of seven units and three stream corridors. The two congressmen simply took Wilson's bill and added 7,000 acres to the Lance Rosier Unit and a 2,000-acre corridor along Menard Creek, a small stream running from the Big Sandy Unit to the Trinity River. The Loblolly Unit, a 550-acre tract of virgin loblolly pine, was deleted in the compromise. The compromise also included a provision for legislative taking. The controversial Village Creek area was excluded in the proposal.[80]

Response to the announced compromise was favorable. Senators Bentsen and Tower congratulated Eckhardt and Wilson for their work.

Texas Governor Dolph Briscoe added his praise in support of the compromise. Wilson also announced that the timber industry would support the settlement. There was, however, some opposition to the new measure. Congressman Steelman announced that he would continue to fight for 100,000 acres, including the Village Creek area, when the subcommittee on Parks and Recreations met to draft the final proposal on October 15. A Steelman aide hinted that the Ft. Worth Republican was miffed at not being consulted by his two Democratic colleagues.[81]

When the subcommittee met to deliberate on the bill, Steelman tried to amend the measure to include 12,000 more acres in the Village Creek area. The amendment failed. Instead, the members endorsed the Wilson-Eckhardt compromise, and sent it to the full House Interior Committee for consideration. Steelman was not easily dissuaded. When the measure was discussed by the full committee on November 13, he again proposed amendments. This time he was more successful. The full committee, at Steelman's request, reinstated the 550-acre Loblolly Unit. After the Interior Committee indicated that it had accepted the compromise, Wilson drafted a new bill incorporating his plan with that of Eckhardt. The new bill included the amendment of the Interior Committee.

On November 15, Wilson, with the entire Texas delegation as cosponsors, introduced HR 11546, entitled "A Bill to Establish a Big Thicket National Preserve." The name was changed from biological reserve to preserve because the Park Service believed it was a more descriptive title for the Thicket. Actually the designation "preserve" was so new that there was not a firm Park Service definition for such a unit.[82] Just two weeks later on November 29, 1973, the Interior Committee issued a favorable report on the bill. On December 3, the House of Representatives passed the proposal and sent it to the Senate.[83]

Wilson had hoped that the preservationists would rally behind the bill. Indeed, the Big Thicket Association's Board of Directors soon voted to endorse the proposal. However, other environmental groups, primarily the Big Thicket Co-ordinating Committee, refused to accept the compromise and continued to agitate for 100,000 acres. Pete Gunter found himself in an awkward position. As president of the Big Thicket Co-ordinating Committee, he had been instrumental in forging the agreement between Wilson and Eckhardt, and now he was faced with the opposition of his own organization. Gunter was in a quandary. If he endorsed the bill, he would lose the support of the Co-ordinating Committee, and if he refused to support the plan, Wilson would be angered. After weighing the options, Gunter chose to support the Co-ordinating Committee. The Co-ordinating Committee then called on Senators Bentsen and Tower to add the Village Creek Unit to the Senate version of the bill, bringing the total acreage to 100,000. By supporting the Co-ordinating Committee, Gunter totally alienated Wilson, who viewed the compromise as the "Holy Grail."[84]

When Wilson learned that some preservationists were urging the senators to add 16,000 acres to his bill, he exploded. "If they raise it one acre," an angry Wilson shouted, "and particularly if they try to put in the Village Creek corridors, I'll oppose it to the very last drop of blood."[85] In fact, Wilson threatened to kill the whole bill if additional acreage were added. Wilson's reaction was predictable. He believed that the preservationists, particularly Pete Gunter, had betrayed him. Wilson had lost some political credibility with his constituency when he compromised above the 75,000-acre maximum he had pledged to support. He was determined not to lose further credibility by accepting a larger Big Thicket bill.[86]

The Senate did not begin its deliberation on the bill until after the Christmas and New Year's holidays. When the Senate reconvened, Senator Alan Bible set February 5 and 6, 1974, as hearing dates for the measure. In addition to reviewing Wilson's bill, Bible also intended to hear testimony for both Bentsen's and Tower's proposals. During his testimony at the hearing, Wilson once again intimated that he might kill the bill if the Senate added more acreage. At one point Wilson stated that he "would advise caution" to those preservationists pushing for a larger preserve.[87] Bible responded, "I understand what you are saying very clearly."[88]

Neither Bentsen nor Tower were impressed by Wilson's implied threat. Both men endorsed a 100,000-acre Big Thicket proposal. Gunter, testifying for the environmentalists, echoed the need for a 100,000-acre preserve. While Gunter admitted that he had helped formulate the Wilson-Eckhardt compromise, he felt justified in trying to gain Senate support for the inclusion of Village Creek because of the ecological uniqueness of the unit.

At one point Bible himself proclaimed that he was favorably inclined to include Village Creek in the final bill. James Webster of the Texas Forestry Association maintained that his organization still supported Wilson's 75,000-acre proposal while Nathaniel Reed of the Interior Department continued to argue for a 68,000-acre national preserve. After listening to the same repetitious arguments of the three prior hearings, Bible adjourned the hearing after stating that he hoped the Senate subcommittee would move on the problem within sixty days.[89]

While the subcommittee was trying to draft the Senate version of a Big Thicket bill, Bentsen and Tower met and drew up their own compromise proposal. The Bentsen-Tower plan dropped 5,459 acres of corridors and added a 14,000-acre Village Creek unit. The Senators then dispatched a joint letter describing their solution to Bible and his subcommittee.[90] On May 16, at a markup session, the Interior Committee ordered that Wilson's bill as amended be favorably reported to the Senate. The committee recommended two major changes in the bill. First, they added a 15,450-acre Village Creek unit, similar to the Bentsen-Tower proposal, bringing the total acreage to 100,000. Also, the committee, at Bible's insistence, deleted the "legislative taking" provision from Wilson's measure. Bible was opposed to "legislative taking" because of the cost. Under "legislative taking," the government was to pay interest to the homeowner at the rate of six percent per annum from the date the property was taken until the homeowner received full payment. Preservationists, on the other hand, argued that "legislative taking" would freeze land prices and prevent speculators from acquiring the land and inflating the price.[91]

On May 23, the Interior Committee reported the measure to the Senate. One week later the Senate passed the bill as amended. When the bill passed, only four senators, including Bentsen, Bible, and Tower, were present. This unusual procedure was allowed under a Senate rule that permitted the Senate to conduct business without a quorum if no one raised a point of order.[92]

Because the Senate and House bills differed, the next legislative step called for a House-Senate conference committee to formulate a compromise acceptable to both Houses of Congress. Since the bill was originated in the House, it was the responsibility of the lower chamber to convene the conference, but due to a variety of reasons, the conference committee never convened. In the summer of 1974 the House was busy discussing the impeachment of Richard Nixon. Also House Interior Committee Chairman Roy Taylor was awaiting Senate action on two other pieces of environmental legislation before calling a conference committee meeting. Wilson's opposition to the Senate measure also contributed to the delay. On one occasion he warned that if the 93rd Congress ended without adopting a Big Thicket bill, it would be the fault of the radical environmentalists.[93]

Eventually, the hurdles to compromise were removed. Nixon's resignation in August 1974, allowed Congress to act on a variety of bottlenecked legislation, including the Big Thicket bill. Additionally, the Senate passed the environmental measures desired by Congressman Taylor. Also, Pete Gunter telephoned both Eckhardt and Bentsen, urging them to accept Wilson's acreage figure. Gunter was finally convinced that a bill would never pass without Wilson's approval. By September, the path appeared to be cleared for final action on the measure.[94]

Instead of calling a conference committee with the Senate, the House Interior Committee simply redrafted Wilson's bill. To appease the Senate, the committee dropped the "legislative taking" provision. In order to soothe Wilson, the measure adopted his 84,550-acre maximum. On September 24, the full House approved the bill as amended, and sent the measure to the Senate. Both Bentsen and Tower agreed to the compromise, and on October 1, the Senate passed the measure without dissent. President Gerald Ford signed the bill establishing the Big Thicket National Preserve on October 11, 1974.[95]

The final bill established eight Preserve units and four stream corridors. (See Map 2.)[96] The bill also offered homeowners within the Preserve the opportunity of remaining in their homes. If the homeowner exercised this option, he could live in his house up to twenty-five years, or until his death or the death of his spouse, whichever occurred last. If the owner decided to remain in his home, the government was to pay the owner "the fair market value of the property on the date of acquisition less the fair market value on that date of the right retained by the owner."[97] For instance, assume that a homeowner with property valued at $15,000 elected to remain in the Preserve. At that time the government would re-assess the value of the property. If the property was re-assessed at $25,000, the homeowner would receive only $10,000. In short, he would be paid only the amount of the increase in the assessed value of his property. Fortunately, only a few homes were included within the boundaries of the Preserve.

The bill stipulated that the Secretary of the Interior could permit hunting, fishing, and trapping within the Preserve. Also, the Secretary was empowered to allow for oil and gas exploration within the units as long as such activities did not endanger the integrity of the Preserve.[98] Finally, the bill charged the Secretary to purchase all land in the Preserve no later than six years from the date of enactment. The bill specified that land acquisition costs were not to exceed $63,812,000. The measure did not, however, offer any federal funds to offset the loss of tax revenue to county governments or school districts once the land was purchased by the federal government.[99]

In all, twenty-eight Big Thicket bills had been presented in Congress between 1966 and 1974. In essence, the final bill was a victory for Charles Wilson. He had forestalled all attempts to create a 100,000-acre preserve. Although his measure did not please the rabid environmentalists or those adamantly opposed to the Preserve, it did satisfy the bulk of his constituency. Without Wilson's support, a Big Thicket National Preserve would have remained only a dream of the Big Thicket Association and its allies.

CHAPTER XI

Conclusion

The Big Thicket National Preserve now moved from the legislative to the administrative phase, but it was a stage no less critical. A shortage of federal land acquisition funds delayed the purchase of all the Preserve units for a number of years. Meanwhile, timber interests, hunters, fishermen, cattlemen, land developers, farmers, and oil prospectors continued to compete for the natural resources of the Thicket until title to the land passed to the federal government. Nevertheless, by creating the Big Thicket National Preserve, Congress ensured that the Big Thicket would continue to exist and to influence, as it always has, the way man lives in southeast Texas.

More than any other group, the Texas congressional delegation must shoulder the responsibility for permitting the struggle over the Thicket to last for nearly a decade. Both the timber industry and preservationists desired to save the timber resources of the Big Thicket, although for vastly different reasons. The desire to conserve the timber resources of the region was a common denominator, which the Texas congressmen could have exploited to forge a compromise solution.

The initial failure of the Texas delegation in uniting behind a Big Thicket measure forced the preservationists and timber industry into stronger than normal adversary roles. When it became apparent that the Texas congressmen and senators were unwilling to act together to solve the problem, both preservationists and timber firms turned to propaganda campaigns in the hopes that an aroused public would bring immense pressure on their congressmen to resolve the problem. The bitterness and divisiveness of the campaign obscured the common objectives of the two groups, and merely served to intensify their differences. The ill-feeling engendered by the contest lingered among the groups, and created a reservoir of mistrust, which could prevent any meaningful cooperation between the preservationists and timber firms for years to come. Of the Texas congressional delegation, only Charles Wilson and Bob Eckhardt worked to achieve the consensus necessary to resolve the Thicket controversy. One of the lessons of the Big Thicket legislative controversy proved to be that if the natural resources of Texas are to be saved for both economic and recreational uses, then Texas congressmen and senators must take a more active role in designing balanced compromises among those factions competing for the land.

On April 26, 1975, the Big Thicket Association gathered at Bill Daniel's Plantation Ranch in Liberty County to celebrate the establishment of the Preserve. The political leaders who had been most instrumental in the battle to save the Thicket, Yarborough, Eckhardt, Wilson, and Price Daniel, were on hand to enjoy the festivities. Over 3,500 people joined in the celebration.[1]

The Association's rejoicing was, in fact, premature, for the assault on the Big Thicket continued even after President Ford signed the bill into law on October 11, 1974. Although the large timber firms maintained a cutting moratorium on Preserve land, many small timber operators continued to log the land in the Preserve units. Since the federal government had merely created the Preserve but failed to secure title to the land, the owners were within their legal right to cut the timber. Some of the preservationists claimed that these new timber operations were "spite cutting" by people who were opposed to the Preserve. However, many of the small timber operators had to cut the wood or go out of business. Unlike the large landowners, they could not afford to wait for several years for the government to pay them for their timber land.[2]

Congressmen Wilson and Eckhardt were particularly disturbed by this newest attack. Wilson, with Eckhardt as cosponsor, introduced a bill in the 94th Congress that called for legislative taking of the Preserve land. Lloyd Bentsen submitted a similar bill to the Senate. Congress, however, was reluctant to act on the proposals for fear of setting a precedent. The legislators reasoned that if they adopted "legislative taking" for the Big Thicket, then other preservationists across the nation would clamor for similar action on their pet proposals. As an alternative, Alan Steelman proposed that the Interior Department exercise its seldom-used power of condemnation. "Condemnation" differs from "legislative taking" in several ways. Under "legislative taking" the entire Preserve would be seized by the government. "Condemnation," on the other hand, allows the Secretary of the Interior to seize only those portions of the Preserve that are in immediate danger of being cut by timber operators or destroyed by real estate developers. As an additional plus, "condemnation" does not require congressional approval. It is an executive power, resting in the Secretary of the Interior.[3]

In addition to the continuing human assault on the Preserve, insects have also attacked the region. By the time the Preserve was established, the southern pine beetle infestation in East Texas had reached alarming proportions. The southern pine beetle is the most serious pest in the southern pine forest. The beetle, which bores into the bark of pine trees, carries a blue stain fungus which attacks the sapwood, killing the tree. If left uncontrolled, the pine beetle will spread over thousands of acres. Paradoxically, and unsettling to the preservationists, the most effective method of controlling the pest calls for the immediate cutting and removal of all infested trees.[4]

The pine beetle had existed within the Big Thicket for a number of years. An aerial survey of the region by the U.S. Forest Service in 1973 revealed heavy pine beetle infestations in the Lance Rosier, Turkey Creek, Big Sandy, and Beech Creek units of the Preserve. By 1975, the infestation had reached crisis proportions, and the Texas Forest Service ordered some of the timber firms to cut their beetle-infested trees. Several acres within the Preserve were cut to prevent the pest from spreading to adjacent woodlands. Predictably, the Big Thicket Association protested the salvage operations. The preservationists maintained that the destruction caused by the beetle was preferable to the damage inflicted on the Preserve by the salvage operations. One preservationist maintained that up to 1,000 acres in the 4,856-acre Beech Creek Unit were destroyed by timber firms attempting to eradicate the pine beetle. In all, Park Service officials estimated that from October 1974, to January 1975, approximately 2,500 to 3,000 acres of the Preserve were destroyed by small timber operators, real estate developers, and pine beetle salvage operations. Preservationists argued that the figure was nearer 4,000 acres.[5]

In an effort to halt the so-called "spite cutting" and salvage operations against the pine beetle, the Big Thicket Association united behind the "legislative taking" bills of Eckhardt, Wilson, and Bentsen. They were joined in this venture by the large timber firms. This "strange alliance" of erstwhile enemies was predicated on self-interest. The preservationists naturally supported "legislative taking" in order to stop the cutting of Preserve land. The timber companies, on the other hand, wanted the federal government to seize title to the land to relieve them of the tax burden and to hasten the transfer of title. The Kirby Lumber Corporation alone paid over $117,000 in taxes between 1967 and 1976, on Preserve land that they had agreed not to cut.[6]

Shortly after President Ford signed the bill creating the Preserve, the National Park Service opened Preserve headquarters in Beaumont. Park Service officials quickly began drawing boundaries for the Preserve, which were published in the *Federal Register* on March 17, 1975. Additionally, the Park Service initiated a survey of property owners within the Preserve. Once the owners were identified, negotiations for land acquisition began. In the negotiating process, the National Park Service had a professional appraiser assess the property. Next, the government made an offer to the owner. If the owner accepted the offer, he received his money, and title to the property was transferred to the government. However, if the landowner contested the offer, the price for the property was settled in court.[7]

The Big Thicket National Preserve became the only entity composed of widely dispersed units within the entire National Parks System; and this configuration presented many managerial problems for the National Park Service. Preserve officials believed that it would be nearly impossible to patrol the miles of narrow corridors to insure that hunters, timber owners, or cattle did not illegally wander onto Preserve land. The smallness of some of the units within the Preserve also presented more problems. Of particular concern was the 550-acre Loblolly Unit and the Hickory Creek Savannah Unit of 668 acres. Such small units would be unable to survive heavy tourist traffic. Preservationists realized that a large influx of tourists could alter the fragile ecosystems that they were trying to preserve, but as one president of the Big Thicket Association states, "anything is better than a bulldozer."[8] To forestall such an occurrence, Preserve officials would be forced to monitor the units carefully to determine how many tourists the resources could tolerate and still survive. If tourist pressure were to become too great, then selective units of the Preserve were to be closed to insure their survival.

Preserve officials established a priority for acquiring the units. Since Hickory Creek Savannah Unit was being rapidly decimated by real estate developers, it was scheduled to be the first unit acquired. Next was to be the Beech Creek Unit, the site of heavy pine beetle salvage and control operations. Other units were to be acquired in relation to the threats to their survival. The first Preserve unit was slated to open April 1, 1977, and the Preserve was scheduled to be fully operational by October 11, 1980. Eventually, forty employees were to be utilized to ensure that the Preserve was properly maintained. The primary policy of Preserve officials was and continues to be the protection of the flora of the region. There was to be little recreational development within the Preserve except along the Neches River.[9]

The establishment of the Preserve served as an elixir for the Big Thicket Association. Proud of its accomplishments, the Association emerged from the ten-year struggle determined to continue its efforts to acquire even more land. The Association established a "Save an Acre" project to purchase small tracts of land that contained the ecosystems that were not included in Wilson's bill. Land acquisition funds for their project were boosted by two gifts totaling $13,900 from two anonymous donors. These and other donations enabled the Association to purchase thirty acres of longleaf pine and a seven-acre tract of virgin prairie.[10]

The Association also urged the Texas government to establish a small state park in the Thicket. The Association hoped to persuade the state to locate the park in the Village Creek area to insure the protection of the arid-sandyland plant community. Also, since the National Park Service was not going to provide large-scale camping facilities in the Preserve, the Association asked the Texas Parks and Wildlife Department to secure land for camping purposes.[11]

In addition to these projects, the Association hoped to rejuvenate the Big Thicket Museum at Saratoga. The Association planned to make the museum an educational center to instruct area students in natural history and ecology. In addition, the museum was to house numerous displays to interpret the Big Thicket to the public. The Association planned to provide a home at Saratoga for scholars, artists, poets, and writers. The preservationists believed that such a home in this wilderness surrounding would offer some creative inspiration to these intellectuals. Additionally, the Association continued to maintain its traditional "watchdog" role on the timber firms until the Preserve was completely owned by the government.[12] At the first sign of renewed cutting in the Preserve, one preservationist announced, "We can howl our heads off."[13] Spurred on by the past success of the Association, and its ambitious plans for the future, the active membership rolls rose to over 900 by mid-1975.[14]

Following the establishment of the Preserve, the large timber firms displayed some willingness to cooperate with the Big Thicket Association in order to insure that the Preserve land was not cut. In one instance, Arthur Temple, whose firm merged with Eastex in March 1974, announced that Temple-Eastex would not cut a 410-acre tract of timber it had purchased within the Preserve. The land had been purchased before the final boundaries were published, and Temple-Eastex had believed the tract would be outside the Preserve. However, once the firm learned of its mistake Temple announced, "We paid $34,000 for the timber but we would rather lose the money than cut the trees."[15] After Arthur Temple became chairman of Temple-Eastex, the rhetoric between preservationists and timber operators cooled. Temple became a moderating influence. Large timber firms started notifying the Big Thicket Association and other preservationist organizations before they undertook pine beetle control measures on Preserve land. Preservationists were invited to witness the salvage operations to see firsthand that the pine beetle threat was not merely a ruse to log the area.[16] The heated passions and distrust kindled by the battles over the Big Thicket were slowly dampened.

The political struggle over the Big Thicket presents a case study of the conflicting rural and urban views of wilderness and its value. It is significant that the strongest political support for the Thicket came from politicians from urban areas. Ralph Yarborough of Austin, Bob Eckhardt and Lloyd Bentsen of Houston, Alan Steelman of Ft. Worth, and Jack Brooks of Beaumont were the leading proponents of a large preserve. Their constituency lived and worked in the glass and steel confines of metropolitan Texas. Undoubtedly, many of these people savored a few days' contact with a wilderness environment to escape the crime, pollution, and other pressures of urban living. To such people, the Big Thicket region offered a place to commune with nature and to refresh the spirit. Most of them probably did not grasp the ecological significance of the area, but they realized that if the Thicket perished, there would be one less region offering an escape-valve for city life. As the Thicket shrank, more and more city dwellers became concerned, and the urban congressmen responded to their pleas to save the Thicket.

Politicians such as Wilson and Dowdy represented the rural values of their constituency. Most of the lifelong residents of the Big Thicket did not view the region with the same reverence as those people who lived in the urban environment. To the inhabitants of the region, the Big Thicket represented an economic livelihood. Logging was the life blood of the economy in many East Texas towns, and preservation was only the concern of those who were economically secure. Since many of the people were lifelong residents of the region, they took the Big Thicket and the surrounding forest for granted. It had always been there, and in their view it would continue to exist without federal government action. Since they were not subjected to the same pressures as their urban counterparts, they could not understand the "hue and cry" to save something that was commonplace to them.

Additionally, the battle over the Big Thicket represented a microcosm of the land-use struggle in the United States. Spurred on by a growing Texas population, the competition for land in the Big Thicket became more intense during the 1960s and early 1970s. Four competing groups wanted the land for their use. Farmers in the southern region of the Thicket wanted to clear the area to make room for more rice fields; real estate

167

operators wanted to develop and sell the land to people seeking to purchase their very own acre of wilderness. Timber companies, fearful of shrinking timber supplies, fought desperately to retain their holdings. Preservationists, seeking to remove the land entirely from man's influences, were uncompromising in their idealism.

Although these four groups were competing for the land, the major struggle was really a contest between timber owners and preservationists. More than any other issue, the multiple-use concept represented the primary philosophical and economic gap separating the timber firms from those seeking to preserve the Thicket. The foresters believed that the Big Thicket should be utilized for a multitude of purposes such as wood production, erosion and flood control, grazing, and hunting. The main motive of the Texas timber industry was to manage the Thicket so as to produce the greatest amount of wood products from the smallest acreage at the lowest possible cost. To the timber men it was anathema to set aside such a large section of land strictly for the single-use of preservation.

The preservationists maintained that the Big Thicket should be allowed to develop its own unique characteristics without the intrusive influence of man. Left alone, much of the Preserve will eventually revert to the hardwood forest that greeted the Anglo settlers who ventured into the region in the 1820s. To the preservationists, the Big Thicket was more than just a place to grow wood products or graze cattle. It was a place to breathe fresh air, and to enjoy a few hours of peaceful solitude away from the pressures of industrial America. Also, the preservationists viewed the Thicket as one of the last remaining symbols in Texas of man's struggle with the wilderness, a struggle which many people believe was one of the dominant influences in molding the American character.

The preservationists prevailed because they were better able to translate their philosophy into understandable terms for the general public. They were aided in their cause by the rising "environmental consciousness" of the American people in the 1960s and 1970s. The failure of the timber firms hinged on their inability to grasp the meaning of wilderness as symbolized by the Big Thicket, or to appreciate the impact of this symbolism on the urban Texas mind. The preservationists convinced the Texas people that to lose the Big Thicket would be to lose either a vital part of

Texas' past, or a needed part of Texas' future, and to do either was un-thinkable.

NOTES TO CHAPTERS I–IX

Notes to Chapter I

[1] Richard G. Lillard, *The Great Forest* (New York: Alfred A. Knape, 1947), 4.

[2] Berton Roueche, "The Witness Tree," *New Yorker,* August 31, 1968, 64.

[3] *Texas Observer* 70 (November 27, 1970), 18.

[4] Ibid.

[5] *The New Encyclopedia of Texas,* ed. Elias A. Davis and Edwin H. Grabe, 2 vols. (Dallas: Texas Development Bureau, n.d.), I:32; *The Handbook of Texas,* ed. Walter Prescott Webb, 2 vols. (Austin: TSHA, 1952), I:160–61.

[6] Frederick W. Simonds, *The Geography of Texas, Physical and Political* (Boston: Ginn and Co., 1914), 52; U.S. Department of Agriculture, Division of Biological Survey, *Biological Survey of Texas,* Vernon Bailey. Bulletin No. 25 (Washington, DC: Government Printing Office, 1905), 107; Texas, University of Texas, *The Natural Regions of Texas,* Elmer H. Johnson. University of Texas Bulletin No. 3113 (Austin: University of Texas, 1931), 62.

[7] Hal B. Parks, Victor L. Cory, et al., *The Fauna and Flora of the Big Thicket Area* (n.p., 1936), 4, 6, 10. The fourteen counties were: Newton, Jasper, Polk, Hardin, Liberty, Tyler, Angelina, Montgomery, San Jacinto, Grimes, Walker, Trinity, San Augustine, and Sabine.

[8] Hal B. Parks, "The Big Thicket," *Texas Geographic Magazine* 2 (Summer 1938): 17.

[9] Aline House, *The Big Thicket: Its Heritage* (San Antonio: Naylor, 1967), 74.

[10] Claude A. McLeod, *The Big Thicket Forest of Eastern Texas, A Brief Historical, Botanical and Ecological Report* (Huntsville: Sam Houston State University, 1972), 2, 15–17.

[11] Geraldine Watson, "The Big Thicket, An Ecological Summary" (unpublished manuscript, n.d.), 1.

[12] *Texas Observer* 62 (November 27, 1970): 18.

[13] Parks and Cory, *Fauna and Flora*, 11.

[14] Ibid.

[15] Claude A. McLeod, *The Big Thicket of East Texas: Its History, Location and Description* (Huntsville: Sam Houston Press, 1967), 8.

[16] Ibid., 30–31.

[17] Ibid., 9.

[18] Ibid., 10. For a list of the major subordinate trees and lowerstory plants see pages 10–11.

[19] Pete Gunter, *The Big Thicket: A Challenge for Conservation* (Austin and New York: Jenkins, 1971), 48.

[20] For example, see Howard Bloomfield, "Big Thicket, The Biological Crossroads of America," *American Forest* 78 (September 1972): 24–27, 45–46; and Orrin H. Bonney, "Big Thicket—Biological Crossroads of North America," *Living Wilderness* 33 (Summer 1969): 19–21.

[21] Edwin W. Teale, "Big Thicket, Crossroads of Nature," *Audubon* 73 (May 1971): 12.

[22] Ibid.

[23] Watson, "Big Thicket," 3.

[24] Bloomfield, "The Biological Crossroads of America," 26; Teale, "Crossroads of Nature," 25.

[25] Parks, "The Big Thicket," 17; Texas, Texas Agricultural Experiment Station, *The Soils of Texas*, William T. Carter. Bulletin No. 431 (n.p., 1931), 15, 35, 43.

[26] T. C. Richardson, *East Texas: Its History and Its Makers* (New York: Lewis Historical Publishing, 1940), I:29–30; *The Natural Regions of Texas*, 61. Also see figure number three located in the pocket at the end of this bulletin.

[27] U.S. Department of Agriculture, Bureau of Chemistry and Soils, *Soil Survey of Polk County, Texas*, H. H. Smith, T. C. Reitch, and others. Bulletin

No. 36 (Washington: Government Printing Office, 1930), 3, 16; Watson, "Big Thicket," chapter entitled "Arid Sandyland," 1; Pete Gunter, "The Big Thicket," *Living Wilderness* 31 (Autumn 1967): 5.

[28] Public Law 93-439, 93 Congress, 2 sess., HR 11546, October 11, 1974.

[29] U.S. Congress, Senate, Committee on Interior and Insular Affairs, *Big Thicket National Preserve, Texas, Report to Accompany H.R. 11546*, 93 Cong., 2 Sess., 1974, S. Rept. 93-875, 4-5; Public Law 93-439, 93 Congress, HR 11546, October 11, 1974; U.S. Department of the Interior, National Park Service, *The Big Thicket National Preserve*, Pamphlet No. 681-103 (Washington, DC: Government Printing Office, 1976), np.

[30] U.S. Congress, Senate, *Report to Accompany H.R. 11546*, 3; Big Thicket Co-ordinating Committee and Big Thicket Association, prep., "Big Sandy Unit," in *Big Thicket National Preserve, A Report to National Park Service* (n.p., 1975), 1-6; U.S. Department of the Interior, National Park Service, *The Big Thicket*, Pamphlet No. 681-103, n.p.

[31] U.S. Congress, Senate, *Report to Accompany H.R. 11546*, 3-4; BTCC, and BTA, prep., "'Hickory Creek Savannah Unit," in *Big Thicket National Preserve, A Report to National Park Service*, 1-2; BTCC and BTA, prep., "Loblolly Unit" in ibid., 1-2; Public Law 93-439, 93 Congress, HR 11546, October 11, 1974, 1.

[32] BTCC and BTA, prep., "Turkey Creek Unit" in *Big Thicket National Preserve, A Report to National Park Service*, 1-4; BTCC and BTA, prep., "Beech Creek Unit," in ibid., 1–4; U.S. Department of the Interior, National Park Service, *The Big Thicket National Preserve*, Pamphlet No. 681-103, n.p.

[33] Public Law 93-439, 93 Congress, HR 11546, October 11, 1974, 1–2; U.S. Congress, Senate, *Report to Accompany H.R. 11546*, 4.

[34] BTCC and BTA, prep., "Neches Bottom and Jack Gore Baygall Unit," in *Big Thicket National Preserve, A Report to National Park Service*, 1–7; BTC and BTA, prep., "Beaumont Unit," in ibid., 1–4 ; U. S. Department of Interior National Park Service, *The Big Thicket National Preserve*, Pamphlet No. 681-103, n.p.; U.S. Congress, Senate, *Report to Accompany H.R. 11546*, 16.

Notes to Chapter II

[1] U.S. Smithsonian Institution, Bureau of American Ethnology, *The Indian Tribes of North America*, John R. Swanton, Bulletin No. 145 (Washing-

ton, DC: Government Printing Office 1952), 315. The Tejas Indians were also called the Assinay and Cenis Indians.

[2] Mrs. Lee C. Harby, "The Tejas: Their Habits, Government and Superstition," *Annual Report of the American Historical Association for the Year 1894* (Washington, DC: Government Printing Office, 1895), 63. The tribes that composed the Hasinai or Tejas Confederation were: the Anadarko, Guasco, Hainai, Nebedaches, Nacochau, Nacanish, Nacao, Nacogdoches, Nacono, Namidish, Nasoni, Nechaui, and Neches. For their location see Smithsonian, *The Indian Tribes of North America*, 315–16.

[3] Harby, "The Tejas," 75; William T. Chambers, "The Redlands of Central East Texas," *Texas Geographic Magazine* 5 (August 1941): 3.

[4] Mattie A. Hatcher, trans., "Description of the Tejas or Asinai Indians, 1691–1722," *Southwestern Historical Quarterly* 30 (January–June 1927): 209.

[5] Ibid., 31 (July 1927): 55.

[6] Smithsonian, *The Indian Tribes of North America*, 198; W. W. Newcomb, Jr., *The Indians of Texas from Prehistoric to Modern Times* (Austin: University of Texs Press, 1961), 328; Marvin C. Burch, "The Indigenous Indians of the Lower Trinity Area of Texas," *Southwestern Historical Quarterly* 60 (July 1956): 39.

[7] Smithsonian, *Indian Tribes of North America*, 308; Burch, "The Indigenous Indians," 49.

[8] U.S. Smithsonian Institution, Bureau of American Ethnology, *The Indians of the Southeastern United States*, John R. Swanton, Bulletin No. 137 (Washington, DC: Government Printing Office, 1969), 820–21.

[9] Burch,"The Indigenous Indians," 41; J. E. Pearce, "The Archaeology of East Texas," *American Anthropologist* 34 (March 1932): 679; Smithsonian, *Indians of the Southeastern United States*, 96.

[10] Smithsonian, *Indian Tribes of North America*, 316; U.S. Smithsonian Institution, *The Aboriginal Population of America North of Mexico*, James Mooney, Smithsonian Miscellaneous Collection 80, No. 7, Publication No. 2955 (Washington, DC: Government Printing Office, 1928), 12–13.

[11] U.S. Smithsonian Institution, Bureau of American Ethnology, *Early History of the Creek Indians*, John R. Swanton, Bulletin No. 73 (Washington, DC: Government Printing Office, 1922), 11, 192–93, 196, 198; Harriet Smithers, "The Alabama Indians of Texas," *Southwestern Historical Quarterly* 36 (October 1932): 85.

[12] Smithsonian, *Early History of the Creek Indians*, 198–204.

[13] Smithers, "The Alabama Indians," 89–90; Prairie View Malone, *Sam Houston's Indians* (San Antonio: Naylor, 1960), 12.

[14] Burch, "The Indigenous Indians," 50; Smithsonian, *Early History of the Creek Indians*, 199.

[15] U.S. Smithsonian Institution, Bureau of American Ethnology, *Handbook of American Indians North of Mexico*, ed. Frederick W. Hodge, Bulletin No. 30, 2 vols. (Washington, DC: Government Printing Office, 1907), I:43.

[16] Smithers, "The Alabama Indians," 92.

[17] Ibid., 94–95, 100; Malone, *Sam Houston's Indians*, 27–28; Smithsonian, *Early History of the Creek Indians*, 206–8.

[18] Howard N. Martin, "Texas Redskins in Confederate Gray," *Southwestern Historical Quarterly* 70 (April 1967): 588–89.

[19] Ibid., 591.

[20] Smithers, "The Alabama Indians," 104–6.

[21] Ibid.; U.S. Congress, House, *Alabama Indians of Texas: Report of William Toker and Letters to the Indian Department Relative to the Alabama Indians of Texas*, H. Doc. 866, 62nd Cong., 2 Sess., 1912, 11–12.

[22] J. C. Feagin to C. A Culberson, January 18, 1912; C.A. Culberson to Samuel Adams, February 15, 1912, H. Doc. 866, 62 Cong., 2 Sess., 1912, 11–12.

[23] Samuel Adams to C. A. Culberson, February 15, 1912, H. Doc. 866, 62 Cong., 2 Sess., 15-16.

[24] J. C. Feagin to C. A Culberson, February 19, 1912; J. C. Feagin to C. A Culberson, April 9, 1912, H. Doc. 866, 62 Cong., 2 Sess., 14-15.

[25] J. H. Stephen to Samuel Adams, May 1, 1912; Samuel Adams to J. H. Stephens, May 1, 1912, H. Doc. 866, 62 Cong., 2 Sess., 3-4.

[26] Malone, *Sam Houston's Indians*, 45, 47–52; Dorman Winfrey, Rupert Richardson, et al., *Indian Tribes of Texas* (Waco: Texian, 1971), 13.

[27] Winfrey, *Indian Tribes of Texas*, 13; Tim Lane, "East Texas Indians Build Future Out of the Past," *East Texas* 39 (March 1965): 8.

Notes to Chapter III

[1] Carlos E. Castaneda, *Our Catholic Heritage in Texas, 1519-1936*, vol. 1, *The Mission Era: The Finding of Texas, 1519–1699* (Austin: Von Boeckmann-Jones, 1936): 289–96; Herbert E. Bolton, "The Location of LaSalle's Colony

on the Gulf of Mexico," *Mississippi Valley Historical Review* 2 (September 1915): 177; Frank W. Johnson, *A History of Texas and Texans*, 4 vols., edited and brought to date by Eugene C. Barker (Chicago: American Historical Society, 1914), 1:2.

[2] George Louis Crocket, *Two Centuries in East Texas: A History of San Augustine County and Surrounding Territory from 1685 to the Present Time* (Dallas: Southwest Press, 1962), 3.

[3] Ibid.; Johnson, *A History of Texas and Texans*, 1:3.

[4] Castaneda, *The Mission Era: The Finding*, 302; Hubert Howe Bancroft, *The Work of Hubert Howe Bancroft, History of North Mexican States and Texas*. 39 vols. (1884; repr., New York: Arno, n.d.), 15:399.

[5] Isaac J. Cox, "The Louisiana-Texas Frontier," *Quarterly of the Texas State Historical Society* 10 (July 1906): 5; Bancroft, *The Work of Hubert*, 15:399.

[6] Bancroft, *The Work of Hubert*, 15:399; Herbert E. Bolton, ed., *Spanish Exploration in the Southwest, 1542–1706* (New York, 1946), 348–49; Crocket, *Two Centuries in East Texas*, 13.

[7] Bolton, *Spanish Exploration*, 357. The Spanish decided to establish their missions among the Tejas because they were the largest and most influential tribe in East Texas. The Spanish knew that if they could control the Tejas, that the French would be unable to penetrate Texas. Johnson, *A History of Texas and Texans*, 1:3.

[8] Bolton, *Spanish Exploration*, 367–69; Castaneda, *The Mission Era: The Finding*, 353; Crocket, *Two Centuries*, 14.

[9] Crocket, *Two Centuries*, 15.

[10] For a full discussion of the re-establishment of the mission see, Carlos Castaneda, *Our Catholic Heritage in Texas, 1519-1936*, vol. 2, *The Mission Era: The Winning of Texas 1693–1731* (Austin: Von Boeckmann-Jones, 1936), 30–67; Crocket, *Two Centuries*, 20.

[11] Castaneda, *The Mission Era: The Winning*, 114–18; Crocket, *Two Centuries*, 24–26.

[12] Castaneda, *The Mission Era: The Winning*, 135, 144.

[13] Carlos Castaneda, *Our Catholic Heritage in Texas, 1519-1936*, vol. 4, *The Mission Era: The Passing of the Missions, 1762–1782* (Austin: Von Boeckmann-Jones, 1939), 46–47.

[14] Crocket, *Two Centuries*, 40; Castaneda, *The Mission Era: The Passing*, 49.

[15] Castaneda, *The Mission Era: The Passing*, 51.

[16] Ibid., 52–55.

[17] Ibid., 72. Crocket, *Two Centuries*, 40–41; Herbert Bolton, *Texas in the Middle Eighteenth Century* (repr., New York: Russell and Russell, 1962), 353; Herbert Bolton, "Spanish Activities on the Lower Trinity River, 1746–1771," *Southwestern Historical Quarterly* 16 (April 1913): 362–64.

[18] Mary McMillan Asburn, "The Atascosita Census of 1826," *Texana* 1 (Fall 1963): 299.

[19] Crocket, *Two Centuries*, 41; Castaneda, *The Mission Era: The Passing*, 223–25.

[20] Lawrence Kinnaird, trans., *The Frontier of New Spain: Nicholas De La Fora's Description, 1776–1768* (Berkeley: Quivira Society, 1958), 168.

[21] Ibid., 169.

[22] Castaneda, *The Mission Era: The Passing*, 231; Kinnaird, *Frontier of New Spain*, 170–71.

[23] Castaneda, *The Mission Era: The Passing*, 242–45; Crocket, *Two Centuries*, 43.

[24] Castaneda, *The Mission Era: The Passing*, 273, 301–2.

[25] Bolton, *Texas in the Middle Eighteenth*, 407, 434–37; Crocket, *Two Centuries*, 53.

[26] Carlos Castaneda, *Our Catholic Heritage in Texas, 151–1936*, vol. 5, *The Mission Era: The End of the Spanish Regime, 1780–1810* (Austin: Von Boeckmann-Jones, 1942), 324–25; Rosalie Fincher, "A History of Liberty County" (master's thesis, University of Texas, 1937), 15–16.

[27] J. Villasana Haggard, "The Neutral Ground between Louisiana and Texas, 1806–1821," *Louisiana Historical Quarterly* 28 (October 1945): 1001, 1020, 1023.

[28] Ibid., 1039–40, 1049–53. Several filibustering expeditions such as the McGee-Gutierrez expedition in 1813 and the James Long expedition in 1819 used the "neutral ground" as a rallying point for their attacks on Texas.

[29] Philip Coolidge Brooks, *Diplomacy and the Borderlands, The Adam-Onis Treaty of 1819* (Berkeley: University of California Press , 1939), 121–22.

[30] Jack Autrey Dabbs, trans. and ed., "Additional Notes on the Champ-d'Asile," *Southwestern Historical Quarterly* 54 (January 1951): 347, 352–54; Brooks, *Diplomacy and the Borderlands*, 121–22.

[31] Brooks, *Diplomacy and the Borderlands*, 123; Dabbs, "Additional Notes," 355.

[32] Haggard, "The Neutral Ground," 1054.

Notes to Chapter IV

[1] Eugene C. Barker, *The Life of Stephen F. Austin, Founder of Texas 1793–1836* (repr; New York: Da Capo, 1968), 26-30, 39-41. Austin began issuing grants in his colony to settlers in November, 1821. Also in November, 1821, Austin commissioned a ship, the *Lively* to carry settlers from New Orleans to the mouth of the Colorado River. Johnson, *History of Texas and Texans*, 1:11–13.

[2] Johnson, *History of Texas and Texans,* 1:14, 17–18.

[3] Mary Virginia Henderson, "Minor Empresario Contracts for the Colonization of Texas, 1825–1834," *Southwestern Historical Quarterly* 31 (April 1928): 296.

[4] Henderson, "Minor Empresario Contracts," 297–98; Barker, *Life of Stephen F. Austin*, 137–38.

[5] McLeod, *Big Thicket of East Texas*, 2–3.

[6] Austin and Josiah Bell, December 6, 1823, Eugene C. Barker, ed., *The Austin Papers* (Washington, DC: Government Printing Office, 1922), vol. 1, pt. 1, 716–17.

[7] Austin to Governor of Coahuila and Texas, August 26, 1824, Barker, *The Austin Papers*, vol. 1, pt. 2, 1034-35.

[8] Baron de Bastrop to Legislature of Coahuila and Texas, March 6, 1825, Barker, *The Austin Papers*, vol. 1, pt. 1, 948.

[9] H. Johnson to Austin, December 29, 1825, Barker, *The Austin Papers*, vol. 1, pt. 2, 1243.

[10] Wanda A. Landrey, "Lawlessness in the Big Thicket" (master's thesis, Lamar State University, 1971), 8–11.

[11] Henderson, "Minor Empresario," 303–4.

[12] Ibid., 305, 311.

[13] Ibid., 306, 309; Anthony Dey and George Curtis to Austin, December 16, 1830; Barker, *The Austin Papers*, vol. 2, 559.

[14] Anthony Dey and George Curtis to Austin, December 6, 1830, Barker, *The Austin Papers*, vol. 2, 559; Anonymous, *A Visit to Texas: Being the Journal of a Traveller Through Those Parts Most Interesting to American Settlers with Description of Scenery, Habits* (Repr.; Austin: Steck Co., 1952), 8.

[15] *A Visit to Texas*, 98; Henderson, "Minor Empresario," 311.

[16] *A Visit to Texas*, 98–101.

[17] Ibid., 102.

[18] Ibid., 103; Henderson, "Minor Empresario," 311–12.

[19] Henderson, "Minor Empresario," 313; Carlos E. Castaneda, trans., "Statistical Report on Texas," by Juan N. Almonte, *Southwestern Historical Quarterly* 28 (January 1925): 177, 206, 208–10; Mary McMillan Osburn, "The Atascosita Census of 1826," *Texana* 1 (Fall 1963): 301.

[20] Castaneda, "Statistical Report on Texas," 207.

[21] A. L. Bradford and T. N. Campbell, eds., "Journal of Lincecum's Travels in Texas, 1835," *Southwestern Historical Quarterly* 53 (October, 1949): 180.

[22] Ibid., 185.

[23] David Woodman, *Guide to Texas Emigrants* (Boston: M. Howes, 1835), iii.

[24] Ibid., 56.

[25] Ibid., 28.

[26] Ibid., 31.

[27] Kate Mason Rowland, "General John Thompson Mason, An Early Friend of Texas," *Quarterly of the Texas State Historical Association* 11 (January 1908): 191; Henderson, "Minor Empresario," 314; Anthony Dey and G. W. Curtis to D. G. Burnet, June 28, 1837, William C. Binkley, ed., *Official Correspondence of the Texas Revolution, 1835–1836* (New York: D. Appleton-Century, 1936), 2:825–27.

[28] Henderson, "Minor Empresario," 314–15.

[29] *An Abstract of the Original Titles of Record in the General Land Office* (Repr., Austin: Pemberton Press, 1964), 129–34; Texas, General Land Office, *Abstract of all Original Texas Land Titles Comprising Grants and Locations to August 31, 1941* (Austin: np, 1941), 1:354–55, 538, 624–26, 708, 768–69, 982; Walter Prescott Webb, ed., *The Handbook of Texas* (Austin: Texas State Historical Ass'n, 1952), 1:132, 867, 906.

[30] George W. Bonnell, *Topographical Description of Texas to Which is Added an Account of the Indian Tribes* (Repr.; Waco: Texian, 1964), iii, 9–16, 22–25; Francis Moore, Jr., *Map and Description of Texas, containing sketches of its History, Geology and Statistics: with concise statements relative to the soil, climate, production, facilities o-f transportation, population of the country, and some brief remarks upon the character and customs of inhabitants* (Repr.; Waco: Texian, 1965), IV A, 89–95.

[31] William Kennedy, *Texas, The Rise, Progress and Prospects of the Republic of Texas* (Repr.; Ft. Worth: Molyneaux, 1925), xx.

[32] Ibid., 193.

[33] Ibid., 194. Some of the other well-known guide books of the period were: Arthur Akin, *Texas: Its History, Topography, Agriculture, Commerce and General Statistics to which is Added a Copy of the Treaty of Commerce Entered into by the Republic of Texas and Great Britain* (Reprint, Waco: 1964; and Orceneth Fisher, *Sketches of Texas in 1840* (Repr., Waco: Texian, 1964).

[34] Dermot H. Hardy and Robert Ingham, eds., *Historical Review of South-East Texas and the Founders, Leaders, and Representative Men of its Commerce, Industry and Civic Affairs* (Chicago: Lewis, 1910), 1: 417, 452, 468; *Texas Almanac and State Industrial Guide, 1974–1975* (Dallas: Dallas Morning News, 1974), 348.

[35] U.S. Bureau of the Census, *The Seventh Census of the United States, 1850, Embracing a Statistical View of Each of the States and Territories Arranged by Counties, Towns, Etc.* (Washington, DC: GPO, 1853), 503–4.

[36] Webb, *Handbook of Texas,* 1:769; Ibid., 2:68, 130, 512, 933; U.S. Bureau of the Census, *Twelfth Census of the United States Taken in 1900* (Washington, DC: GPO, 1901), Vol. 1, pt. 1, 41–42; U.S. Bureau of the Census, *Population of the United States in 1860* (Washington, DC, 1860), 1: 216–17.

[37] Ronald L. Benjamin, "East Texas in the Civil War" (master's thesis, Lamar State College, 1970), 23; Macklyn Zuber, "Fire at the Union Wells," *Frontier Times* 40 (October/November, 1963): 29–62.

[38] Zuber, "Fire," 29, 62; Pete Gunter, "The Big Thicket," *Living Wilderness* 31 (Autumn 1967): 5.

[39] *Twelfth Census,* Vol. 1, pt. 1, 41–42.

[40] Soloman A. Wright, *My Rambles as East Texas Cowboy, Hunter, Fisherman, Tie Cutter,* edited J. Frank Dobie (Austin: Texas Folklore Society, 1942), 158.

[41] Ibid., 159.

[42] Sue Watkins, ed., *One League to Each Wind, Accounts of Early Surveying in Texas* (Austin: Von Boeckmann-Jones, 1964), 192.

[43] McLeod, *The Big Thicket of East Texas,* 4.

Notes to Chapter V

[1] Eugene C. Barker, contr., "Description of Texas by Stephen F. Austin, in 1828," *Southwestern Historical Quarterly* 28 (October 1924): 106.

[2] Rosalie Fincher, "The History of Liberty County" (master's thesis, University of Texas, 1937), 74; Hamilton Pratt Easton, "The History of the Texas Lumbering Industry" (Ph.D. dissertation, University of Texas, 1947), 32, 68.

[3] Easton, "Texas Lumbering," 45.

[4] Fincher, "Liberty County," 75; Easton, "Texas Lumbering," 45.

[5] Robert S. Maxwell, "East Texas Forgotten Logging Railroads," *Texas Forestry* 14 (August 1973): 6; Robert S. Maxwell, "Whistle in the Piney Woods: Paul Bremond and the Houston, East and West Texas Railway," *Texas Gulf Coast Historical Association Publication* 7 (November 1963): 3. Transporting lumber by ox-cart cost approximately twenty times more than by railroad. See Easton, "Texas Lumbering," 68.

[6] Easton, "Texas Lumbering," 36, 57; Frederick Law Olmsted, *A Journey Through Texas: a Saddle Trip on the Southwestern Frontier* (New York: Dix, Edwards and Co., 1857), 373.

[7] Jacob De Cordova, *Texas: Her Resources and Her Public Men* (Repr., Waco: Texian, 1969), 39.

[8] U.S. Bureau of the Census, *Manufacturers of the United States in 1860: Compiled from the Original Returns of the Eighth Census* (Washington, DC: GPO, 1865), 3: 586–87, 594; Vera L. Dugas, "Texas Industries, 1860–1880," *Southwestern Historical Quarterly* 59 (October 1955): 154; James L. Rock and W. I. Smith, *Southern and Western Guide for 1878* (St. Louis: A. H. Granger, 1878), 111.

[9] Maxwell, "Whistle in the Piney Woods," 4.

[10] William Brady, *Glimpses of Texas* (1870. Repr., Louisville: Lost Cause Press, 1964), 26.

[11] Texas, University of Texas, *Railroad Transportation in Texas* by Charles S. Potts, University of Texas Bulletin No. 119, Humanistic Series, No. 7 (Austin: University of Texas Press, 1901), 50–51.

[12] Maxwell, "Whistle in the Piney Woods," 5–6, 9.

[13] Ibid., 10, 11, 17; Easton, "Texas Lumbering," 131.

[14] Maxwell, "Whistle in the Piney Woods," 37, 67.

[15] Ibid., 67.

[16] Robert S. Maxwell, "Researching Forest History in the Gulf Southwest: The Unity of the Sabine Valley," *Louisiana Studies* 10 (Summer 1971): 116.

[17] The railroad was originally named the East Texas Railroad Company, but the name was changed in 1881 to the Sabine and East Texas Railroad Company. Saint Clair Griffin Reed, *A History of Texas Railroads and of Transportation Conditions under Spain and Mexico and the Republic and the State* (Houston: Saint Clair Pub., 1941), 230; House, *Big Thicket: Its Heritage*, 10; Richardson, *East Texas: Its History*, 1:374.

[18] University of Texas, *Railroad Transportation in Texas*, 50.

[19] Reed, *History of Texas Railroads*, 292; Mary Lasswell, *John Henry Kirby, Prince of the Pines* (Austin: Encino, 1967), 52, 63.

[20] Webb, *Handbook of Texas*, 1:966; Reed, *History of Texas Railroads*, 292–93; Lasswell, *John Henry Kirby*, 68.

[21] Texas, Texas Railroad Commission, *Fourth Annual Report of the Railroad Commission of the State of Texas for the Year 1895* (Austin: Ben C. Jones, 1896), 348–49; Ibid., *Fifth Annual Report of the Railroad Commission of the State of Texas for the Year 1896* (Austin: Ben C. Jones, 1897), 266–78; Texas, Texas Forest Service, *Forest Resources of Eastern Texas* by J. H. Foster, Bulletin Number 5 (College Station: Texas A&M College, 1917), 18, 25, 29, 36, 39, 52.

[22] Webb, *Handbook of Texas*, 1: 271, 274, 336, 377, 390, 575, 966, 974; 2:47, 498, 610, 847.

[23] Manager of Mills and Logging to W. T. Hancock, December 17, 1907, Box 112 Kirby Lumber Corporation Records, Special Collections, Stephen F. Austin State University Library, Nacogdoches, Texas. Hereafter cited as Kirby Lumber Corporation SFASU; Reed, *History of Texas Railroads*, 500, 503.

[24] Roger Sheldon, "Texas Big Thicket," *American Forest* 58 (September 1952): 24.

[25] Robert S. Maxwell, "The Pines of Texas: A Study in Lumbering and Public Policy," *East Texas Historical Journal* 2 (October 1964): 77; Robert S. Maxwell, "Lumbermen on the East Texas Frontier," *Forest History* 9 (April 1965): 12.

[26] Maxwell, "Lumbermen," 13; Blueprint of Lutcher and Moore's holdings in Louisiana and Texas, Box 70, Lutcher and Moore Lumber Company Records, Special Collection, Stephen F. Austin State University, Nacogdoches, Texas; Maxwell, "The Pines of Texas," 78.

[27] Maxwell, "The Pines of Texas," 78. During the 1880s, W. T. Carter amassed timber holdings of 300,000 acres near Barnum, Texas, in Polk County. See Flossie Tyson Beck, "Development of W. T. Carter and Brothers Lumber Company" (master's thesis, Stephen F. Austin State College, 1950), 4.

[28] Texas, Texas Planning Board, *A Review of Texas Forestry and Its Industries* (Austin: np, 1937), 11.

[29] Maxwell, "Lumbermen," 12.

[30] U.S. Bureau of the Census, *Report on Manufacturing Industries in the United States at the Eleventh Census: 1890, Selected Industries* (Washington, DC: Government Printing Office, 1895), Vol. 12, Book 13, pt. III, 611; Easton, "History of Texas Lumbering," table between pages 3 and 4.

[31] The longleaf pine generally grew in soil that was too dry to support an understory of plants and subordinate trees. Also the frequent fires in the longleaf district kept the forest floor cleared of any brush, thus giving the longleaf forest its parklike appearance. U.S. Department of Agriculture, Bureau of Forestry, *Forest Resources of Texas*, William L. Bray, Bulletin No. 47, (Washington, DC: GPO, 1904), 21; Texas, Texas A&M College, Department of Forestry, *General Survey of Texas Woodlands, including a Study of the Commercial Possibilities of Mesquite*, by J. H. Foster, H. B. Rrausz, A. H. Leidigh, Bulletin No. 3 (College Station: Texas A&M College, 1917), 15–17. The Big Thicket region contained billions of board-feet of both pine species in 1880. Hardin, Jasper, Liberty, Polk, Newton, and Tyler counties boasted a combined total of over eleven billion board-feet of longleaf and over three billion board-feet of loblolly pine. Texas, Department of Insurance, Statistics and History, *The Resources, Soil and Climate of Texas*, by A. W. Spaight (Galveston: A. H. Belo, 1882), 133, 161, 192, 236, 255, 313.

[32] The loblolly pine was able to grow in association with hardwoods because it was shade tolerant and preferred a moist soil. The longleaf pine, on the other hand, must have sunlight to prosper, and seeks dry soil. For these reasons, longleaf pines are generally found growing in pure stands. TX Dept. of Forestry, *General Survey of Texas Woodlands*, 17–22; US Dept. of Agri., *Forest Resources of Texas*, 20–23; Texas, University of Texas, *The Trees of Texas*, Isaac M. Lewis, University of Texas Bulletin No. 22 (Austin: University of Texas Press, 1915), 34.

[33] U.S. Department of Agriculture, Bureau of Forestry, *Loblolly Pine in Eastern Texas with Special References to the Production of Cross-Ties*, Raphael Zon, Bulletin No. 64 (Washington DC: Government Printing Office, 1905), 79 27–28. Much to the horror of homeowners, loblolly pine that was not kiln-dried was often attacked by a fungus that stained it blue.

[34] US Dept. of Agri., *Forest Resources of Texas*, 19.

[35] Easton, "History of the Texas Lumbering Industry," 154–55; Texas, Stephen F. Austin State University, School of Forestry, *A Short History of Con-*

servation in Texas 1880-1940, Robert S. Maxwell and James W. Martin, Bulletin No. 20 (Nacogdoches: School of Forestry, 1970), 10–11.

[36] James W. Martin, "History of Forest Conservation in Texas 1900-1935" (master's thesis, Stephen F. Austin State University, 1966), 26, 217; Easton, "History of the Texas Lumbering Industry," 44.

[37] US Dept. of Agriculture, *Loblolly Pine in Eastern Texas*, 34–37, 42. The average tie was eight feet long, six inches thick, and eight inches wide. Each tie contained thirty-two board-feet. The tie-maker, who usually produced twenty to twenty-five ties a day, received between eleven to thirteen cents per tie.

[38] As quoted in Martin, "History of Forest Conservation in Texas 1900-1935," 218.

[39] TX Dept. of Forestry, *General Survey of Texas Woodlands*, 18. Martin, "History of Forest Conservation in Texas 1900-1935," 150; Texas Planning Board, *A Review of Texas Forestry*, 21.

[40] *Texas Almanac and State Industrial Guide, 1911* (Galveston: A. H. Belo, 1911), 129.

[41] Ibid.

[42] Martin, "History of Forest Conservation," 36–38, 72.

[43] George Creel, the journalist, was one of the first to refer to the timber operators as feudal lords. See George Creel, "The Feudal Towns of Texas," *Harper's Weekly*, January 23, 1915, 76–77.

[44] Kirby won his nickname because of his tremendous holdings in East Texas. See Lasswell, *John Henry Kirby*, ix-xi.

[45] John Henry Kirby, *Timber Resources of East Texas: Their Recognition and Development* (Chicago: American Lumberman, 1902), 22.

[46] John O. King, "The Early History of the Houston Oil Company of Texas, 1901–1908," *Texas Gulf Coast Historical Association Publication* 3 (April 1959): 5–6.

[47] Lasswell, *John Henry Kirby*, 45–46, 53–69; King, "The Early History," 7.

[48] King, "The Early History," 8–15.

[49] Ibid., table 1, 55. Kirby had originally hoped to obtain sixteen mills, but two owners were asking too high a price, and the oil company only purchased fourteen mills. The mills were located at Beaumont, Orange, Silsbee, Lillard, Call, Kirbyville, Roganville, Sharon, Village Mills, Mobile, Woodville, and Fuqua. Easton, "A History of the Texas Lumbering Industry," 220; Lasswell, *John Henry Kirby*, 80; Maxwell, "The Pines of Texas," 79.

[50] Maxwell, "Lumbermen," 14; Assistant to the President to Mr. F. Bell, May 21, 1902, Box 10 Kirby Lumber Corporation Records, SFASU; William T. Chambers, "Pine Woods Regions of Southeastern Texas," *Economic Geography* 10 (July 1934): 307.

[51] Maxwell, "The Pines of Texas," 79; *Notes on Investigation of Three Texas Lumber Towns* by Peter A. Speck for John R. Commons and Associates. "Reports of the United States Commission on Industrial Relations" from the General Records of the Department of Labor (microfilm, Special Collections, Stephen F. Austin State University Library); Commissary Operations for the Year Ended December 31, 1902, Box 19 Kirby Lumber Corporation Records, SFASU; W. F. Mantooth to G. T. Davidson, July 16, 1920, Box 349 Kirby Lumber Corporation Records, SFASU.

[52] *Notes on Investigation of Three Texas Lumber Towns*. The federal investigator claimed the company opposed incorporation because it would loosen the company's hold on the town.

[53] Maxwell, "The Pines of Texas," 79; *Notes on Investigation of Three Texas Towns*; Ruth H. Allen, *East Texas Lumber Workers: An Economic and Social Picture 1870-1950* (Austin: University of Texas Press, 1961), 117; Aetna Life Insurance Company to Receivers, August, 1907, Box 115 Kirby Lumber Corporation Records, SFASU, 1-2.

[54] Letter to B. F. Bonner, December 23, 1907, Box 115 Kirby Lumber Corporation Records, SFASU, Attached is a wage scale of three companies. *Notes on Investigation of Three Texas Lumber Towns*; B. F. Bonner to W. A. Shields, October 3, 1908; B. F. Bonner to Thomas J. Foster, October 8, 1908, Box 115 Kirby Lumber Corporation Records, SFASU.

[55] *Notes on Investigation of Three Texas Lumber Towns*.

[56] Ibid. For an example of such speculation see B. F. Bonner to W. F. Mantooth, October 17, 1907; W. F. Mantooth to Dr. D. S. Wier, October 17, 1907, Box 115 Kirby Lumber Corporation Records, SFASU.

[57] *Notes on Investigation of Three Texas Lumber Towns*.

[58] Ibid.

[59] Creel, "The Feudal Towns of Texas," 76.

[60] Maxwell, "Lumbermen," 13.

[61] Allen, *East Texas Timber Workers*, 182; Maxwell, "The Pines of Texas," 80; Sangster to all mill managers August 27, 923; Copy of total number of children at Kirby's mills by age, sex, and race, signed by W. N. Sangster, Octo-

ber 15, 1923; J. M. Seale to J. H. Link, December 18, 1923; W. N. Sangster to J. M. Seale, July 10, 1924, Box 280 Kirby Lumber Corporation Records, SFASU.

[62] R. W. Berkman to J. W. Link, December 26, 1923, Box 280 Kirby Lumber Corporation Records, SFASU. Gifts for the children included such items as books, stationery sets, manicure sets, and toilet sets. Sadie and Thelma Biskamp to J. H. Kirby, December 29, 1923, ibid.

[63] File letter to H. B. Hildreth and T. O. Matcalfe, December 1, 1922; R. F. Ford to all mill managers and store managers, December 7, 1922, Box 280 Kirby Lumber Corporation Records, SFASU.

[64] Letter to all mill managers, December 4, 1922, Box 280 Kirby Lumber Corporation Records, SFASU.

[65] Mr. John H. Kirby's Christmas Day Address Over the Radio, December 25, 1922, Box 280 Kirby Lumber Corporation Records, SFASU. All of Kirby's actions were not aimed at enhancing his personal image. On occasions he gave sums of money to Houston and Woodville. In addition, he donated land for a state park and sent many intelligent but poor boys to college. See Maxwell, "The Pines of Texas," 80.

[66] George T. Morgan, Jr., "No Compromise—No Recognition: John Henry Kirby, the Southern Lumber Operators' Association and Unionism in the Piney Woods, 1906–1916," *Labor History* 10 (Spring 1969): 194; Charles R. McCord, "A Brief History of the Brotherhood of Timber Workers" (master's thesis, University of Texas, 1959), 14–16.

[67] McCord, "A Brief History," 18–20.

[68] Ibid., 38.

[69] Allen, *East Texas Lumber Workers*, 180–81; Morgan, "No Compromise —No Recognition," 196–97.

[70] C. P. Myers to all mill managers, August 19, 1911, Box 196 Kirby Lumber Corporation Records, SFASU.

[71] C. P. Myers to mill managers, October 23, 1911, Box 196 Kirby Lumber Corporation Records, SFASU. Also Box 197 of Kirby Lumber Corporation Records contains several letters from mill managers listing union men and union sympathizers.

[72] Ross Williams to J. W. Lewis, September 10, 1911; J. A. Herndon to C. P. Myers, May 10, 1911, Box 197 Kirby Lumber Corporation Records, SFASU; McCord, "A Brief History," 32.

[73] McCord, "A Brief History," 3, 38–64, 96–106.

[74] Maxwell, "The Pines of Texas," 82–83.

[75] Martin, "History of Forest Conservation in Texas 1900–1935," 41; Maxwell and Martin, *A Short History of Forest Conservation in Texas*, 20.

[76] Maxwell and Martin, *A Short History of Forest Conservation in Texas*, 21.

[77] Ibid., 22–24; Bray, *Forest Resources of Texas*, 23.

[78] Maxwell and Martin, *A Short History of Forest Conservation in Texas*, 25–26.

[79] Ibid.

[80] Ibid., 27.

[81] Ibid., 28–29; Martin, "History of Forest Conservation in Texas 1900–1935," 94–95.

[82] Robert S. Maxwell, "The Impact of Forestry in the Gulf South," *Forest History*, 17 (April 1973): 33.

[83] Bray, *Forest Resources of Texas*, 22-23.

[84] *Beaumont Enterprise*, March 20, 1974, section D. In the 1960s, forty-three mills were still operating in the region. *Texas Almanac and State Industrial Guide 1970-71* (Dallas: Dallas Morning News, 1969), 137. The following figures represent the acreage owned by the largest timber firms in the preserve: Temple-Eastex, 27,000 acres; Kirby Lumber Corporation, 12,800 acres; Champion International, 7,100 acres; International Paper, 4,000 acres. The figures were furnished by Thomas Lubbert, Superintendent of the Big Thicket National Preserve.

Notes to Chapter VI

[1] Alexander Deussen, "Oil Producing Horizons of the Gulf Coast in Texas and Louisiana," in *Gulf Coast Oil Fields,* ed. Donald C. Coston and George Sawtelle (Tulsa: American Association of Petroleum Geologist, 1963), 3 .

[2] U.S. Congress, House, *Hearing before a Subcommittee of the Committee on Interior and Foreign Commerce on H.R. 441* 73 Cong., Recess (4 parts, Washington, 1934), II, 1045; William Kennedy, "Coastal Salt Domes," *American Association of Petroleum Geologist Bulletin* 1 (1917); J. A. Udden, "Oil Bearing Formations in Texas," *American Association of Petroleum Geologist Bulletin* 3 (1919): 87.

[3] Ina May Rowe, "A Study of the Development of Oil at Sour Lake" (master's thesis, Southwest Texas State Teachers College, 1939), 33–35.

[4] Ibid., 37–44; Carl C. Rister, *Oil! Titan of the Southwest* (Norman: University of Oklahoma Press, 1949), 8.

[5] C. A. Warner, *Texas Oil and Gas Since 1543* (Houston: Gulf Publishing, 1939), 3; Rowe, "A Study of the Development of Oil at Sour Lake," 52.

[6] U.S. Department of the Interior, U.S. Geological Survey, *Oil Fields of the Texas-Louisiana Gulf Coastal Plains* by W. S. Fenneman, Bulletin Number 282 (Washington, DC: Government Printing Office, 1906), 38; Warner, *Texas Oil and Gas*, 23.

[7] Rister, *Oil!*, 75.

[8] *Beaumont Enterprise*, September 4, 1901, 8.

[9] *Beaumont Enterprise*, September 14, 1901, 2.

[10] Warner, *Texas Oil and Gas*, 190.

[11] *Beaumont Enterprise*, July 12, 1902, 6.

[12] Ibid.

[13] Rister, *Oil!*, 76; U.S. Dept. of the Interior, *Oil Fields of the Texas-Louisiana Gulf Coast Plains*, 39.

[14] Rowe, "A Study," 60–62; U.S. Dept. of Interior, *Oil Fields of the Texas-Louisiana Gulf Coastal Plains*, 39.

[15] U.S. Dept. of Interior, *Oil Fields of the Texas-Louisiana Gulf Coastal Plains*, 39-45.

[16] *Houston Daily Post*, July 10, 1903, 7; Rowe, "A Study," 71, 74–75; U.S. Dept. of Interior, *Oil Fields of the Texas-Louisiana Gulf Coastal Plains*, 45.

[17] Rowe, "A Study," 74–75.

[18] U.S. Dept. of Interior, *Oil Fields of the Texas-Louisiana Gulf Coastal Plains*, 57; Warner, *Texas Oil and Gas Since 1543*, 8.

[19] U.S. Dept. of Interior, *Oil Fields of the Texas-Louisiana Gulf Coastal Plains*, 57.

[20] Ibid.; Warner, *Texas Oil and Gas Since 1543*, 190.

[21] U.S. Dept. of Interior, *Oil Fields of the Texas-Louisiana Gulf Coastal Plains*, 48.

[22] George Sawtelle, "The Batson Oil Field, Hardin County, Texas," *American Association of Petroleum Geologist Bulletin* 9 (December 1925): 1277.

[23] U.S. Dept. of Interior, *Oil Fields of the Texas-Louisiana Gulf Coastal Plains*, 56; William A. Owens, "Boom in Batson: The Birth of an Oil Field," *Drilling* 19 (December 1957): 105.

[24] D. A. Willey, "New Texas Oil Deposits," *Scientific American*, January 30, 1904, 96; *Houston Daily Post*, July 16, 1903, 3.

[25] Rowe, "A Study," 83-34; *Southwestern Reporter* 104 (St. Paul, 1908), 420–24.

[26] Rowe, "A Study," 84.

[27] In 1904, there were 210 miles of pipeline between the three boom towns and Beaumont. *Texas Almanac and State Industrial Guide*, 1904 (Galveston: A. H. Belo, 1904), 155; U.S., Congress, House, *Hearing on H.R. 441*, 73 Cong., Recess, 11, 1192, Texas, Texas Railroad Commission, *Rules and Regulations of the Texas Railroad Commission*, prepared by R. W. Byram (Austin: np, 1937), 1: 7–8; Gunter, *The Big Thicket: A Challenge*, 91.

[28] U.S. Dept. of Interior, *Oil Fields of the Texas-Louisiana Gulf Coastal Plains*, 60.

[29] Texas, University of Texas, *Subsidence in Gulf Coastal Plains Salt Domes* by E. H. Sellards, University of Texas Bulletin Number 3001 (Austin: University of Texas, 1930), 13–28.

[30] Ibid.

[31] *Houston Daily Post*, July 10, 1903, 7; Rister, *Oil!*, 76; Rowe, "A Study of the Development of Oil at Sour Lake," 71; Warner, *Texas Oil and Gas Since 1543*, 196.

[32] Willey, "New Texan Oil Deposits," 96; Rowe, "A Study," 66–67; *Houston Daily Post*, July 16, 1903, 3.

[33] Interview with James Donohoe, August 1, 1952, transcript of tape number 23; Interview with W. H. Bryant, July 29, 1952, transcript of tape number 27, Oral History of Texas Oil Pioneers, University of Texas Archives, Austin, Texas. Hereafter cited as UTA.

[34] L. P. Teas, "Natural Gas of Gulf Coast Salt Dome Areas," in *Geology of Natural Gas*, ed. Henry A. Ley (Tulsa: American Association of Petroleum Geologist, 1935), 707; Interview with William E. Cotton, May 23, 1956, Oral History of Texas Oil Pioneers, UTA.

[35] Charlie Jeffries, "Reminisces of Sour Lake," *Southwestern Historical Quarterly* 50 (July 1964): 32–33.

[36] Ibid.

[37] Rowe, "A Study," 63–64; Owens, "Boom in Batson: The Birth of an Oil Field," *Drilling* 19, 104.

[38] Rowe, "A Study," 64–69; Mody C. Boatright and William A. Owens, *Tales from the Derrick Floor, A People's History of the Oil Industry* (Garden City, NY: Doubleday, 1970), 76.

[39] Interview with James Donohoe, August 1, 1952, transcript of tape number 23; Interview with William E. Cotton, May 23, 1956, transcript of tape number 185; Interview with Frank Hamilton, July 29, 1952, transcript of tape number 33, Oral History of Texas Oil Pioneers, UTA.

[40] Interview with W. A. Owen, July 29, 1952, transcript of tape number 27, Oral History of Texas Oil Pioneers, UTA.

[41] Interview with Mr. and Mrs. V. B. Daniels, July 3, 1952, transcript of tape number 22, Oral History of Texas Oil Pioneers, UTA.

[42] Ibid.; *Houston Daily Post*, July 15, 1903, 2.

[43] Interview with James Donohoe, August 1, 1952, transcript of tape number 23, Oral History of Texas Oil Pioneers, UTA.

[44] Interview with Mr. and Mrs. V. B. Daniels, July 3, 1952, transcript of tape number 22, Oral History of Texas Oil Pioneers, UTA.

[45] Owens, "Boom in Batson," 104.

[46] Ibid.; Boatright and Owens, *Tales from the Derrick Floor*, 95; Interview with James Donohoe, August 1, 1952, transcript of tape number 23; Interview with William E. Cotton, May 23, 1956, transcript of tape number 185, Oral History of Texas Oil Pioneers, UTA.

[47] Interview with James Donohoe, August 1, 1952, transcript of tape number 23; Interview with William E. Cotton, May 23, 1956, transcript of tape number 185, Oral History of Texas Oil Pioneers, UTA; Owens, "Boom in Batson," 104.

[48] Boatright and Owens, *Tales from the Derrick Floor*, 71.

[49] Owens, "Boom in Batson," 106.

[50] Deussen, "Oil Producing Horizons," 6; Rister, *Oil!*, 105; Texas, Texas Railroad Commission, The *Railroad Commission of Texas: Oil and Gas Annual Production by Active Fields* (Austin: np, 1974), 24–34; George H. Fancher, Robert L. Whiting and James H. Cretsinger, *The Oil Resources of Texas, A Reconnaissance Survey of Primary and Secondary Reserves of Oil* (Austin and College Station: University of Texas and Texas A&M College, 1954), 78.

[51] In 1975, the refinery capacity in Texas was 1,881,124,000 barrels of oil per year. *Texas Almanac and State Industrial Guide, 1975-1976* (Dallas: Dallas Morning News, 1975), 415.

Notes to Chapter VII

[1] Eugene C. Barker, ed., *The Austin Papers* (Washington, DC: Government Printing Office, 1928), 2: 678. This volume appeared as Volume II of the Annual Report of the *American Historical Association 1922*.

[2] Gunter, *The Big Thicket*, 69.

[3] Ibid., 71; Hal B. Parks, Victor L. Cory and others, *The Fauna and Flora of the Big Thicket Area* (n.p., 1936), 4–6; "The Big Thicket of East Texas," *Beaumont Business* (May 1938), n.p.

[4] Parks and Cory, *The Fauna and Flora*, 8.

[5] Lois Williams Parker, *Big Thicket Bibliography* (Saratoga: Big Thicket Association, 1970), 14.

[6] Weekly/Monthly Reports for Texas Agricultural Experiment Stations, Field Stations and Laboratories, 1936, San Antonio, State Apicultural Laboratory, Box 12, file 12-36, Texas A& M University Archives and Manuscript Collection, Texas A & M University Library, College Station, Texas. (hereinafter cited as TAMU Archives and Manuscripts.); Annual Reports Texas Agricultural Experiments Stations, 1936 Annual Report of the State Apicultural Laboratory, Box 21, file 21-2, 9, TAMU Archives and Manuscripts.

[7] Annual Reports Texas Agricultural Experiment Station, 1936 Annual Report of the State Apicultural Laboratory, Box 21, file 21-2, 3, 9, TAMU Archives and Manuscripts; Victor L. Cory and Hal B. Parks, *Catalogue of the Flora of Texas* Texas Agricultural Experiment Extension Bulletin Number 550 (July, 1937), n.p.; H. B. Parks to V. L. Cory, July 3, 1936, The Correspondence of V. L. Cory and H. B. Parks (11 vols., n.p.), VI, TAMU Archives and Manuscripts. (Hereinafter cited as Correspondence of Cory and Parks.) The Cory and Parks letters are in hand bound volumes. The volumes are numbered by calendar year. For example, volume VI is 1936, volume VII is 1937, etc. Parks and Cory, *The Fauna and Flora*, 4.

[8] H. B. Parks to V. L. Cory, July 28, 1936, Correspondence of Cory and Parks, VI, TAMU Archives and Manuscripts.

[9] Ibid.

[10] Parks to Cory, August 6, 1936; R. E. Jackson to A. B. Conner, August 5, 1936; Cory to Parks, August 11, 1936, Correspondence of Cory and Parks, VI, TAMU Archives and Manuscripts.

[11] Weekly/Monthly Reports for Texas Agricultural Experiment Stations, Field Stations, and Laboratories, 1936, San Antonio, State Apicultural Labo-

ratory, Box 12, file 12-36; Box 12, file 12-13, TAMU Archives and Manuscripts.

[12] Ibid.; Box 12, file 12-37, TAMU Archives and Manuscripts.

[13] Ibid.

[14] Ibid.; Annual Reports, Texas Agricultural Experiment Stations, 1936 Annual Report of Substation #1, Sonora, Texas, Box 22 , File 22-8, TAMU Archives and Manuscripts.

[15] Parks to Cory, November 1, 1936, Correspondence of Cory and Parks, VI, TAMU Archives and Manuscripts; Parks and Cory, *The Fauna and Flora*, 10.

[16] Parks to Cory, November 1, 1936, Correspondence of Cory and Parks, VI, TAMU Archives and Manuscripts. Parks used the following works in compiling his list: Vernon Bailey's *The Biological Survey of Texas*, published as a bulletin by the U.S.D.A.; *A Checklist of the Mammals of Texas, Exclusive of the Sirenia and Cetacea* by J. K. Strecker; *The Birds of Texas* by J. K. Strecker; *The Fish of Texas and the Rio Grande Basin* by Evermann and Kensall; *The Land and Freshwater Snails and the Naeades or Pearly Freshwater Mussels of Texas* by J. K. Strecker. For the plant list Parks used his own publication, *The Catalogue of the Flora of Texas*.

[17] Parks to Cory, November 1, 1936; Parks to Cory, November 16, 1936, Correspondence of Cory and Parks, VI TAMU Archives and Manuscripts.

[18] Cory to Parks, December 3, 1936, ibid.

[19] Parks to Cory, December 14, 1936, ibid.

[20] Parks to Cory, January 5, 1937, ibid., VII, TAMU Archives and Manuscripts.

[21] Parks to Cory, December 14, 1936, ibid., VI, TAMU Archives and Manuscripts.

[22] Parker, *Big Thicket Bibliography*, 14; Annual Reports, Texas Agricultural Experiment Station, 137 Annual Report of the State Apicultural Laboratory Box 21, file 21-3, TAMU Archives and Manuscripts; *Proceedings of the Texas Academy of Science 1937–38* 20 (Austin, 1938), 7.

[23] James E. Gow, "An Ecological Study of the Sabine and Neches Valleys, Texas," *Proceedings of the Iowa Academy of Science for 1904* 12 (1905): 39.

[24] Ibid., 41–47.

[25] Roland M. Harper, "A Week in Eastern Texas," *Bulletin of the Torrey Botanical Club* 97 (June 1920): 293, 305–6.

[26] Ibid., 307.

[27] Ibid., 309.

[28] Ibid., 307.

[29] R. M. Harper to Cory, February 3, 1938, Correspondence of Cory and Parks, VII, TAMU Archives and Manuscripts.

[30] Cory to Harper, February 11, 1938, ibid.

[31] Ibid.

[32] Gunter, *The Big Thicket: A Challenge for Conservation*, 69; *Beaumont Journal*, June 25, 1937, 1.

[33] *Beaumont Enterprise*, January 22, 1938, 11.

[34] Texas, Texas Railroad Commission, *The Railroad Commission of Texas: Oil and Gas Annual Production by Active Fields, 1974* (Austin: np, 1974), 30-34. Item from *Beaumont Journal* February 17, 1942 in Larry Jene Fisher Collection, Lamar State University Library, Beaumont, Texas; "War Stimulated 20 Percent Rise in Timber Cut," *Texas Forest News* 22 (January–February, 1942): 1.

[35] Carolyn F. Hyman, "A History of Texas National Forest" (master's thesis, University of Texas, 1948), 18, 25–26, 28.

[36] Big Thicket Morgue File, *Houston Chronicle*, February 8, 1954; House, *Big Thicket: Its Heritage*, 80–81.

[37] Big Thicket Morgue File, *Houston Chronicle*, February 8, 1954.

[38] Gunter, *The Big Thicket: A Challenge for Conservation*, 72.

[39] Big Thicket Morgue File, *Houston Chronicle*, June 21, 1959.

[40] Interview with Price Daniel, Sr. Austin, Texas, March 11, 1976. The number of tourists visiting Texas had been declining since 1957. Daniel hoped a strong park system would reverse the trend. The Price Daniel Papers Box 194, file "Texans for Tourist" Texas State Archives, Austin, Texas.

[41] Ibid.; Memo from W. C. Latham to George Stanley, October 9, 1961, Big Thicket File, Kirby Lumber Corporation, Houston, Texas.

[42] Interview with Price Daniel, Sr. Austin, Texas, March 11, 1976. For an excellent sketch of Lance Rosier see Gunter, *The Big Thicket: A Challenge for Conservation*, 87–102.

[43] Interview with Price Daniel, Sr. Austin, Texas, March 11, 1976.

[44] Ibid.

[45] Ibid., U.S. Department of the Interior, National Park Service, *Proposed Big Thicket National Monument, Texas: A Study of Alternatives* (Washington, DC: Government Printing Office, 1967), 1.

[46] *Dallas Morning News*, February 23, 1962, 1 sec. 1.

[47] Interview with Price Daniel, Sr.

[48] *Dallas Morning News*, March 24, 1962, 10, sec. 1.

[49] Ibid.

[50] Big Thicket Morgue File, *Houston Chronicle*, March 27, 1962.

[51] *Houston Post*, March 20, 1962, sec. 1.

[52] Ibid.

[53] Ibid.

[54] Ibid.

[55] Interview with Price Daniel, Sr.

[56] *Houston Post*, March 30, 1962, sec. 1.

[57] Big Thicket Morgue File, *Houston Chronicle*, March 30, 1962; Interview with Price Daniel Sr.

[58] *Houston Post*, March 30, 1962, 12, sec. 1; Big Thicket Morgue File, *Houston Chronicle*, March 20, 1962; *Dallas Morning News*, March 22, 1962, 9, sec. 1.

[59] Interview with Price Daniel, Sr.

[60] Price Daniel to Dempsie Henley and others, October 31, 1962, The Price Daniel Papers, Box 97, file entitled Big Thicket Study Commission, Texas State Archives, Austin, Texas.

[61] Ibid.

[62] Ibid.

[63] Interview with Price Daniel, Sr.; Big Thicket Morgue File, *Houston Chronicle*, November 20, 1962.

[64] Big Thicket Morgue File, *Houston Chronicle*, December, 1962; Dempsie Henley, *The Murder of Silence: The Big Thicket Story* (Waco: Texian, 1976), 40–42; Texas, Report to the Legislature, Governor Price Daniel 1957–1963 (Austin, 1963), 153.

[65] Henley, *The Murder of Silence*, 49–51.

[66] Ibid., 47–48; Gunter, *The Big Thicket: A Challenge*, 72; The Big Thicket Morgue File, *Houston Chronicle*, March 28, 1965.

[67] Big Thicket Morgue File, *Houston Chronicle*, October 22, 1968; Maxine Johnston, ed., *Big Thicket Association's Handbook for Members* (Saratoga: Big Thicket Association, 1970), 25.

[68] Johnston, ed., *Big Thicket Association's Handbook*; Henley, *The Murder of Silence*, 78–82.

[69] Ibid., 98–100.

[70] Ibid., 101, 111.

[71] Ibid., 111–13.

[72] Ibid., 105, 115.

[73] Ibid., 126.

[74] Interview with Dempsie Henley, Liberty, Texas, February 20, 1975.

[75] Ibid.; Henley, *The Murder of Silence*, 129–32.

Notes to Chapter VIII

[1] Interview with Ralph Yarborough, Austin, Texas, February 26, 1976.

[2] Ibid.

[3] Ibid.

[4] Ibid.

[5] Ibid.; *Congressional Record*, 89 Cong., 2d Sess., 27887 (Oct. 20, 1966).

[6] Interview with Ralph Yarborough; Mary Lasswell, *I'll Take Texas* (Boston: Houghton Mifflin, 1958), 229–300.

[7] Interview with Ralph Yarborough.

[8] Big Thicket Morgue File, *Houston Chronicle*, November 2, 1963.

[9] Big Thicket Morgue File, *Houston Chronicle*, July 2, 1963.

[10] Interview with Ralph Yarborough.

[11] Dempsie Henley, *The Murder of Silence*, 138–40; Interview with Dempsie Henley, Liberty, Texas, February 20, 1976.

[12] Henley, *The Murder of Silence*, 140.

[13] *Houston Post*, October 10, 1965, 22, sec. 4.

[14] Ibid.

[15] Ollie Crawford to George Stanley, October 20, 1965, Big Thicket File, Kirby Lumber Corporation, Houston, Texas.

[16] Memorandum to File by George Stanley, November 2, 1965; Ollie Crawford to Thomas Carter, Hugh Patterson, and George Stanley, December 20, 1965, Big Thicket File, Kirby Lumber Corporation, Houston, Texas.

[17] Memorandum to File by John Wood, January 12, 1966, Big Thicket File, Kirby Lumber Corporation, Houston, Texas.

[18] Ibid.

[19] Ibid.

[20] Ibid.; Memorandum from John Herndon to George Stanley, March 7, 1966, Big Thicket File, Kirby Lumber Corporation, Houston, Texas.

[21] Hugh Patterson to Ollie Crawford, Tom Carter, Lud King and George Stanley, undated, Big Thicket File, Kirby Lumber Corporation, Houston, Texas.

[22] Ibid.

[23] Ibid.

[24] Memorandum from George Stanley to James Herndon, February 14, 1966; Memorandum to File by George Stanley, March 21, 1966, Big Thicket File, Kirby Lumber Corporation, Houston, Texas.

[25] Henley, *Murder of Silence*, 202; Memorandum to File by George Stanley, March 21, 1966, Big Thicket File, Kirby Lumber Corporation, Houston, Texas.

[26] Henley, *Murder of Silence*, 202–8; Memorandum from George Stanley to John Herndon, May 17, 1966; Memorandum to File by George Stanley, March 21, 1966, Big Thicket File, Kirby Lumber Corporation, Houston, Texas.

[27] Ollie Crawford to John Connally, March 23, 1966, Big Thicket File, Kirby Lumber Corporation, Houston, Texas.

[28] Henley, *Murder of Silence*, 160–94; Big Thicket Morgue File, *Houston Chronicle*, April 6, 1966.

[29] Henley, *Murder of Silence*, 172–74; Big Thicket Morgue File, *Houston Chronicle*, March 15, 1966.

[30] William O. Douglas, *Farewell to Texas, A Vanishing Wilderness* (New York: McGraw-Hill, 1967), viii–ix, 35.

[31] Ollie Crawford to J. R. Singleton, August 7, 1967, Big Thicket File, Kirby Lumber Corporation, Houston, Texas.

[32] Henley, *Murder of Silence*, 196–97; Texas, Parks Wildlife Department, Transcript of Parks and Wildlife Commission Hearing, Austin, Texas, May 31, 1966, Minute Book Number 7, 25.

[33] Texas, Parks and Wildlife Department, Transcript of Parks and Wildlife Commission Hearing, Austin, Texas, May 31, 1966, Minute Book Number 7, 25-54.

[34] *Houston Post*, June 21, 1966, 6, sec. 4; Interview with Price Daniel, Austin, Texas, March 11, 1976; Memorandum to File by W. R. McDonald, January 25, 1967, Big Thicket File, Kirby Lumber Corporation, Houston, Texas.

[35] *Congressional Record*, 89 Cong., 2d. Sess., 27887 (Oct. 30, 1966).

[36] Interview with Ralph Yarborough.

[37] Ibid.

[38] Ibid.

[39] Ibid.

[40] *Congressional Record*, 89 Cong., 2 Sess., 27887 (Oct. 20, 1966).

[41] Ibid.

[42] U.S. Department of the Interior, National Park Service, *Proposed Big Thicket National Monument Texas, A Study of Alternatives* (Washington, 1967), 1–2.

[43] Ibid.

[44] Claude A. McLeod, *Big Thicket of Eastern Texas*, 1–11.

[45] U.S. Department of Interior, *Proposed Big Thicket*, 3–4.

[46] Ibid.

[47] Ibid., 5.

[48] Ibid., 6–8.

[49] Ibid., 9.

[50] Ibid., 10.

[51] Ibid., 10–11.

[52] Ibid., 11–12.

[53] Ibid., 12.

[54] Ibid., 13–14.

[55] Ibid., 12, 14.

[56] Ibid., 15, 46.

[57] Ibid., 46–47.

[58] *Congressional Record*, 90 Cong., 1st sess., 209 (Jan. 11, 1967).

[59] Big Thicket Morgue File, *Houston Chronicle*, May 11, 1968.

[60] Interview with Ralph Yarborough.

[61] *Congressional Record*, 90 Cong., 1st Sess., 17618 (June 27, 1967).

[62] Memorandum to File by George Stanley, August 22, 1967, Big Thicket File, Kirby Lumber Corporation, Houston, Texas.

[63] Ibid.

[64] Eugene A. Walker to R. M. Buckley, August 23, 1967; John Herndon to George Stanley, May 31, 1968, Big Thicket File, Kirby Lumber Corporation, Houston, Texas.

[65] Interview with Ralph Yarborough; Big Thicket Morgue File, *Houston Chronicle*, March 17, 1968.

[66] Stewart Udall to O. R. Crawford, September 27,1967, Big Thicket Correspondence File 1967–1972, Congressman Bob Eckhardt's office, Houston, Texas; *Texas Forest and Texas* (Lufkin), March–April, 1968, 1; Arthur

Temple to T. L. Carter, May 1, 1968, Big Thicket File, Kirby Lumber Corporation, Houston, Texas.

[67] Interview with James Webster, Houston, Texas, February 17, 1976.

[68] Transcript of a Press Conference by Secretary of Interior Stewart Udall, July 2, 1968, reprinted in Congressional Record 90 Cong., 2 Sess., 20294 (July 9, 1968).

[69] Big Thicket Morgue File, *Houston Chronicle*, July 3, 1968.

[70] Memorandum from Chief, Division of Park Planning to Mr. Brooks, Southwest Keyman, September 23, 1968, Big Thicket Collection, Big Thicket National Preserve Headquarters, Beaumont, Texas.

[71] Ibid., Follow-up Slip to Director, September 23, 1968, Big Thicket Collection, Big Thicket National Preserve Headquarters, Beaumont, Texas.

[72] *Dallas Morning News*, October 25, 1968, 4, sec. D; Myrl G. Brooks to Assistant Director, Cooperative Activities, November 12, 1968, Big Thicket Collection, Big Thicket National Preserve Headquarters, Beaumont, Texas.

[73] Big Thicket Morgue File, *Houston Chronicle*, December 13, 1968.

Notes to Chapter IX

[1] John C. Meyers to John Herndon, December 16, 1968, Big Thicket File, Kirby Lumber Corporation, Houston, Texas; Interview with Maxine Johnston, Batson, Texas, February 28, 1976.

[2] Ibid., Big Thicket Morgue File, *Houston Chronicle*, December 15, 1968.

[3] Ibid.

[4] Interview with Maxine Johnston.

[5] Memorandum to File by George Stanley, June 6, 1968, Big Thicket File, Kirby Lumber Corporation, Houston, Texas.

[6] The new leaders were E. C. Fritz, Dallas attorney, Orrin Bonney, Houston attorney, Charles Wilbanks, professor at Lamar State University in Beaumont, Maxine Johnston, librarian at Lamar State University, Pete Gunter, professor of philosophy at North Texas State University in Denton, and Howard Peacock, Houston attorney and administrator of the Bates School of Law, University of Houston. In an interview, Gunter said that clear-cutting and pine plantations were the major issues. Yarborough echoed these sentiments as did Maxine Johnston and Howard Peacock.

[7] "Slash Pine in Texas," *Texas Forest News* 19 (May–June 1939), 3; *Texas Almanac and State Industrial Guide*, 1955 (Dallas: Dallas Morning News, 1955), 222.

[8] *Texas Almanac and State Industrial Guide*, 1971 (Dallas: Dallas Morning News, 1971), 112.

[9] U.S. Congress, Senate, Subcommittee on Parks and Recreation of the Committee on Interior and Insular Affairs, Hearing on S. 4, To Establish a Big Thicket National Park in Texas, 91 Cong., 2 Sess., 12 June 1970, 101; R. L. Young to Bob Eckhardt, April 21, 1971, Big Thicket Correspondence 1967-1971, Congressman Bob Eckhardt's office, Houston, Texas; Gunter, *Big Thicket: A Challenge*, xvi.

[10] U.S. Congress, Senate, Hearing on S. 4, 75–77; Pete A. Gunter, "The Rural Southern Mentality and the Environmental Crisis," in *Population and Environmental Crisis*, ed. Stephen White (Johnson City, TN: East Tennessee State Univ. Research Advisory Council, 1975), 15–16; *The Texas Observer*, August 29, 1969, 1–2; Interview with Pete Gunter, Denton, Texas, March 19, 1976.

[11] Interview with Alan Miller, Diboll, Texas, March 4, 1976; R. L. Young to Bob Eckhardt, April 21, 1971, Big Thicket Correspondence 1967-1971, Congressman Bob Eckhardt's office, Houston, Texas; U.S., Congress, Senate, Hearing on S. 4, 73-74.

[12] Interview with Ralph Yarborough.

[13] Memorandum to Mr. Sanders, January 14, 1969, Ralph Yarborough Name File, Lyndon Baines Johnson Presidential Library, Austin, Texas.

[14] Ibid. The reply was stapled to the memorandum.

[15] On January 8, 1969, President Johnson issued a statement urging preservation of some of the Big Thicket. He did not specifically endorse Yarborough's bill. *Public Papers of the President of the United States, Lyndon B. Johnson, Containing the Public Messages, Speeches and Statements of the President 1968–1969* (Washington, DC: Government Printing Office, 1970), 2: 1366.

[16] *Congressional Record*, 91 Cong., 1 sess., 777–778 (Jan. 15, 1969); U.S., Congress, Senate, Hearing on S. 4, 93; *Congressional Record*, 91 Cong., 1 Sess., 5851 (Mar. 11 , 1969).

[17] U.S., Congress, Senate, Hearing on S. 4, 44-45; *Texas Forest and Texas* (Lufkin), March–April 1969, 1–2; Interview with Alan Miller, Diboll, Texas.

[18] *Stewards of the Land* (Lufkin: Texas Forest Service, 1968), 21.

[19] Interview with Pete Gunter; Orrin Bonney, "The Big Thicket: The Biological Crossroads of North America," *Living Wilderness* 32–33 (Summer 1969): 19; Orrin Bonney, "The Big Thicket: The Biological Crossroads of

North America," *Sierra Club Bulletin* 53 (May, 1968, 7; article by Dennis Forney in *Wall Street Journal*, July 1, 1968, reprinted in *Congressional Record*, 90 Cong., I Sess., 34477 (Dec. 1, 1967).

[20] Interview with Pete Gunter; Gunter, "The Rural Southern Mentality," 21–22.

[21] *The Texas Observer* (Austin) August 29, 1972, 1–2.

[22] Interview with Ralph Yarborough; *Congressional Record*, 91 Cong., 1 Sess., 30443 (Oct. 16, 1969); *Houston Post*, June 4, 1971, 16, sec. A.

[23] Interview with Ralph Yarborough.

[24] *Dallas Morning News*, April 16, 1970, 7, sec. A.

[25] Interview with Ralph Yarborough; *Dallas Morning News*, May 17, 1970, 31, sec. A; Big Thicket Morgue File, *Houston Chronicle*, June 15, 1970.

[26] U.S. Congress, Senate, Hearing on S. 4., 1-2.

[27] Ibid., 7–8.

[28] Ibid., 7–8.

[29] Ibid., 10.

[30] Ibid., 37.

[31] Ibid., 37.

[32] Ibid., 39.

[33] Ibid., 44–45, 57–61, 71–74, 104–7.

[34] Ibid., 30–36, 51–56, 79, 106–10.

[35] Ibid., 79–85.

[36] Ibid., 83.

[37] Ibid., 83–84, 86–87. Yarborough and Daniel maintained that Senator Bible was impressed that a states-right advocate such as Price Daniel endorsed a 100,000-acre National Park. Interview with Ralph Yarborough. Interview with Price Daniel, Austin, Texas, March 11, 1976.

[38] Ibid., 131–32; *Houston Post*, June 13, 1970, 24, sec. B.

[39] *Dallas Morning News*, June 24, 1970, 8, sec. B; *Dallas Morning News*, July 9, 1970, 24, sec. A; *Congressional Record*, 91 Cong., 2 Sess., 24614-24615 (July 16, 1970), 25001 (July 20, 1970); *Dallas Morning News*, July 17, 1970, 14, sec. A.

[40] *Congressional Record*, 91 Cong., 2 Sess., 25546 (July 23, 1970); *Dallas Morning News*, July 17, 1970, 14, sec. A.

[41] *Dallas Morning News*, July 26, 1970, 18, sec. A.

[42] Big Thicket Morgue File, *Houston Chronicle*, October 14, 18, November 24, 1970.

[43] Big Thicket Morgue File, *Houston Chronicle*, November 14, 1970; U.S., Congress, Senate, Subcommittee on Parks and Recreation of the Committee on Interior and Insular Affairs, *Hearing on S. 4 a Bill to Establish a Big Thicket National Park and S. 4149 and H.R. 10874 a Bill to Provide for the Establish of the Gulf Islands National Seashore*, 91 Cong. 2 Sess., 24 November 1970; 2 -7.

[44] Ibid., 6.

[45] Ibid.

[46] Ibid., 8–9.

[47] *Dallas Morning News*, November 26, 1970, 1, sec. 1; Interview with Ralph Yarborough.

[48] O. R. Crawford to Alan Bible, December 2, 1970, Olin E. Teague Papers, Box 193, Texas A & M University Archives and Manuscript Collection, Texas A & M University Library, College Station, Texas.

[49] Ibid.

[50] Yarborough claims that Bible amended the bill to show his anger at being forced to report on the bill. Interview with Ralph Yarborough; U.S., Congress, Senate, Committee of Interior and Insular Affairs, *Big Thicket National Park, Texas; Report to Accompany S. 4*, 91 Cong., 2nd Sess., 1970, Rept. 91-1415, 4: *Congressional Record*, 91 Cong., 2nd Sess., 40317 (Dec. 17, 1970); *Houston Post*, December 17, 1970, 1, sec. A.

[51] *Houston Post*, December 7, 1970, 2, sec. AA.

[52] *Congressional Record*, 92 Cong., 1st Sess., 7 (Jan. 21, 1971).

Notes to Chapter X

[1] *Congressional Record*, 92nd Cong., 1st Sess., 354 (Jan. 25, 1971).

[2] Ibid., 738 (Jan. 27, 1971).

[3] Ibid.

[4] The following congressmen introduced Big Thicket bills from 1971–1974: Jake Pickle, Jack Brooks, Bob Eckhardt, Earle Cabell, Wright Patman, Robert Roe, Charles Wilson, Alan Steelman, and John Saylor. Some of the men introduced two or more bills. *Congressional Record*, 92nd Cong., 1st Sess., 1778–1779 (Feb. 4, 1971).

[5] *Houston Post*, February 5, 1971, 9, sec. A; *Texas Observer* (Austin) March 26, 1971, 9.

[6] *Texas Observer* (Austin), March 26, 1971, 9; Interview with Ralph Yarborough.

[7] Interview with Pete Gunter.

[8] *Congressional Record*, 92nd Cong., 1st Sess., 2391 (Feb. 10, 1971), 4696 (Mar. 2, 1971), 7641 (Mar. 23, 1971).

[9] *Big Thicket Bulletin* (Summer 1971): 1–2.

[10] Interview with Pete Gunter.

[11] Interview with Maxine Johnston.

[12] Interview with Pete Gunter; *Big Thicket Bulletin* (Fall 1971): 4.

[13] Interview with Pete Gunter.

[14] Ibid.

[15] Ibid.

[16] Vita for Dr. Pete A. Y. Gunter. For an example of the postcards and letters to Texas congressmen see Olin E. Teague Papers, Box 193, Texas A&M University Archives and Manuscript Collection, Texas A&M University Library, College Station, Texas. Also see Graham Purcell Papers, Unprocessed Collection, ibid.

[17] Interview with Pete Gunter; Vita of Dr. Pete A. Y. Gunter.

[18] For example see Howard Bloomfield, "Big Thicket, The Biological Crossroads of America" *American Forest* 78 (September 1972): 24–27, 45–46; and Edwin W. Teale, "Big Thicket, Crossroads of Nature," *Audubon* 73 (May 1971): 12, 25–32; Vita of Dr. Pete A. Y. Gunter; Pete Gunter, *The Big Thicket: A Challenge for Conservation* (Austin and New York: Jenkins Publishing Company, 1972).

[19] *Big Thicket Bulletin* (Fall 1971).

[20] Interview with James Webster, Houston, Texas, February 17, 1976.

[21] Ibid. In the process of completing this work, the author interviewed four representatives of the timber industry. All four men felt that Gunter's attacks were the most aggressive. Gunter, himself, admits that he may have been too harsh on occasion, but he feels his actions gained the needed publicity for the movement. He hoped to scare the timber firms into negotiating with Emil Kindschy, the moderate leader of the Big Thicket Co-ordinating Committee.

[22] Interview with James Webster, Houston, Texas, February 17, 1976; Interview with Erich Krumm, Huntsville, Texas, 1976; Interview with Alan Miller, Diboll, Texas, 1976. For an example of the timber industry's position see Oliver R. Crawford's statement in U.S., Congress, House, Committee on Interior and Insular Affairs, *Big Thicket National Park Texas, Hearing on H.R. 12034*, 92nd Cong., 2nd Sess., 10 June 1972, 51–56.

[23] Most of the timber industry's arguments appeared in such publications as *Texas Forestry*, published by the Texas Association at Lufkin.

[24] Interview with Pete Gunter.

[25] Ibid.; Big Thicket Morgue File, *Houston Chronicle*, July 23, 1971.

[26] Memorandum from Management Assistant to Director, Southwest Region, October 14, 1971; National Park Service Map NP-BT-91, 002, July, 1970, Big Thicket Collection, Big Thicket National Preserve Headquarters, Beaumont, Texas.

[27] Memorandum from Management Assistant to Director, Southwest Region, October 14, 1971, Big Thicket Collection, Big Thicket National Preserve Headquarters, Beaumont, Texas.

[28] Ibid.

[29] Bob Eckhardt to Pete Gunter, August 30, 1971; Bob Eckhardt to Alfred Knapf, November 23, 1971, Big Thicket Correspondence File August-December 1971, Congressman Bob Eckhardt's office, Houston, Texas; Memorandum from Assistant Secretary Reed to Director, National Park Service, October 14, 1971, Big Thicket Collection, Big Thicket National Preserve Headquarters, Beaumont, Texas; *Big Thicket Bulletin* (Fall 1971): 1; Interview with Maxine Johnston.

[30] Interview with Maxine Johnston; Interview with Pete Gunter; Emil O. Kindschy to Frank Hradisky, E. C. Fritz, and Geraldine Watson, October 25, 1971, Big Thicket Background File 1967-1972, Congressman Bob Eckhardt's office, Houston, Texas; *Big Thicket Bulletin* (Fall 1971): 1.

[31] Bob Eckhardt to Lloyd Bentsen, November 15, 1971, Big Thicket Correspondence File August-December 1971, Congressman Bob Eckhardt's office, Houston, Texas.

[32] Bob Eckhardt to Wright Patman, December 8, 1971, Big Thicket Background File 1967-1972, Congressman Bob Eckhardt's office, Houston, Texas.

[33] Ibid.; *Congressional Record*, 92nd Cong., 1st Sess., 44374 (Dec. 2, 1971).

[34] Big Thicket Morgue File, *Houston Chronicle*, December 9, 1971.

[35] *Congressional Record*, 92nd Cong., 1st Sess., 47236 (Dec. 15, 1971).

[36] Big Thicket Morgue File, *Houston Chronicle*, January 16, 1971.

[37] Ibid.

[38] Big Thicket Morgue File, *Houston Chronicle*, January 21, 1972.

[39] Follow-up-slip from Homer Rouse to T. Flynn, January 25, 1972, Big Thicket Collection, Big Thicket National Preserve Headquarters, Beaumont, Texas.

[40] Big Thicket Morgue File, *Houston Chronicle*, May 4, 1972.

[41] U.S. Congress, House, Committee on Interior and Insular Affairs, *Big Thicket National Park, Texas, Hearing on H.R. 12034*, 92nd Cong., 1st Sess., 10 June 1972, 1.

[42] Ibid., 72–75, 95–98, 154–56.

[43] Director, Denver Service Center to Occupant, February 25, 1972, Big Thicket Collection, Big Thicket National Preserve Headquarters, Beaumont, Texas.

[44] Acting Director, Denver Service Center to Occupant, April 11, 1972, Big Thicket Collection, Big Thicket National Preserve Headquarters, Beaumont, Texas.

[45] Big Thicket Morgue File, *Houston Chronicle*, May 14, 1972.

[46] See testimony of Dick Watkins, W. C. Vanderwater, and James Dorman in U.S., Congress, House, *Hearing on H.R. 12034*, 72–75, 95–98, 154–56.

[47] Ibid., 103.

[48] Ibid., 108.

[49] U.S. Congress, House, *Hearing on H.R. 12034*, 195–96.

[50] Memorandum from Keith Osmore to Bob Eckhardt, August 25, 1972, Big Thicket Background File 1967-1972, Congressman Bob Eckhardt's office. Houston, Texas; Bob Eckhardt to Ralph Yarborough, September 20, 1972, Big Thicket Correspondence July–December 1972, Congressman Bob Eckhardt's office, Houston, Texas; Nathaniel Reed to Edward Fritz, September 11, 1972, Big Thicket Correspondence, Big Thicket National Preserve Headquarters, Beaumont, Texas.

[51] *Texas Observer* (Austin), October 20, 1975, 14.

[52] *Congressional Record*, 93rd Cong., 1st Sess., 754 (Jan. 11, 1973), 3955 (Feb. 8, 1973), 8932 (Mar. 21, 1973), Big Thicket Morgue File, *Houston Chronicle*, March 22, 1973.

[53] *Congressional Record*, 93rd Cong., 1st Sess., 19394 (June 13, 1973); U.S. Congress, Senate, Committee on Interior and Insular Affairs, *Big Thicket National Park, Texas, Hearing on S. 314, S. 1981, S. 2286, H.R. 11546*, 93rd Cong., 2nd sess., 5 and 6 February, 1974, 226; Interview with Maxine Johnston; Big Thicket Morgue File, *Houston Chronicle*, February 15, 1973.

[54] Follow-up-slip from H. L. Rouse to Associate Director, Legislation February 2, 1972; Follow-up-slip from Homer L. Rouse to Mike and Dean, March 6, 1973, Big Thicket Collection, Big Thicket National Preserve

Headquarters, Beaumont, Texas. In a letter dated April 17, 1972, to Mr. Stanley Hulett, associate director of the Department of Interior, Ollie Crawford proclaimed that the timber industry was ready to assist in "putting together a park of 100,000 acres or larger if needed." The letter is located at the Big Thicket National Preserve Headquarters in Beaumont, Texas.

[55] Follow-up-slip from Homer L. Rouse and Mike and Dean, March 6, 1973, Big Thicket Collection, Big Thicket National Preserve Headquarters, Beaumont, Texas; U.S. Congress, House, Committee on Interior and Insular Affairs, *Big Thicket National Reserve in Texas, Hearing on H.R. 4270, et al.*, 93rd Cong., 1st Sess., 16 and 17 July, 1973, 74–76.

[56] Memorandum from Acting New Area Keyman, Southwest Region to Associate Director Legislation, June 1, 1973, Big Thicket Collection, Big Thicket National Preserve Headquarters, Beaumont, Texas.

[57] James Webster to T. M. Orth, June 6, 1973, Big Thicket File, Kirby Lumber Corporation, Houston, Texas.

[58] Ibid, Memorandum from New Area Keyman, Southwest and Western Regions to Associate Director, Legislation, June 25, 1973, Big Thicket Collection, Big Thicket National Preserve Headquarters, Beaumont, Texas.

[59] *Congressional Record*, 93rd Cong., 1st Sess., 22167 (June 28, 1973).

[60] U.S. Congress, House, *Hearing on H.R. 4270*, 15–16.

[61] Ibid., 4.

[62] Ibid., 6–8.

[63] Big Thicket Morgue File, *Houston Chronicle*, June 27, 1973.

[64] Memorandum to file by James Webster, June 26, 1973, Big Thicket File, Kirby Lumber Corporation, Houston, Texas.

[65] Congressman Steelman had introduced his first Big Thicket bill on June 28, 1973. This second bill, introduced on July 12, was nearly identical to the first measure. The only difference in the two bills was some changes in wording and the fact that the second bill had eleven co-sponsors. *Congressional Record*, 93 Cong., 1 Sess., 23770 (July 12, 1973).

[66] U.S. Congress, House, *Hearing on H. R. 4270*, 23–37, 66.

[67] Ibid., 55–57. *Houston Post*, July 16, 1973, sec. A.

[68] U.S. Congress, House, *Hearing on H. R. 4270*, 64–72, 73–84, 87–108, 204–8.

[69] U.S. Congress, House, *Hearing on H. R. 4270*, 75–77.

[70] Ibid., 77.

[71] Ibid., 76.

[72] See statements of Orrin Bonney, Edward Fritz, and Geraldine Watson for their view of the importance of Village Creek to the reserve. Ibid., 170, 176–77, 262–64.

[73] Ibid., 108.

[74] Ibid., 111–18.

[75] Ibid., 209–12.

[76] Ibid., 217.

[77] Ibid., 229.

[78] U.S. Congress, House, *Hearing on H.R. 4270*, 331; Big Thicket Morgue File, *Houston Chronicle*, July 18, 1973. Although the Department of Interior's 68,000-acre proposal was never seriously considered, it was introduced in both houses of Congress. On July 25, John Saylor introduced the measure in the House while Henry Jackson introduced the companion bill in the Senate just five days later.

[79] Interview with Pete Gunter.

[80] *Big Thicket Bulletin* (November/December 1973): 1; *Houston Post*, October 4, 1973, 19, sec. A.

[81] *Houston Post*, October 5, 1971, 1, 17, sec. A.

[82] *Houston Post*, October 16, 1973, 1, 21, sec. A; Big Thicket Morgue File, *Houston Chronicle*, November 4, 1973; *Congressional Record*, 93rd Cong., 1st Sess., 37191-37192 (Nov. 15, 1973).

[83] U.S. Congress, House, Committee on Interior and Insular Affairs, *Big Thicket National Preserve Texas; Report to Accompany H.R. 11546*, 93 Cong., 1 Sess., 1973, H. Rept. 93-676, 1–14; *Congressional Record*, 93 Cong., 1 sess., 39220 (Dec. 3, 1973).

[84] *Big Thicket Bulletin* (January/February 1974): 1; Interview with Pete Gunter.

[85] Big Thicket Morgue File, *Houston Chronicle*, December 19, 1973.

[86] Interview with Maxine Johnston.

[87] U.S. Congress, Senate, Committee on Interior and Insular Affairs, *Big Thicket National Park, Texas; Hearing on S. 314, S. 1981, S. 2286, H.R. 11546*, 93rd Cong., 2nd Sess., 5 and 6 February, 1974, 80.

[88] Ibid.

[89] U.S. Congress, Senate, *Hearing on S. 314*, 48–49, 59063, 64–72, 73–75, 120–24, 156–57; Big Thicket Morgue File, *Houston Chronicle*, February 6, 1976.

[90] *Houston Post*, April 5, 1974, 2, sec. A.

[91] U.S. Congress, Senate, Committee on Interior and Insular Affairs, *Big Thicket National Preserve, Texas, Report to Accompany H.R. 11546*, 93rd Cong., 2nd Sess., 1974, S. Rept. 93-875, 5-6; U.S. Congress, House, *Hearing on H.R. 4270*, 34-35; Big Thicket Morgue File, *Houston Chronicle*, September 25, 1974; *Big Thicket Bulletin* (July/August, 1974): 1.

[92] *Congressional Record*, 93rd Cong., 2nd Sess., 89355 (May 30, 1974); *Houston Post*, May 31, 1974, 1, 15, sec. A.

[93] Big Thicket Morgue File, *Houston Chronicle*, August 4, 1974.

[94] Big Thicket Morgue File, *Houston Chronicle*, September 10, 1974; Interview with Pete Gunter.

[95] Big Thicket Morgue File, *Houston Chronicle*, September 24, 25, 1974; *Congressional Record*, 93rd Cong., 2nd Sess., H9501 (Sept. 24, 1974), S17946 (Oct. 1, 1974); Big Thicket Morgue File, *Houston Chronicle*, October 12, 1974.

[96] Public Law 93-439, 93 Congress, H.R. 11546, October 11, 1974, 1.

[97] Ibid., 3.

[98] Ibid., 3.

[99] Ibid., 4.

Notes to Chapter XI

[1] *Big Thicket Bulletin* (May/June, 1975): 1.

[2] Big Thicket Morgue File, *Houston Chronicle*, January 31, March 12, August 22, 1975; Interview with Maxine Johnston; Interview with Alan Miller, Diboll, Texas, March 4, 1976.

[3] *Congressional Record*, 94th Cong., 1st Sess., H 427 (Jan. 31, 1975), and 17750 (Oct. 8. 1975); Big Thicket Morgue File, *Houston Chronicle*, September 19, December 17, 1975.

[4] Texas, Texas Forest Service, *A Manual of Forestry*, ed. Howard E. Weaver, Bulletin Number 45 (College Station: Texas Forest Service, 1952), 198–99; "Pine Bark Beetle Invades Thicket," *Texas Forestry* 13 (October 1972): 6.

[5] Donald Pierce to Monte Fitch, March 13, 1973, Big Thicket Collection, Big Thicket National Preserve Headquarters, Beaumont, Texas; Big Thicket Morgue File, *Houston Chronicle*, November 14, 1975; Interview with Howard Peacock, Houston, Texas, February 17, 1976; Interview with Thomas Lubbert, Beaumont, Texas, February 20, 1976.

[6] *Big Thicket Bulletin* (January/February, 1975): 1; Interview with Howard Peacock, Houston, Texas, February 17, 1976; interview with James Webster, February 17, 1976.

[7] Interview with Thomas Lubbert, Beaumont, Texas, February 20, 1976.

[8] Interview with Pete Gunter.

[9] Interview with Thomas Lubbert.

[10] *Big Thicket Bulletin* (November/December 1974): 1; *Big Thicket Bulletin* (January/February 1975): 2–3.

[11] Clayton Garrison to Maxine Johnston, May 5, 1975, Big Thicket Collection, Big Thicket National Preserve Headquarters, Beaumont, Texas; Interview with Maxine Johnston; Interview with Dempsie Henley, Liberty, Texas, February 20, 1976.

[12] Interview with Howard Peacock.

[13] Ibid.

[14] *Big Thicket Bulletin* (May/June, 1975): 4.

[15] Big Thicket Morgue File, *Houston Chronicle*, January 28, 1976.

[16] Interview with Erich Krumm, Huntsville, Texas, February 25, 1976.

BIBLIOGRAPHY TO CHAPTERS I–IX

I. PRIMARY SOURCES

A. Public Documents

1. Federal Documents

Bailey, Vernon. *See* U. S. Department of Agriculture.

Bray, W. L. *See* U. S. Department of Agriculture.

Fenneman, N. S. *See* U. S. Geological Survey.

Hodge, Frederick W. *See* U. S. Smithsonian Institution.

Mooney, James. *See* U. S. Smithsonian Institution.

Reitch, T. C. *See* U. S. Department of Agriculture.

Smith, H. H. *See* U. S. Department of Agriculture.

Swanton, John R. *See* U. S. Smithsonian Institution.

U.S. Bureau of the Census. *Manufacturers of the United States in 1860: Compiled from the Original Returns of the Eighth Census.* 4 vols. Washington, DC: Government Printing Office, 1865.

———. Bureau of the Census. *Population of the United States in 1860.* 4 vols. Washington, DC: Government Printing Office, 1864.

———. Bureau of the Census. *Report on Manufacturing Industries in the United States at the Eleventh Census: 1890, Selected Industries.* 12 vols. Washington, DC: Government Printing Office, 1895.

————. Bureau of the Census. *The Seventh Census of the United States, 1850, Embracing a Statistical View of Each of the States and Territories Arranged by Counties, Towns, Etc.* Washington, DC: Government Printing Office, 1853.

————. Bureau of the Census. *Twelfth Census of the United States Taken in 1900.* 10 vols. Washington: Government Printing Office, 1901.

U. S. Congress. *Congressional Record.* 1966–1975.

U.S. Congress. House. *Alabama Indians of Texas: Report of William Toker and Letters to the Indian Department Relative to the Alabama Indians of Texas.* H. Doc. 866. 62nd Cong., 2nd Sess., 1912.

————. Subcommittee on National Parks and Recreation of the Committee on Interior and Insular Affairs. *Hearing on H.R. 12034, Big Thicket National Park, Texas.* 92nd Cong., 2nd Sess., 1972.

————. Subcommittee on National Parks and Recreation of the Committee on Interior and Insular Affairs. *Hearing on H.R. 4270 et al. Proposed Big Thicket National Reserve, Texas.* 93rd Cong., 1st Sess., 1973.

————. Subcommittee of the Committee on Interstate and Foreign Commerce. *Hearing on H. Res. 441, Petroleum Investigations.* 4 parts. 73rd Cong., Recess, 1904.

U.S. Congress. Public Law 93-439. 93 Cong., H.R. 11546, October 11, 1974.

U.S. Congress. Senate. Committee on Interior and Insular Affairs. *Big Thicket National Park Texas, Report to Accompany S. 4.* 91st Cong., 2nd Sess., 1970, H. Rept. 1415.

————. Committee on Interior and Insular Affairs. *Big Thicket National Preserve Texas, Report to Accompany H. R. 11546.* 93rd Cong., 2nd Sess., 1974, H. Rept. 93-676.

————. Subcommittee on Parks and Recreation of the Committee on Interior and Insular Affairs. *Hearing on S. 4, To Establish a Big Thicket National Park in Texas.* 91st Cong., 2nd Sess., 1970.

————. Subcommittee on Parks and Recreation of the Committee on Interior and Insular Affairs. *Hearing on S. 4, S. 4149, and H. R. 10874, Big Thicket National Park and Gulf Island National Seashore.* 91st Cong., 2nd Sess., 1970.

————. Subcommittee on Parks and Recreation of the Committee on Interior and Insular Affairs. *Hearing on S. 314, S. 1981, S. 2286 and H. R. 11546, Big Thicket National Park.* 93rd Cong., 2nd Sess., 1974.

U.S. Department of Agriculture. Bureau of Chemistry and Soils. *Soil Survey of Polk County Texas.* H. H. Smith, T. C. Reitch and others. Bulletin No. 36. Washington, DC: Government Printing Office, 1930.

———. Bureau of Forestry. *Forest Resources of Texas.* W. L. Bray. Bulletin No. 47. Washington, DC: Government Printing Office, 1904.

———. Bureau of Forestry. *Loblolly Pine in Eastern Texas with Special Reference to the Production of Cross-Ties.* Raphael Zon. Bulletin No. 64. Washington, DC: Government Printing Office, 1905.

———. Bureau of Soils. *Soil Survey of Polk County, Texas* H. H. Smith, et al. Bulletin No. 581. Washington, DC: Government Printing Office, 1930.

———. Division of Biological Survey. *Biological Survey of Texas.* Vernon Bailey. Bulletin No. 25. Washington, DC: Government Printing Office, 1905.

U.S. Department of the Interior. National Park Service. *Proposed Big Thicket National Monument, Texas: A Study of Alternatives.* Washington, DC: n.p., 1967.

———. National Park Service. *The Big Thicket National Preserve.* Pamphlet No. 681-103. Washington, DC: Government Printing Office, 1976.

U.S. Geological Survey. *Oil Fields of the Texas Louisiana Gulf Coast Plain.* N. S. Fenneman. Bulletin No. 282. Washington, DC: Government Printing Office, 1906.

U.S. Smithsonian Institution. *The Aboriginal Population of America North of Mexico.* James Mooney. Smithsonian Miscellaneous Collection Vol. 80. No. 7. Publication No. 2955. Washington, DC: Smithsonian Institution, 1928.

——— Bureau of American Ethnology. *Early History of the Creek Indians and Their Neighbors.* John R. Swanton. Bulletin No. 73. Washington, DC: Government Printing Office, 1922.

———. Bureau of American Ethnology. *Handbook of American Indians North of Mexico.* Frederick W. Hodge. Bulletin No. 30. 2 vols. Washington, DC: Government Printing Office, 1907.

———. Bureau of American Ethnology. *The Indian Tribes of North America.* John R. Swanton. Bulletin No. 145. Washington, DC: Government Printing Office, 1952.

———. Bureau of American Ethnology. *The Indians of the Southeastern United States.* John R. Swanton. Bulletin No. 137. Washington, DC: Government Printing Office, 1946.

Zon, Raphael. *See* U.S. Department of Agriculture.

2. Texas Documents

Texas. Department of Insurance, Statistics and History. *The Resources, Soil and Climate of Texas*. A. W. Spaight. Galveston: A. H. Belo and Company, 1882.

Texas. General Land Office. *Abstract of all Original Texas Land Titles Comprising Grants and Locations to August 31, 1941*. 8 vols. Austin: n.p., 1941.

Texas. *Report to the Legislature, Governor Price Daniel 1957–1963*. Austin: n.p., 1963.

Texas. Parks and Wildlife Department. Transcript of Parks and Wildlife Commission Hearing. Austin, Texas, May 31, 1966. Minute Book No. 7.

Texas. Stephen F. Austin State University. School of Forestry. *A Short History of Forest Conservation in Texas, 1880-1940*. Robert S. Maxwell and James W. Martin. Bulletin No. 20. Nacogdoches: School of Forestry, 1970.

Texas. Texas A&M College. Department of Forestry. *Forest Resources of Eastern Texas*. J. H. Foster, H. B. Krausz and George W. Johnson. Bulletin No. 5. College Station: Texas A&M College, 1917.

———. Department of Forestry. *General Survey of Texas Woodlands, including a Study of the Commercial Possibilities of Mesquite*. J. H. Foster, H. B. Krausz and A. H. Leidigh. Bulletin No. 3, Third Series. College Station: Texas A&M College, 1917.

Texas. Texas Agricultural Experiment Station. *Catalogue of the Flora of Texas*. Hal B. Parks and Victor L. Cory. Bulletin No. 550. College Station: Texas Agricultural Experiment Station, 1936.

———. Texas Agricultural Experiment Station. *The Soils of Texas*. William T. Carter. Bulletin No. 431. College Station: Texas Agricultural Experiment Station, 1931.

Texas. Texas Forest Service. *A Manual of Forestry*. Ed. Howard E. Weaver. Bulletin No. 45. College Station: Texas Forest Service, 1972.

Texas. Texas Planning Board. *A Review of Texas Forestry*. Austin: n.p., 1937.

Texas. Texas Railroad Commission. *Fifth Annual Report of the Railroad Commission of the State of Texas for the Year 1896*. Austin: Ben C. Jones and Company, 1897.

———. Texas Railroad Commission. *Fourth Annual Report of the Railroad Commission of the State of Texas for the Year 1895*. Austin: Ben C. Jones and Company, 1896.

————. Texas Railroad Commission. *Rules and Regulations of the Texas Railroad Commission: Oil and Gas.* Prepared by R. W. Byram and Company. 11 Vols. Austin: n.p., 1937.

_____. Texas Railroad Commission. *The Railroad Commission of Texas: Oil and Gas Annual Production by Active Fields, 1974.* Austin: n.p., 1974.

Texas. University of Texas. Bureau of Business Research. *The Natural Regions of Texas.* Elmer H. Johnson. University of Texas Bulletin No. 3113. Austin: University of Texas, 1931.

_____. University of Texas. *Railroad Transportation in Texas*, by Charles S. Potts. University of Texas Bulletin No.19, Humanistic Series No. 7. Austin: University of Texas Press, 1901.

————. University of Texas. *Subsidence in Gulf Coastal Plains Salt Domes*, by E. H. Sellards. University of Texas Bulletin Number 3001. Austin: University of Texas, 1930.

————. University of Texas. *The Trees of Texas.* Issac M. Lewis. University of Texas Bulletin No. 22. Austin: University of Texas Press, 1915.

B. Manuscripts

Big Thicket Background File 1967–1972. Congressman Bob Eckhardt's office, Houston, Texas.

Big Thicket Collection. Big Thicket National Preserve Headquarters, Beaumont, Texas.

Big Thicket Correspondence File. Congressman Bob Eckhardt's office, Houston, Texas.

Big Thicket Correspondence File August–December 1971. Congressman Bob Eckhardt's office, Houston, Texas.

Big Thicket Correspondence July–December 1972. Congressman Bob Eckhardt's office, Houston, Texas.

Big Thicket File. Kirby Lumber Corporation, Houston, Texas.

Correspondence of Victor L. Cory and Hal B. Parks. 13 Vols. Texas A&M University Archives and Manuscript Collections, Texas A&M Library, College Station, Texas.

Daniel, Price, Papers. Texas State Archives, Austin, Texas.

Fisher, Larry Jene, Collection. Lamar State University Library, Beaumont, Texas.

Kirby Lumber Corporation Records. Special Collections, Stephen F. Austin State University Library, Nacogdoches, Texas.

Lutcher and Moore Lumber Company Records. Special Collections. Stephen F. Austin State University Library, Nacogdoches, Texas.

"Notes on Investigation of Three Texas Lumber Towns." Peter A. Speck for John R. Commons and Associates. "Report of the United States Commission on Industrial Relations." From the General Records of the Department of Labor. microfilm. Special Collections, Stephen F. Austin State University Library.

Oral History of Texas Oil Pioneers. University of Texas Archives, Austin, Texas.

Purcell, Graham, Papers. Texas A&M University Archives and Manuscript Collections, Texas A&M University Library, College Station, Texas.

Teague, Olin E., Papers. Texas A&M University Archives and Manuscript Collections Texas A&M University Library.

Texas Agricultural Experiment Station. 1936 Annual Report of the State Apicultural Laboratory. Texas A&M University Archives and Manuscript Collections. Texas A&M University Library.

Texas Agricultural Experiment Station. 1936 Annual Report of Substation No. 11, Sonora, Texas. Texas A&M University Archives and Manuscript Collections. Texas A&M University Library.

Texas Agricultural Experiment Station. 1937 Annual Report of the State Apicultural Laboratory. Texas A&M University Archives and Manuscript Collections. Texas A&M University Library.

Vita of Pete Gunter. In possession of the author.

Weekly/Monthly Reports for Texas Agricultural Experiment Stations, Field Stations and Laboratories, 1936. San Antonio State Apicultural Laboratory. Texas A&M University Archives and Manuscript Collections. Texas A&M University Library.

Yarborough, Ralph, Name File. Lyndon Baines Johnson Presidential Library, Austin, Texas.

C. Published Memoirs, Personal Accounts, and Letters

An Abstract of the Original Titles of Record in the General Land Office. Reprint, Austin: Pemberton Press, 1964.

Anonymous. *A Visit to Texas: Being the Journal of a Traveller Through Those Parts Most Interesting to American Settlers with Description of Scenery, Habits.* 1834. Reprint, Austin: Steck Co., 1952.

Barker, Eugene C., ed. *The Austin Papers.* 3 vols. Washington, DC: Government Printing Office, 1922–1928.

Binkley, William C., ed. *Official Correspondence of the Texas Revolution 1835–1836.* 2 vols. New York: D. Appleton-Century Company, 1936.

Boatright, Mody, and William A. Owens. *Tales from the Derrick Floor, A People's History of the Oil Industry.* Garden City, NY: Doubleday, 1910.

De Cordova, Jacob. *Texas, Her Resources and Public Men.* 1858. Reprint, Waco: Texian Press, 1969.

Henley, Dempsie. *The Murder of Silence, The Big Thicket Story.* Waco: Texian Press, 1970.

Kinnaird, Lawrence, trans. *The Frontier of New Spain: Nicholas De La Fora's Description, 1766-1768.* Berkeley: Quivira Society, 1958.

Olmsted, Frederick Law. *A Journey Through Texas: or a Saddle Trip on the Southwestern Frontier.* New York: Dix, Edwards and Company, 1857.

Public Papers of the Presidents of the United States, Lyndon B. Johnson, Containing the Public Messages, Speeches, and Statement of the President 1968-1969. 2 vols. Washington: Government Printing Office, 1970.

Watkins, Sue., ed. *One League to Each Wind: Accounts of Early Surveying in Texas.* Austin: Von Boeckmann-Jones, 1964.

White, Gifford. *The 1840 Census of the Republic of Texas.* Austin: The Pemberton Press, 1966.

Wright, Soloman A. *My Rambles as East Texas Cowboy, Hunter, Fisherman, Tie-Cutter.* Ed. J. Frank Dobie. Austin: Texas Folklore Society, 1942.

D. Articles

Castaneda, Carlos E., trans. "Statistical Report on Texas by Juan N. Almonte." *Southwestern Historical Quarterly* 28 (January 1925): 177–222.

Barker, Eugene C., contr. "Description of Texas by Stephen F. Austin." *Southwestern Historical Quarterly* 28 (October 1924): 98–121.

Bradford, A. L. and T. N. Campbell, ed. "Journal of Lincecum's Travels in Texas, 1835." *Southwestern Historical Quarterly* 53 (October 1949): 180–201.

Dabbs, Jack Autrey. ed., and trans. "Additional Notes on the Champ-d'Asile." *Southwestern Historical Quarterly* 54 (January 1951): 347–58.

Gow, James E. "An Ecological Study of the Sabine and Neches Valleys, Texas." *Proceedings of the Iowa Academy of Science for 1904* 12 (1905): 39–47.

Harper, Roland M. "A Week in Eastern Texas." *Bulletin of the Torrey Botanical Club* 97 (July 1920): 289–317.

Jeffries, Charlie. "Reminiscences of Sour Lake." *Southwestern Historical Quarterly* 50 (July 1946): 26–35.

Osburn, Mary McMillan. "The Atascosita Census of 1826." *Texana* 1 (Fall 1963): 299–321.

E. Interviews Conducted by the Author

Daniel, Price. Austin, Texas. March 11, 1976.

Gunter, Pete. Denton, Texas. March 19, 1976.

Henley, Dempsie. Liberty, Texas. February 20, 1976.

Johnston, Maxine. Batson, Texas. February 28, 1976.

Krumm, Erich. Huntsville, Texas. February 25, 1976.

Lubbert, Thomas. Beaumont, Texas. February 20, 1976.

Miller, Alan. Diboll, Texas. March 4, 1976.

Peacock, Howard. Houston, Texas. February 17, 1976.

Webster, James. Houston, Texas. February 17, 1976.

Yarborough, Ralph. Austin, Texas. February 26, 1976.

F. Newspapers

Austin Texas Observer. 1969–1975.

Beaumont Enterprise. 1901–1974.

Dallas Morning News. 1962–1970.

Houston Chronicle. 1954–1976.

Houston Daily Post. 1903

Houston Post. 1962–1974.

Lufkin Texas Forest and Texans. 1968–1969.

G. Almanacs

Texas Almanac and State Industrial Guide, 1904. Galveston: A. H. Belo and Company, 1904.

Texas Almanac and State Industrial Guide, 1911. Galveston: A. H. Belo and Company, 1911.

Texas Almanac and State Industrial Guide, 1970–1971. Dallas: *Dallas Morning News*, 1969.

Texas Almanac and State Industrial Guide, 1974–1975. Dallas: *Dallas Morning News*, 1974.

Texas Almanac and State Industrial Guide, 1975–1976. Dallas: *Dallas Morning News*, 1975.

H. Proceedings and Reports

Big Thicket Bulletin. Saratoga: Big Thicket Association, 1971–1975.

Big Thicket Co-ordinating Committee and Big Thicket Association, prep. *Big Thicket National Preserve, A Report Submitted to National Park Service*. n..p., January, 1975.

Johnston, Maxine, ed. *Big Thicket Association's Handbook for Members*. Saratoga: Big Thicket Association, 1970.

Proceedings of the Texas Academy of Science 1937–1938. Vol. 20. Austin: Texas Academy of Science, 1938.

Southwest Reporter. Vol. 104. St Paul: West Publishing Company, 1908.

II. SECONDARY SOURCES

A. Books

Allen, Ruth A. *East Texas Lumber Workers: An Economic and Social Picture, 1870–1950*. Austin: University of Texas Press, 1961.

Bancroft, Hubert H. *The Works of Hubert Howe Bancroft*. Vol. 15, *History of the North Mexican States and Texas. Vol. I 1531–1800*. 1884. Reprint, New York: Arno Press, n.d.

Barker, Eugene C. *The Life of Stephen F. Austin, Founder of Texas, 1793–1836*. 1925. Reprint, New York: Da Capo Press, 1968.

Bolton, Herbert E. *The Spanish Borderlands: A Chronicle of Old Florida and the Southwest*. New Haven, CT: Yale University Press, 1901.

———. ed. *Spanish Exploration in the Southwest 1542–1706*. 1908. Reprint, New York: Barnes and Noble Inc., 1946.

———. *Texas in the Middle Eighteenth Century*. 1915. Reprint, New York: Russell and Russell Inc., 1962.

Bonnell, George W. *Topographical Description of Texas: To Which is Added an Account of the Indian Tribes.*1840. Reprint, Waco: Texian Press, 1964.

Brady, William. *Glimpses of Texas.* ca. 1870. Reprint, Louisville: Lost Cause Press, 1964.

Brooks, Philip Coolidge. *Diplomacy and the Borderlands, The Adams-Onis Treaty of 1819.* Berkeley: University of California Press, 1939.

Castaneda, Carlos E. *Our Catholic Heritage in Texas 1519–1936.* Vol. 1, *The Mission Era: The Finding of Texas, 1519–1699.* Austin: Von Boeckmann-Jones Company, 1936.

———. *Our Catholic Heritage in Texas 1519–1936.* Vol. 2, *The Mission Era: The Winning of Texas, 1693–1731.* Austin: Von Boeckmann-Jones Company, 1936.

———. *Our Catholic Heritage in Texas 1519–1936.* Vol. 4, *The Mission Era: The Passing of the Missions, 1762–1782.* Austin: Von Boeckmann-Jones Company, 1939.

———. *Our Catholic Heritage in Texas 1519–1936.* Vol. 5, *The End of the Spanish Regime, 1780–1810.* Austin: Von Boeckmann-Jones Company, 1942.

Crocket, George Louis. *Two Centuries in East Texas: A History of San Augustine County and Surrounding Territory from 1685 to the Present Time.* Dallas: Southwest Press, 1962.

Davis, Ellis A., and Edwin H. Grobe, eds. *The New Encyclopedia of Texas.* 2 vols. Dallas: Texas Development Bureau, n.d.

Douglas, William O. *Farewell to Texas: A Vanishing Wilderness.* New York: McGraw-Hill Book Company, 1967.

Fancher, George H., Robert L. Whiting., and James H. Cretsinger. *The Oil Resources of Texas, A Reconnaissance Survey of Primary and Secondary Reserves of Oil.* Austin and College Station: University of Texas and Texas A&M College, 1954.

Fisher, Orceneth. *Sketches of Texas in 1840.* 1841. Reprint, Waco: Texian Press, 1964.

Folmer, Henri. *Franco-Spanish Rivalry in North America.* Glendale: Arthur H. Clark Company, 1953.

Gunter, Pete. *The Big Thicket: A Challenge for Conservation.* Austin and New York: Jenkins Publishing Company, 1971.

Hardy, Dermot H., and Robert Ingham, eds. *Historical Review of South East Texas and Founders, Leaders and Representative Men of Its Commerce,*

Industry and Civic Affairs. 2 vols. Chicago: Lewis Publishing Company, 1910.

House, Aline. *Big Thicket: Its Heritage*. San Antonio: The Naylor Company, 1967.

Johnson, Frank W. *A History of Texas and Texans*. 4 vols. Edited and brought to date by Eugene C. Barker. Chicago: American Historical Society, 1914.

Kennedy, William. *Texas, the Rise, Progress and Prospects of the Republic of Texas*. 1841. 2 vols. Reprint, 2 vols. in 1, Ft. Worth: Molyneaux Craftsmen, Inc., 1925.

Kirby, John Henry. *Timber Resources of East Texas: Their Recognition and Development*. Chicago: American Lumberman, 1902.

Lasswell, Mary. *I'll Take Texas*. Boston: Houghton Mifflin, 1958.

———. *John Henry Kirby, Prince of the Pines*. Austin: The Encino Press, 1967.

Lillard, Richard G. *The Great Forest*. New York: Alfred A. Knape, 1947.

McLeod, Claude A. *The Big Thicket Forest of Eastern Texas, A Brief Historical, Botanical, and Ecological Report*. Huntsville: Sam Houston State University, 1972.

———. *The Big Thicket of East Texas: Its History, Location, and Description*. Huntsville: Sam Houston Press, 1968.

Malone, Prairie View. *Sam Houston's Indians*. San Antonio: The Naylor Company, 1960.

Moore, Francis, Jr. *Map and Description of Texas Containing Sketches of its History, Geology, Geography and Statistics*. 1840. Reprint, Waco: Texian Press, 1965.

Newcomb, W. W. Jr. *The Indians of Texas from Prehistoric to Modern Times*. Austin: University of Texas Press, 1961.

Parker, Lois Williams. *Big Thicket Bibliography*. Saratoga: Big Thicket Association, 1970.

Parks, Hal B., V. L. Cory and others. *Biological Survey of the East Texas Big Thicket Area*. n.p., 1936.

———. *The Fauna and Flora of the Big Thicket Area*. (n.p., 1936).

Pickett, Arlene. *Historic Liberty County*. Dallas: Tardy Publishing Company, 1936.

Reed, Saint Clair Griffin. *A History of Texas Railroads and of Transportation Conditions Under Spain and Mexico and the Republic and the State*. Houston: St. Clair Publishing Company, 1941.

Richardson, T. C. *East Texas: Its History and Its Makers*. 4 vols. New York: Lewis Historical Publishing Company, 1940.

Rister, Carl Coke. *Oil! Titan of the Southwest*. Norman: University of Oklahoma Press, 1949.

Rock, James L., and W. I. Smith. *Southern and Western Guide for 1878*. St. Louis: A. H. Granger, 1878.

Simonds, Frederic W. *The Geography of Texas, Physical and Political*. Boston: Ginn and Company, 1914.

Warner, C. A. *Texas Oil and Gas Since 1543*. Houston: Gulf Publishing Company, 1939.

Webb, Walter Prescott, ed. *The Handbook of Texas*. 2 vols. Austin: Texas State Historical Association, 1952.

Winfrey, Dorman, Rupert Richardson, et al. *Indian Tribes of Texas*. Waco: Texian Press, 1971.

Woodman, David. *Guide to Texas Emigrants*. Boston: M. Howes, 1835.

B. Articles

Bloomfield, Howard. "Big Thicket, The Biological Crossroads of America." *American Forest* 78 (September 1972): 24–27, 45–46.

Bolton, Herbert. "Spanish Activities on the Lower Trinity River, 1746–1771." *Southwestern Historical Quarterly* 16 (April 1913): 362–64.

Bonney, Orrin H. "Big Thicket—Biological Crossroads of North America." *Living Wilderness* 32–33 (Summer 1969): 19–21.

———. "The Big Thicket: The Biological Crossroads of North America." *Sierra Club Bulletin* 53 (May 1968): 7–11.

Bolton, Herbert E. "The Location of LaSalle's Colony on the Gulf of Mexico." *Mississippi Valley Historical Review* 2 (September 1915): 165–82.

———. "The Native Tribes About the East Texas Missions." *Southwestern Historical Quarterly* 11 (April 1908): 249–76.

Burch, Marvin C. "The Indigenous Indians of the Lower Trinity Area of Texas." *Southwestern Historical Quarterly* 60 (July 1956): 36–52.

Chambers, William T. "Division of the Pine Forest Belt of East Texas." *Economic Geography* 6 (January 1930): 94–103.

———. "Pine Woods Regions of Southeastern Texas." *Economic Geography* 10 (July 1934): 302–18.

———. "The Redlands of Central Eastern Texas." *Texas Geographic Magazine* 5 (August 1941): 1–15.

Cox, Issac J. "The Louisiana-Texas Frontier." *The Quarterly of the Texas State Historical Society* 10 (July, 1906): 1–75.

Creel, George. "Feudal Towns of Texas." *Harper's Weekly*. January 23, 1915, 76–78.

Deussen, Alexander. "Oil Producing Horizons of the Gulf Coast in Texas and Louisiana." In *Gulf Coast Oil Fields*, edited by Donald C. Barton and George Sawtelle. Tulsa: American Association of Petroleum Geologist, 1936.

Dugas, Vera Lea. "Texas Industry, 1860–1880." *Southwestern Historical Quarterly* 59 (October 1955): 151–83.

Gunter, P. A. "The Rural Southern Mentality and the Environmental Crisis." In *Population and Environmental Crisis*, edited by Stephen White. Johnson City, TN: East Tennessee State University Research Advisory Council, 1975.

Gunter, Pete. "The Big Thicket." *Living Wilderness* 31 (Autumn 1967): 3–9.

Haggard, J. Villasana. "The Neutral Ground Between Louisiana and Texas, 1806–1821." *Louisiana Historical Quarterly* 28 (October 1945): 1001–128.

Hatcher, Mattie A., trans. "Description of the Tejas or Asinai Indians, 1691–1722." *Southwestern Historical Quarterly* 30 (January–June 1927): 206–19, 283–304; 31 (July 1927): 50–62.

Henderson, Mary Virginia. "Minor Empresario Contracts for the Colonization of Texas, 1825-1834." *Southwestern Historical Quarterly* 31 (April 1928): 295–324; 32 (July 1928): 1–28.

King, John O. "The Early History of the Houston Oil Company of Texas, 1901–1908." *Texas Gulf Coast Historical Association Publication* 3 (April 1959): 1–97.

Lane, Tim E. "East Texas Indians Build Future Out of the Past." *East Texas* 39 (March 1965): 8.

Martin, Howard N. "Texas Redskins in Confederate Gray." *Southwestern Historical Quarterly* 70 (April 1967): 586–92.

Maxwell, Robert S. "East Texas Forgotten Logging Railroad." *Texas Forestry* 14 (August 1973): 6.

———. "Lumbermen on the East Texas Frontier." *Forest History* 9 (April 1965): 12–16.

————. "Researching Forest History in the Gulf Southwest." *Louisiana Studies* 10 (Summer 1971): 109–22.

————. "The Pines of Texas: A Study in Lumbering and Public Policy." *East Texas Historical Journal* 2 (October 1964): 77–85.

————. "Whistle in the Piney Woods: Paul Bremond and the Houston, East and West Texas Railway." *Texas Gulf Coast Historical Association Publication* 7 (November 1963): 75.

Morgan, George T., Jr. "No Compromise—No Recognition: John Henry Kirby, The Southern Lumber Operators' Association and Unionism in the Piney Woods, 1906-1916." *Labor History* 10 (Spring 1969): 193–204.

Owens, William A. "Boom in Batson: The Birth of an Oil Field." *Drilling Magazine* 19 (December 1957).

Parks, Hal B. "The Big Thicket." *Texas Geographic Magazine* 2 (1938): 16–28.

Pearce, J. E. "The Archaeology of East Texas." *American Anthropologist* 34 (March 1932): 670–87.

"Pine Bark Beetle Invades Thicket." *Texas Forestry* 13 (October 1972): 6.

Roueche, Berton. "The Witness Tree." *New Yorker*, August 31, 1968, 56–64.

Rowland, Kate Mason. "General John Thompson Mason, An Early Friend of Texas." *The Quarterly of the Texas State Historical Association* 11 (January 1908): 163–98.

Sawtelle, George. "The Batson Oil Field, Hardin County, Texas." *American Association of Petroleum Geologist Bulletin* 9 (December 1925): 1277–82.

Sheldon, Roger. "Texas Big Thicket." *American Forest* 58 (September 1952): 22–24, 46.

"Slash Pine in East Texas." *Texas Forest News* 19 (May/June 1939): 3–4.

Smithers, Harriet. "The Alabama Indians of Texas." *Southwestern Historical Quarterly* 36 (October 1932): 83–108.

Suman, John R. "The Saratoga Oil Field." *American Association of Petroleum Geologist Bulletin* 9 (March/April 1925): 263–85.

Teale, Edwin W. "Big Thicket—Crossroads of Nature." *Audubon* 73 (May 1971): 12–32.

Teas, L. P. "Natural Gas of Gulf Coast Salt Dome Area." In *Geology of Natural Gas*, edited by Henry A. Ley. Tulsa: American Association of Petroleum Geologist, 1935.

"The Big Thicket of East Texas." *Beaumont Business*, n.v. (May 1938): n.p.

Udden, J. A. "Oil Bearing Formations in Texas." *American Association of Petroleum Geologist Bulletin* 3 (1919): 82–98.

"War Stimulates 20 Percent Rise in Timber Cut." *Texas Forest News* 22 (January/February 1942): 1, 7.

Willey, D. A. "New Texan Oil Deposits." *Scientific American* 90 (January 30, 1904): 96.

Zuber, Macklyn. "Fire at Union Wells." *Frontier Times* 40 (October/November, 1962): 28–29, 62.

C. Theses, Dissertations and Typescripts

Beck, Flossie Tyson. "Development of W. T. Carter and Brothers Lumber Company." Master's thesis, Stephen F. Austin State College, 1950.

Benjamin, Ronald L. "East Texas in the Civil War." Master's thesis, Lamar State College of Technology, 1970.

Burch, Marvin C. "A History of the Lower Trinity Region of Texas to 1836." Master's thesis, University of Texas, 1950.

Easton, Hamilton Pratt. "The History of the Texas Lumbering Industry." Ph.D. dissertation, University of Texas, 1940.

Fincher, Rosalie. "The History of Liberty County." Master's thesis, University of Texas, 1937.

Hyman, Carolyn. "A History of Texas National Forest." Master's thesis, University of Texas, 1948.

Landrey, Wanda A. "Lawlessness in the Big Thicket." Master's thesis, Lamar State University, 1971.

Martin, James W. "History of Forest Conservation in Texas 1900-1935." Master's thesis, Stephen F. Austin State College, 1966.

McCord, Charles R. "A Brief History of the Brotherhood of Timber Workers." Master's thesis, University of Texas, 1959.

Rowe, Ina May. "A Study of the Development of Oil at Sour Lake." Master's thesis, Southwest Texas State Teachers College, 1939.

Watson, Geraldine. "The Big Thicket, An Ecological Summary." Unpublished manuscript in hands of Professor Henry Dethloff. Texas A&M University.

D. Pamphlets

Stewards of the Land. Lufkin: Texas Forest Service, 1968.

AFTERWORD

What follows is an effort to complete James Cozine's narrative, taking off roughly from the point at which he ends his account and bringing it up to the present time. To write such a concluding narrative is to confront serious problems. The creation of the Big Thicket National Preserve was a single event, one which tied together innumerable strands of history. The development of the Preserve was, and is, a many-sided series of events, which branch out, grow, and only occasionally interact. In the first case, one has many strands of history becoming a single strand; in the second, one has the Preserve becoming many strands of events.

It would seem at first glance that these events could be approached as a simple chronology: that is, as a series of dates of significant events listed according to the order in which they took place. The apparent simplicity of such a rubric, however, conceals its weakness. The history of the Big Thicket National Preserve is too complex to be constructed as a single series. Too many of its factors are contemporaneous, taking place at the same time but without affecting each other. Too many take place in areas outside the Preserve. Too many culminate at different times—if they do indeed culminate. All of these must be described in the present essay. Their sheer diversity in time, place, and character forbids their being nailed down on a "time line." Inevitably what follows must be like the Neches River: a free-flowing stream with definite beginnings, but with many loops, bends, and cutoff channels along the way.

It is useful to begin with a moral, or at least a practical admonition. Most environmentalists engaged in the effort to "save" something—a forest, river, or mountain—believe that once the feature in question is set aside, the task is over. Thus one would: 1. Get possession of the land. 2. Put a fence around it 3. Put up a no entrance sign. Nothing, however, is farther from the truth. The end of an environmental campaign is the beginning of a phalanx of problems. Some can be quickly solved; some will rankle on for decades. Some will be bureaucratic, some political, some economic. The Big Thicket National Preserve provides examples of all of these. They continue to unroll today, as diverse and tangled as the Big Thicket itself.

1. Bureaucratic Beginnings

When President Gerald R. Ford signed the Big Thicket National Preserve into existence on October 11, 1974, his signature created a paper park. The real one was to be long in the making—far longer than its protagonists could have imagined. The first land purchase was to take place fourteen months later, just before Christmas, 1975.[1] It came not too soon, but too late. As James Cozine points out, though large lumber companies had faithfully observed a moratorium on cutting inside the Preserve, some smaller timber operators continued to log the land in Preserve units.[2] Meanwhile, cutting to control pine beetle infestations caused the felling of extensive stands of pine trees inside the Preserve. The results were dramatic. Timber cutting by small landowners and big lumber companies destroyed some 2500 to 3000 acres of the Preserve. (Some conservationists put the figure as high as 4000 acres.) Not until emergency land purchase bills could be gotten through Congress in 1976 by Congressman Charles Wilson and Senator Lloyd Bentsen was the onslaught halted.

Subsequently, land purchase funding was to move ahead by uneven increments. From a beginning of $7,000,000 in 1976, funding reached $47,000,000 in 1977; $9,000,000 in 1978; $5,000,000 in 1979; $2,100,000 in 1980; $5,100,000 in 1981; and $7,600,000 in 1982.[3] The *Beaumont*

Enterprise pointed out that at that time (1982) 18% of the Preserve was still unacquired, and no funds were authorized for the current fiscal year.[4] Funding had ceased in 1982 due to a new Land Protection Plan imposed by the Reagan administration. The new plan required that all lands acquired by the National Park Service be subject to extremely stringent accounting procedures.[5] The plan, stigmatized by its detractors as "paralysis through analysis," managed to slow down but not quite halt land purchase. For the next decade, purchase funds were to be doled out to the Preserve in increments of a million dollars or less. Not until 1992—eighteen years after the creation of the Preserve—was land purchase finally completed.

But the sheer difficulty of finding funding was minor compared to the problems of actually purchasing the separate tracts of land that made up the Preserve. The task of processing these many purchases fell to William Jewell of the U.S. Corps of Engineers. Besides the problem of dealing with a multitude of small land parcels, Jewell found himself, as he recounted to a *Texas Lawyer* reporter, beset with "a nightmare of convoluted title searches and time-consuming detective work to track down the heirs of long-departed oil field speculators."[6] Foot-dragging by local title companies and the tendency of landowners to reject government land value estimates and take their cases to court did not make the task any easier.[7] Widely credited with skillful handling of difficult cases and with keeping funding moving in spite of bureaucratic roadblocks, Jewell was given an award in 1994 by the Big Thicket Association.[8]

Meanwhile, other sorts of questions were being posed and struggled with. Whereas earlier components of the National Park System had been set aside for their scenery, the Big Thicket National Preserve—the first biological preserve in the history of the Park Service—had been set aside almost exclusively because of its biology. If this meant that its biological integrity had to be protected, it was nonetheless clear that the public had to be allowed access. Equally challenging, hunting was to be allowed in the Preserve along with oil exploration and recovery. The Preserve's matrix of often isolated units and sprawling stream corridors further complicated an already complex situation. To deal with this would require a unique mix of wisdom and common sense.

Among the first of these problems was that of boundaries. When the Big Thicket National Preserve was created, its boundaries were depicted only in the most general terms. A long time Thicket environmentalist, Billy Hallmon, took it on himself to drive down from Dallas weekend after weekend and walk the boundaries of Preserve units mapping them step by step, mile after mile, here leaving out a residence or weekend retreat, there including a seep or oxbow lake. He managed this with little more than a topographical map, an ankle-attached yardage gauge, and a hand-held map roller.[9] No one asked him to do it, or paid him, or encouraged him. He simply did it.

Meanwhile, the National Park Service found itself in a quandary. Boundaries had to be established before lands could be bought, but, perennially short on staff and money, NPS found itself unable to begin boundary mapping. Given the nature of bureaucratic mapping, getting the requisite maps would require another year—or two, or three. Preserve superintendent Tom Lubbert solved the problem. Bringing the massive federal establishment with him, he accepted Billy's maps, which with some corrections are those of the present Preserve.[10]

What was to be allowed within these boundaries was to emerge from a seemingly endless series of NPS public meetings, studies, plans and statements. The most important of these were, in order: (1976) Final Environmental Statement, (1977) Proposal and Assessment Visitor Use and General Development, (1979) Wilderness Study, (1979) Land Acquisition Plan, (1980) General Management Plan, (1980) Wilderness Recommendations, (1983) Management Plan, and (1988) Fire Management Plan.[11] Once a plan is completed and filed, it is then subjected to periodic updates. The process of updating continues indefinitely.

As the series of studies and updates took form, the National Park Service began creating trails in the Preserve. In 1978, an Information Center (a log cabin next to a parking lot) was opened at the foot of the Turkey Creek Unit. This was to be the Preserve's de facto visitor center until a full-fledged visitor center opened to the public on October 6, 2001.[12] The causes of the twenty-five year wait for this center were many and will be discussed below.

Not until 1978 was the first trail opened in the Preserve. It was the first nine miles of the Turkey Creek Trail, at the north end of the Turkey

Creek Unit, far removed from the visitor's center at the unit's south end.[13] In 1979, the Beech Wood Trail opened in the Beech Creek Unit,[14] and in 1980 the Sundew Trail opened in the Hickory Creek Unit.[15] In 1983 the Youth Conservation Corps began construction of the Woodlands Trail in the Big Sandy Unit. This trail was completed the following year, as were the accessible loop on the Sundew Trail and a similar loop on the Pitcher Plant Trail, in the north part of the Turkey Creek Unit.[16] The Woodlands Trail was completed in 1990 by the addition of the Big Sandy Horse Trail.[17] This trail system was now nine miles long and was available for hiking, all-terrain bicycling, and horseback riding. In 1991, the Boy Scouts opened a path (the Birdwatcher's Trail) to the confluence of Menard Creek and the Trinity River. This half-mile-long trail offers a panoramic view of broad sandbars on the Trinity River from high bluffs on its east side. The Preserve's over forty miles of trails sketched above have subsequently been added to by the 1.5 mile Beaver Slide Trail in the southeast corner of the Big Sandy Unit.[18] In the future, an R. E. Jackson Trail will traverse the Big Sandy Unit from west to east. This trail, blazed by the Big Thicket Association, is already partly completed. A Bear Trail is projected for the Lance Rosier Unit. It will utilize the old Lance Rosier homesite. The NPS has been able to install picnic facilities at the entrances to several of these trails.[19]

The facts presented so far do not complete the Preserve's bureaucratic agenda. Among the other things that it has been called on to do (again, with insufficient personnel) is to administer hunting and trapping within its boundaries. Hunting permits began to be given out in 1980; trapping permits became available soon after.[20] It would be nice to be able to say that all went smoothly. Permits were originally given equally to all comers, producing a situation in which outside hunters far outnumbered local ones. In the beginning, also, local people were not effectively informed about how to obtain hunting permits. Uncertainty over the differences between federal and state hunting regulations added further confusion. Geraldine Watson recounts that local people became bitter about the situation—some nearly to the point of violence. The Park Service discovered that it had to change its stripes:

Each year, changes for the better were made in the hunting program. Registration was held in a public school nearest the unit involved and permits given on a first-come, first-serve basis, which gave the locals an edge. Aside from a few diehards who want everything to be as it was in the old days, people seem to be satisfied with the program.[21]

The Park Service's willingness to change its ways did improve feelings among the locals. But it can not be denied that a residue of resentment remains.

In the midst of these projects, Preserve superintendents and their staffs managed to find time and resources to fund scientific studies of the Preserve's plant growth communities, rare, scarce, and endangered species, archeological sites, birds, reptiles, mammals, as well as the impact, potential and actual, of oil and gas development. Policies for prescribed burning had to be worked out in the midst of sometimes heated controversies among environmentalists.[22] Payments in lieu of taxes needed to be worked out for counties deprived of tax revenues through federal land purchase.[23]

Even this long list of projects barely scratches the surface. Just how much more the Preserve leadership and staff were called on to do is revealed by a speech given in January 1992 to the Big Thicket Association by then-Preserve superintendent Ron Switzer. Switzer stated: 1. Methamphetamine labs on floating houseboats were turning up on Preserve streams. These were being policed by NPS personnel, as were occasional marijuana patches discovered in the woods. Insufficient personnel made it especially hard to police far-flung corridors and units. In 1982 the Preserve had 36 personnel; in 1992 it had 37. 2. Thirty water samples were being taken every two weeks throughout the Preserve. This and the maintenance of an air quality measuring station (in the Turkey Creek Unit) required trained personnel. 3. Because of these factors and because of its sheer complexity, the Big Thicket was a natural training ground for the National Park Service. Unfortunately, once trained, personnel tended to move on, and the Preserve has had to undertake more hiring and training. 4. Environmental education was now a required part of K through 12 curricula in Texas. The Preserve had begun an environmental education program, which, though it received an award from the Environmental Educators of Texas, was still in an embryonic state. 5. The Preserve Visitor Center (he stated optimistically) should begin construction over the next few months. The National Park Service would pay most of the costs for water and gas lines to be installed between the Center and Kountze, to the south. This, happily, put NPS out of the water and the gas business. 6. The church across from the Visitor Center bought four acres next to it to keep a Big Thicket McDonald's from moving in next door. Because of an old railroad right of way, the State of Texas would control frontage on the west side of U. S. Highway 69. Keeping the area around the Visitor Center "green" will be a big problem. 7. Current estimations for nesting pairs of the endangered red-cockaded woodpecker were eight (perhaps nine, given reports of a pair in the Hickory Creek Savannah Unit). 8. The Big Thicket was "the best kept secret in Southeast Texas." Efforts were being made to publicize it through a traveling exhibit, a new tabloid (sponsored by Chevron Oil), a new handbook, and articles in regional media. 9. The Preserve was beginning to rely on and to train volunteers as nature interpreters. 10. Land was beginning to be donated to the Preserve. At that time twenty acres of beautiful cypress sloughs on Pine Island Bayou and another 140-acre plot were in negotiation. 11. Pending legislation (S.1105) to add the Big Sandy-Village Creek Corridor to the Preserve was stalled in congressional committee. 12. The Preserve might be forced to take up drug education in its five-county area. 13. The last 244 acres of the Preserve were about to be purchased. Problems of multiple ownership had delayed the process.[24]

Listeners marveled that Switzer was able to cover all of these issues—and others on which he touched—in less than an hour. They were equally struck by the magnitude of the tasks that the National Park Service set itself, and the degree to which it managed to keep up with them, understaffed and underfunded as it was.

2. Beyond Bureaucracy
Saving Pine Island Bayou and Keeping the Neches River Free

To deal with the "bureaucratic" side of a natural area is to deal primarily (though not even in this case exclusively) with factors inside the area. But if, as John Donne said, no man is an island, then neither is a natural area. Each is situated in a natural and social context that has a very real effect on any island, man, or park. Increasingly, as stated above, attention must be focused on surrounding areas and their effect. This would turn out to be true especially of the stream corridors in and near the Big Thicket National Preserve.

Pine Island Bayou is a peculiar stream. In dry months it and its tributary, Little Pine Island Bayou, consist through their upper reaches of little more than tea-colored water holes strung between low-lying flats of baked black clay. If any alligators live in the upper course of these streams, they must be highly accomplished walkers. Even in their lower reaches, where sluggish dark water flows year-round, these streams seem more like small creeks than bayous. But these appearances are misleading. Tropical storms, thunderstorms, and stalled cold fronts have been known to dump massive rains of ten to twenty inches in a day. These hundred-year floods, which occur every fifteen to twenty years in the region, turn low flats of palmetto palm and live oak into one-half to one-mile-wide moving swamps. To build a home in such areas is to court misery, even if the home is built on stilts: a point real estate developers have been slow to recognize.

Much of the upstream region of Pine Island and Little Pine Island Bayou lies outside the Preserve. But Little Pine Island Bayou lies within the Lance Rosier Unit and Pine Island Bayou from its confluence with Little Pine Island Bayou in the Rosier Unit to its intersection with the Neches River is a Preserve corridor. The bayous and their deep wooded palmetto flats are thus an integral part of the Thicket, and what happens to them is a matter of particular concern to environmentalists.[25]

Though the bayous and their swampy watersheds are implausible places to build subdivisions, they remain tantalizingly close to Beaumont. The result has been the growth of exurbanite communities along their banks. The two largest and most important of these are Bevil Oaks and Pinewoods. Upscale and well kept, these clubhouse communities have a simple drawback: they flood. They flood often and well.

It was understandable—entirely predictable—that the residents of these and other nearby areas would soon join in a chorus of protest against their flood-prone predicament. Beginning in 1967 and reemerging in 1975,

1979, and 1995, the streamside communities pleaded for help from local government, and then from the Texas legislature. This would involve cutting trees and brush along the bayou, removing sunken logs and tree trunks, and straightening (i.e. ditching) its looping bends.[26] One spokesperson for the embattled exurbanites insisted that the problem could only be solved by building a dam upstream on the Neches River (the Rockland Dam, to be discussed below).[27]

Professional opinion was far from encouraging for these projects. In 1976, the U. S. Corps of Engineers had done a "reconnaissance" of the area, and in 1985 completed a much more elaborate feasibility study. Both concluded that no "economically feasible structural or non-structural means" of reducing flooding on the Pine Island Bayou watershed existed.[28] Another way of putting the matter would be to say that any conceivable way of halting flooding in the low, poorly drained area would be exorbitantly expensive, costing many times over the value of the affected subdivisions.[29]

The citizens of Pinewood and Bevil Oaks, however, were adamant. The question of flood control continued to be debated by their representatives in the newspapers and on television, and in 1995 bills to create a Pine Island Bayou Stormwater District were forwarded to the legislature by State Representative Zeb Zbranik and State Senator Michael Galloway. Zbranik's bill passed, but Galloway's was "tagged" at the last minute (i.e. prevented by other senators from being brought to the floor for a vote).[30] If the issue died a temporary death, it was resurrected in 1997, when on March 25 and 26 Galloway reintroduced his bill of two years before (now SB 1899) and Zbranik reintroduced his own (now HB 3546).[31] Both bills quickly passed and were signed into law by Governor Bush.

The lines were now drawn. On one side stood the conservationists, the National Park Service (which, however, could not actively interfere with the election), and the lumber companies, who stood to lose acreage to flood control cutting and ditching. On the other side stood homeowners, their friends and allies, including potential real estate developers. Jeannie Turk, realtor and spokesperson for the Pine Island Bayou Flood Committee, pleaded that her constituents had a right to live wherever they wanted to live, and that their homes and property values were threatened by serious flooding. Did local people want a local entity representing them on issues that affected them, or did they want state and federal agencies representing them? In response Dorothy Griffin, former manager of the Lumberton Chamber of Commerce and spokesperson for the Pine Island Bayou Tax Prevention Committee, said that the stormwater district would impose a new layer of taxes, duplicating those already imposed for local drainage districts, that it would impose a new layer of bureaucracy on top of already existing bureaucracy, and that it would levy taxes on people whose homes would be unaffected by potential flooding. On top of that, the district would not be able to halt floods.[32]

Scheduled for January 17, 1998, the election was forestalled by lawsuits filed by timber companies (chiefly Louisiana-Pacific) protesting the siting of voting places at the far southern end of the drainage district (at Pinewood, Bevil Oaks, and Daisetta). This siting was, they argued, clearly designed to limit voting only to those immediately affected, and not to the voters of the drainage district as a whole. The suits were successful. After continued legal sparring, the elections were held on November 3.[33]

Interestingly, efforts to predict the results were few, and guarded. If anyone had a crystal ball, it seems to have remained clouded. Stormwater district proponents trumpeted impending victory. Environmentalists and their allies said little. If anything, a pall of gloom had settled over the environmental camp. The "us against the Big Guys who are pushing us around" rhetoric of the stormwater spokesmen had a profound appeal to the local people. It had swayed them often before. But when the results came in, the figures were astonishing. Just over two thousand votes (2078) were registered for the district while almost six thousand (5835) were against it: a ratio of three to one. Still more surprising, the stormwater district carried Bevil Oaks and Pinewood by only the narrowest of margins. To almost everyone's surprise, ditching, timbering, and swampland development—and a new round of taxes—had been roundly defeated.[34]

No sooner had the threat to the bayous been removed, than a new threat emerged, this time on the Neches River. If Big and Little Pine Island Bayous are small meandering streams, the Neches is clearly a river: broad, free flowing, and powerful. The Big Thicket National Preserve encompasses a 72-mile as-the-crow-flies corridor stretching from Dam B

(Steinhagen Reservoir) on the north to the Beaumont Country Club to the south.[35] This corridor contains three Preserve units: Jack Gore Baygall Unit, Neches Bottom Unit, and the Beaumont Unit. In its course from Dam B to Beaumont, the Neches rolls through three distinct regions: a northern section in which swift-running water courses between high wooded bluffs, a middle section where banks begin to subside and slow waters begin to deposit their sediments, and a southern section that is far flatter, more alluvial, and increasingly swampy.[36] Particularly in the lower two sections, the river floodplain is carved into terraces. Each terrace sustains its own distinctive plant growth communities. All are dependent on annual river floods, which keep them wet and prevent the intrusion of dryland species. If flooding were halted, these areas would be significantly transformed.

This, of course, portended a problem. Though Dam B does limit flooding downstream on the Neches, it is a comparatively small dam with a minimal impact.[37] The U. S. Corps of Engineers, however, had projected a second, larger dam farther north on the Neches, the Rockland Dam and Reservoir. This structure would inundate at least 110,000 acres of hardwood bottomland forests, would effectively end the Neches' career as a wild, free-flowing river, and would significantly affect downstream water flow through the Big Thicket National Preserve corridor and its three units.[38]

Beginning in 1983, the Big Thicket Association started a drive to deauthorize the Rockland Reservoir, taking it off the Corps of Engineers list of potential projects. The drive was led by Billy Hallmon, at that time president of the Big Thicket Association. Because the dam had never been funded, it was eligible for inclusion in section 12 of Public Law 93-251, the Federal Water Resources Development Act of 1974. The actual process of deauthorization, however, was as tangled and Byzantine as any procedure in the federal bureaucracy. Each year the Chief of the U. S. Corps of Engineers prepares a list of from five to six hundred water projects acceptable for deauthorization, and then chooses a small number of these to be deauthorized. In doing this he has to consult with the states in which the projects were located and forward written comments to the Secretary of the Army, who could halt any deauthorization he might choose to halt.

The end result of this withering process was then sent to the public works committees of the House and Senate where, again, any item could be removed from the list. After ninety days any deauthorization that had not been shot down in the meantime was automatically considered put into law. Amazingly, each year some projects actually did get deauthorized by this process.[39] It is hard to imagine how.

There was an alternative to this labyrinthine scheme: direct congressional action. Given the ease with which legislation can be killed off in Congress, however, this at first seemed the most unlikely path. On June 26, 1983, Billy Hallmon sent a letter to the Corps of Engineers requesting that the Rockland Dam be officially included in the deauthorization process.[40]

If this move started the glacial deauthorization plan in motion, the motion was immediately interrupted. In 1984, the Texas Department of Water Resources had come out in favor of using federal funding to construct Rockland Reservoir.[41] The TDWR, in turn, had been prodded into action by the Lower Neches River Authority, which in 1982 had urged the creation of the federally funded dam.[42] In spite of persistent prodding by Congressman Wilson, the deauthorization process was stalled by state and local resistance. On March 19, 1987, the congressman, tired of waiting, introduced a bill into Congress to deauthorize Rockland Dam.[43] HR 1747 was referred to the House Committee on Public Works and Transportation, where it languished unmoved for two years. Finally the congressman, late in 1989, attached his bill as an obscure and unnoticed amendment to an omnibus bill. The omnibus bill sailed out of committee, was passed by Congress and made into law. On January 1, 1990, the Rockland Dam and Reservoir was officially deauthorized.[44]

This, of course ended the matter, precisely in the way that the Treaty of Versailles ended future wars in Europe. The Lower Neches Valley Authority, which had originally urged federal funding for the Rockland Dam, soon urged that the project be supported not by federal but by state funding. The LNVA's move was to be promoted by the East Texas Water Planning Group, one of sixteen regional water planning groups in the state.[45] In June 2000 the East Texas Water Planning Group proposed the creation of thirteen reservoirs in East Texas, impounding a total of 290,000 acres.

Among these was the Rockland Dam and Reservoir at a conservatively estimated cost of $700,000,000.[46] So significantly was the proposal regarded that it elicited an editorial in the *Beaumont Enterprise* and an extensive article in the *Houston Chronicle*.[47]

Environmentalists, awakened from their momentary happiness, responded with pointed criticisms. The proposed dam, they noted, would involve the condemnation of over 150,000 acres of prime timberland, cost not the projected figure but over a billion dollars when completed, and seriously disrupt water flow downstream.[48] One environmentalist, Richard Donovan of Lufkin, canoed down 200 miles of the Neches in October 1999, describing the beauty of the primitive back country and arguing that the Neches should be declared a National Wild and Scenic River. Such a status, of course, would preclude the creation of any further dams along its length.[49] The idea of a National Wild and Scenic River on the Neches (or of a National Recreational River) began to be seriously developed by conservationists and attracted favorable interest by the newly elected congressman for the district, Democrat Jim Turner.

But just at that moment, as environmentalists and water interests steeled themselves for a very long, hard, noisy battle, a strange silence settled over the Piney Woods. Local people, interestingly, were letting it be known far and wide that they wanted no more reservoirs and, given the chance, would vote against them. Conservationists, caught unaware by the stillness, looked elsewhere for problems to address (and managed to find them). Water interests withdrew and bided their time. Meanwhile, in the background, moves were being made which would change the future of the Neches River. In July 2003, a projected purchase of 33,000 acres of prime timber in the Neches River bottomland was announced. This acreage, purchased from International Paper, lies directly in the path of the proposed Rockland Reservoir and renders its future construction extremely unlikely. The purchase, arranged by the National Land and Conservation Fund, was supported by the Meadows Foundation, the T. L. L. Temple Foundation, and Renewable Resources, LLC. This last plans to manage the area as sustainable production hardwood forest until it can be turned over to public ownership.[50] The land segment, which connects the Davy Crockett National Forest and the

Angelina National Forest, will possibly become part of a Neches River National Wildlife Refuge.

The defeat of efforts to ditch, timber, and de-snag Pine Island and Little Pine Island Bayou was unexpected and, exactly to that degree, dramatic. The creation of a new bottomland wilderness and the simultaneous halting of plans to put a major dam on the Neches River were less dramatic, precisely because events in this case moved quietly and the new wilderness was announced without fanfare. The results, however, were even more astonishing. At one stroke, a vast stretch of land was left wild. And a river—the last such river in East Texas—was left free. It could be hard to believe that such things are possible.

3. A Wider Big Thicket
Parks, Donations, and a New Center

So far this essay has recounted the "bureaucratic" creation of the Big Thicket National Preserve and struggles to defend the area streams that feed into the Preserve and also are part of it. What follows is an expansion of scope. It is a description of the many subsequent additions to the Preserve as well as to the broad area surrounding it. These additions, it will be argued, broaden the very concept of the Big Thicket Preserve. Inevitably one is drawn from thinking of it as one ecological reality to conceiving it as the center of a broad, sprawling Big Thicket Environmental Area.

When the Preserve was created in 1974, it contained all the basic plant growth communities in the Thicket but one. The community not included was the "arid sandland" community, which, though it contained ponds, floodplains and bogs, sits on one- to three-hundred-feet-deep sand deposits. Abundant rainfall there immediately sinks downward, leaving a dry land of dwarfed pine trees, cacti, and West Texas wildflowers. To complete the catalogue of plant growth communities, in 1977 Temple-Eastex (now Temple-Inland) donated 2138 acres of arid sandland to The Nature Conservancy, a national environmental organization mentioned several times in this essay. This tract (the Larsen Sanctuary) lies on the east side of Village Creek and runs from FM418 on the north to FM327 on the south: an easy one-day canoe trip. A 40-acre donation in 1978 by Gulf

State Utilities and a subsequent donation in 1985 by Sun Oil were added to by a Temple-Inland donation in 1991 along FM418. Purchase of several smaller tracts by The Nature Conservancy in 1990 and 1991 brought the total size of the sanctuary to 2400 acres.[51]

But this was not to be the end. In 1994, Temple-Inland conveyed to The Nature Conservancy an additional 380.15 acres on the west side of Village Creek along with an additional 2800-acre "conservation easement" also on the creek's west side. This brought the size of the sanctuary to 5,600 acres: larger than many of the Preserve units and a vital addition to them.[52]

There is more than a little irony in this consummation. The struggle to bring Village Creek into the Preserve in the 1970s had very nearly cost the Preserve its existence. Now an extensive sanctuary had been created on the creek, and by a timber company. But this was not to be the end of the Adventure of Village Creek. At almost the same time as the Larsen Sanctuary was announced, the Village Creek State Park of 1004 acres was opened on the creek to the south, near Lumberton.[53] This park, with its two-mile creek frontage, would be developed for camping in its upland areas while its low areas would remain undeveloped.[54] In January 2001, an additional 45 acres (predominantly longleaf pine upland) were added to the park.[55]

Big Sandy-Village Creek, though not in the Preserve as such, now boasted five protected areas along its sixty-mile length: the Big Sandy Unit, the foot of the Turkey Creek Unit, the Larsen Sanctuary, Village Creek State Park, and the confluence of the creek with the Lower Neches Corridor. It remained to be seen whether more sanctuaries could be added to it, or whether a Big Thicket Addition Bill could bring the whole creek under protection. The unending effort to pass a Big Thicket Addition Bill in Congress will be considered below—at great length.

If this, for the time being, ended the acquisition of land along Village Creek and in the lower Neches drainage basin generally, it did not halt acquisition of new state parks east of the Neches, and on (and west of) the Trinity. The only place where the Big Thicket Preserve directly touches the Trinity River is at the confluence of the Trinity and the Preserve's Menard Creek Corridor. But in 1983 Texas State Parks and Wildlife ac-

quired the 1734-acre Davis Hill State Park, twelve miles south of the
Menard Corridor on the west bank of the river. This picturesque park sits
on a salt dome rising 210 feet above low, swampy bottomlands.[56] The park's
elevation makes for beautiful views, and creates microhabitats supporting
some rare and some unusual plant species.[57]

During the time (roughly from 1964 to 1974) when conservationists
and lumber interests were quarreling over the creation and location of the
Big Thicket National Preserve, a quiet gentleman's agreement was reached
between the combatants. That is, it was agreed to concentrate only on the
land between the Trinity River and the Neches River. Neither party had
the energy or the resources to fight over outlying areas. (This in spite of
the fact that most parties agreed that the "Thicket" sprawled west to the
San Jacinto River and east, with interruptions, to the Sabine River.) With
the creation of Lake Houston State Park (4917 acres) in the San Jacinto
River drainage basin and Tony Houseman State Park (4919 acres) on the
Sabine River, the arbitrary Trinity-Neches Barrier was transgressed.[58] Now
it became possible to think about the Big Thicket throughout its length.

In 1994, ten years after the creation of Davis Hill State Park on the
Trinity, a new and unexpected environmental presence came to the river.
From just south of the Lake Livingston Dam (approximately 12 1/2
crowflight miles northwest of the Menard Creek Corridor) to and beyond
SH90 to the south, the Trinity flows for over 45 straightline miles through
wild, tangled deep-southern bottomland, which in spite of a scattering of
oil wells, occasional weekend subdivisions, and cattle pastures, remains
virtually uninhabited. Except for the proposed Tanner Bayou Unit on the
west side of the river not far south of the dam, none of this area had seriously been considered for inclusion in the Big Thicket National Preserve.
Its wild/semiwild status, its vast size, and its complex of diverse habitats
and plant growth communities, however, made it a natural candidate for
some kind of environmental protection. So did its economic value, which
often involved the production of income only sufficient for payment of
gradually increasing taxes.

The new environmental presence came in the form not of the National Park Service or Texas State Parks and Wildlife, but of the National
Fish and Wildlife Service. The result would be the Trinity River National

Wildlife Refuge. Acquisition of the wildlife refuge was to be piecemeal. The initial land purchase (purchase from willing sellers, not through condemnation) came to 4,400 acres: an area just to the south of and at some points directly adjacent to the Davis Hill State Park.[59] From 1994 through April 2002, parcels of 900, 1500, 600, 1200, 100, 200, and 3100 acres were added to the refuge, bringing the total size to 12,900 acres.[60] As of September 2003, total refuge size had risen to 18,000 acres.[61] Original projections for the TRWR ranged from as low as 20,000 to as high as 80,000 or more acres. The future extent of the refuge is at this moment uncertain. It does seem that the final figure will transcend the minimum figure of 20,000 acres.

Meanwhile, a collection of smaller wild areas were added to the tally, some near (in fact, some directly adjacent to) the Preserve, others far from it. These came from very different sources and had quite different statuses. The first to be sketched here are those that derive from private organizations. Formally dedicated in July 1978, the 40-acre Dujay Sanctuary, contiguous with the northeast section of the Lance Rosier Unit, will be used by Lamar University for educational and scientific purposes.[62] The Nature Conservancy of Texas currently owns the Wier Woods Preserve of 106 acres near Lumberton, the 43-acre J. Cooke and Mary Randolph Wilson Preserve in the north Beaumont city limits near Pine Island Bayou, and the 49-acre Big Thicket Bogs and Pinelands on U. S. Highway 69 near Warren.[63] In addition, the Natural Area Preservation Association (affiliated with the Texas Committee on Natural Resources) has donated 12 acres to the Marysee Prairie, west of Saratoga, and in 1998 came into possession of the 254-acre Gum Bayou Preserve near Liberty and the 69.6-acre J. H. McAfee Preserve in Tyler County east of Woodville.[64]

To these areas (totaling 574 acres) must be added a very odd wildland, created by the Hardin County Commissioners Court in August 1997. From Saratoga, Texas, a county road runs due north to the abandoned village of Bragg, on FM1293. The road, which follows a former logging railroad spur, is surrounded with a mystery. Many years ago a drunken railroad worker was said to have lain down on the railroad track and had his head cut off by a passing locomotive. Since then a strange light has been seen drifting along the road: the ghost, it is said, of the workman looking for his lost head by lantern light. The pencil-straight thoroughfare has come to be called the "Ghost Road." People have come for many years to look for the ghost. For several years the Big Thicket Association sponsored walks on the road at midnight and even gave out t-shirts proclaiming the bravery of those willing to make the trek.

The problem was that the road and its right of way belonged to the county, which periodically threatened to cut the timber that flourished there. The value of the timber has been estimated as high as $86,000—no small sum for a county with a slender tax base.[65] Gradually, however, the value of the road as a historical icon and a tourist attraction began to win converts, who organized and put pressure on the county judges.[66] After many meetings, petitionings, and well-publicized hikes by local groups, the Hardin County Commissioners in 1997 created the Ghost Road Scenic Drive County Park. In the words of Commissioner Ken Pelt, the Ghost Road Planning Committee was charged with working out a "long-range plan for the maintenance, use, and development of Ghost Road".[67] The Big Thicket now boasted a 100-acre nature preserve eight miles long and 110 feet wide.[68]

Many other areas have been set aside. They are both farther than the Ghost Road from the Preserve and by far less dramatic. In the western reaches of the Big Thicket the Natural Area Protection Association established the 74-acre Winter's Bayou Protective Addition in 1991 and 1994. The Houston Audubon Society has also set aside 130.6 acres on Winter's Bayou and more recently has established the 517-acre Damuth Sanctuary. Of equal size and importance is the Houston Outdoor Nature Club's aptly named 665-acre Little Thicket Sanctuary.[69] All of these areas are in or near the southeast section of the Sam Houston National Forest and constitute a kind of Western Big Thicket Nature Complex. It would be pleasant to report that the organizations interested in maintaining this complex are concerned with working out interrelations among its components (that is, stream corridors, game trails, scenic easements). Unfortunately this does not seem to be the case.

Finally, there are the additions to the Preserve itself. These are many, and to deal with them all is, unfortunately, to indulge in a long, not overwhelmingly exciting list. (That is, the listing is not exciting; the nature and value of the added areas is.) In rough chronological order the additions are: 42.37 acres in 1978 by Amoco Production; 10 acres in 1983 by Conoco, Inc.; 12.76 acres in 1994 by the Big Thicket Association; and 1.86 acres in 1995 by the Charles G. Hooks Estate. All of these areas are in or near the Lance Rosier Unit. In 1992 Rebecca Ann Best gave 47.5 acres along Pine Island Bayou to the Preserve, and two years later Mrs. Richard Monro donated 22.98 acres on Village Creek. This botanically rich area, originally the Magnolia Garden Club's Winfred Turner Sanctuary, will be included in the Village Creek Corridor.[70] In 1994 the board of Magnolia Petroleum gave 23.54 acres on the Menard Creek Corridor, and in 2000 the Citgo Pipeline Company donated 26.20 acres to the Beaumont Unit. In 2002 the Lower Neches Valley Authority gave two parcels of land northeast of the Beaumont Unit totaling 361.32 acres. This acreage was given in "mitigation" for a saltwater barrier constructed on the Neches River south of the Beaumont Unit. To these parcels should be added 13.10 acres given by John Blair to increase the size of the proposed Big Thicket National Preserve Visitor Center. As this is written, a 22-acre tract near the Beech Creek Unit is being considered for acceptance by the Preserve. The approximate total of all these additions is 560 acres.[71]

This section must end with a bit of arithmetic, and with a pointed admonition. When the acreage of the Larsen Preserve (5600) is added to the acreage donated directly to the Preserve (560), one has a figure of 6160 acres. When this sum is added to that of the Trinity River National Wildlife Refuge (18,000 acres) and to the smaller holdings of private organizations (2,189.6), the figure comes to 26,349.6 acres. The acreage of new state parks (12,619), added to the preceding, sums up to a grand figure of 38,958 acres. This, viewed in itself, appears as a massive area. Some would argue that such an area is a serious subtraction from the land base that underlies East Texas's economy. When these areas are viewed in their natural context, however, this illusion vanishes. Against the millions of acres that make up southeast Texas, these tens of thousands of acres barely appear against the massive sprawl of prairie and woodland, town and reservoir. They stand out as environmental freckles on the broad face of the land. When each tract is looked at separately, moreover, it turns out that most are of minimal economic value: particularly the swamps, stream corridors, and sandlands. Their best use is not for timbering but for hiking, fishing, hunting, camping, birdwatching, horseback riding or the simple enjoyment of nature. That is, put in terms of the contemporary rubrics, they are best suited to recreational and environmental tourism. Local businessmen and chambers of commerce are beginning to recognize these factors and take them as an additional base for the area's economy, rather than a threat to it.

Finally, there is the matter of a single very small increment to the environmental tracts of southeast Texas: a mere 28.10 acres at the junction of U.S. Highway 69 and FM420, situated between the Hickory Creek Savannah Unit and the Turkey Creek Unit of the Big Thicket National Preserve. This was, after an endless process, the Preserve's Visitor Center.

All those connected with the Preserve had realized from the beginning that such a facility was needed. Visitors needed to know not only where the Preserve and its units were; they needed to know what they were and why the Preserve was created in the first place. The tiny log cabin at the foot of the Turkey Creek Unit could hand out brochures and conversation, but it could do little more. This hardly oriented the public to the region and its biological richness. Under these conditions it was not surprising that visitation to the Preserve remained low.

As it was with everything connected to the Preserve, the process finally leading to the Visitor Center was to be glacially slow. On October 17, 1984, Public Law 98-489 made it possible for the Park Service to buy the Visitor Center land.[72] In fiscal year 1989 Congressman Wilson was able to get a $450,000 appropriation to do the planning for the center.[73] In 1990 he obtained further planning funds plus $3,097,000 for Phase I construction of maintenance facilities. Preserve superintendent Switzer waxed enthusiastic to a local reporter: "We feel this visitor center is the cornerstone to the future of Hardin County. We want to be partners in the future of the county."[74] The new complex, he explained, would include not only maintenance facilities but a new visitor's center and the Preserve's administrative offices, a 13,000-square-foot structure with a massive geodesic dome and geometrical, flat angled roof. All this would be completely built in three years. That is, it would be built by 1992.

Superintendent Switzer, however, failed to reckon with the swampwater temporality and molasses-drip entropy of a Federal bureaucracy. As these words are written, the administrative offices of the Preserve remain in Beaumont, in rented property. The Visitor Center exists and is open to the public. By a lucky quirk of fate, it was redesigned by architect Bill Nelson of Beaumont, who removed the alien geodesic dome and sloping jet wing roof, replacing them with a building reminiscent both of a log cabin and of a Southern plantation home, veranda and all.[75] The Center now "fits" its surroundings, physical and historical.

That it exists at all is a function of local determination. In 1999 the Kountze Economic Development Corporation pledged $150,000 from local tax funds towards the construction of the Visitor Center, with a promise to raise $200,000 in additional funds.[76] Though by early May 2000 they had been able to raise only an additional $47,500, this was enough to break the logjam. On May 13, 2000, Congressman Jim Turner's office was able to announce an additional $300,000 in funding to add to $530,250 already budgeted by the National Park Service. The final amount raised by the Kountze Economic Development Corporation was $330,000.[77] Thus on October 6, 2001, only 26 years after the creation of the Preserve and almost a decade after its announcement to the world as a *fait accompli*, the Visitor Center was dedicated.

Meanwhile another center—a scientific research center—was also taking form. It began as an idea in the mind of Maxine Johnston, a past president of the Big Thicket Association and editor of the *Big Thicket Reporter*. Over a generation earlier when the BTNP was being created, one of the primary arguments in its favor was its scientific and educational value. This belief had led to two Big Thicket Science conferences, the first in Beaumont, October 1996, the second in the same city in October 1999. The proceedings of both were published in special issues of the *Texas Journal of Science*.[78]

Such conferences were useful. But a facility was needed to which scientists and their students could come to pursue their research. Though no such structure existed, a possibility, on the grounds of the Big Thicket Association in Saratoga, did exist. As James Cozine notes in his narrative, these grounds were bought originally by the Big Thicket Association. They consisted of an old brick school building, a wooden gymnasium, and a construction brick-and-tile cafeteria. Broken into by vandals and leached by rain, the school building had to be taken down. Later the gym (which one wit insisted, stood erect only because the termites were holding hands to keep it standing) had to be disassembled also. That left the cafeteria, which, though it had served as a Big Thicket Museum, was showing signs of advanced old age.

Though it seemed hard to imagine that the cafeteria, with its peeling paint, antique roof, and cracked, dusty windows, could serve as an upscale research center, the scarcely imaginable soon began to take shape. In July 1999 the National Park Foundation and Georgia Pacific jointly awarded a $60,000 grant towards the project.[79] This was to be followed by a $5000 grant by the Crawford family,[80] a $1000 grant by the Foundation for Southeast Texas,[81] and by a succession of grants from the Meadows Foundation ($74,000), the Brown Foundation ($67,000) and the Magnolia Garden Club ($6,000).[82] The end result, achieved with overlapping, not always consistent construction projects, is a spacious, clean structure with meeting rooms, a kitchen, scientific research areas, men's and women's dormitories and restroom-shower facilities, and a large entry room equipped with sofas, chairs, and library tables.

If the Visitor Center opened on one day, the Research Center was to have many openings before its completion. In its first year, study groups from Rice University, the University of Texas at Austin, Tarleton College, the University of North Texas, and the University of Illinois were able to utilize the Research Center.[83] When the Center's construction projects were finally completed, it was at last able to open officially. This was without photo-ops, fanfare, or the waving of flags. Perhaps this was because it had not taken decades to achieve.

This account of additions to Big Thicket National Preserve and to the areas around it does not pretend to completeness. For the last four years the author has attempted to put together a "map atlas" of all preserves, parks, hiking trails, and wilderness areas in southeast Texas. These include county parks, city hiking trails, city wildlands, private preserves, and other kinds of protected places. The bizarre unwillingness of most parties involved in these areas to provide maps or plats of their lands has made the process difficult. So has the behavior of two of the three large timber companies in the area, which, as will be detailed below, ceremoniously set aside "special," "unique," beautiful" natural areas in the Big Thicket Nature Area and then sold them and their surrounding lands, leaving the areas with no secure future or perhaps no future at all. No thoroughgoing map atlas of the Thicket region has been attempted here. The aim has been to provide a broad, factual account of permanent additions to the Big Thicket region.

4. The Big Thicket Addition Act, Corporate Sell-offs, and a New Big Thicket Crisis

James Cozine's description of the part played by the Big Sandy-Village Creek Corridor in the struggle to create the Big Thicket National Preserve is convincing.[84] Many were those who did not want its inclusion, both those in or associated with the area timber industry and many of those who simply did not like the idea. Against these protagonists, conservationists pleaded that the creek corridor, which tied together three of the Preserve's units, was the lifeblood of the Preserve. Even if this were not true, they proclaimed, the Big Sandy-Village Creek Corridor was not only beautiful, it was one of the best, if not the best, canoeing streams in East Texas. If it were not saved, sooner or later it would be clearcut and/or picked to pieces by real estate speculators.

It was obvious, however, that in trying against all odds to include the creek corridor in the Preserve, conservationists had overreached themselves. In persisting as they had, environmentalists had broken a de facto pact with Congressman Charles Wilson, with whom they had initially agreed to refrain from seeking the corridor. It was quite understandable that the congressman felt betrayed. It was also understandable that the timber companies believed they had already given up more than they should and should not be required to give up more. In the end, the "anti" faction won out. Conservationists relented. The corridor remained unsaved.

But not for long. In 1978, former Senator Ralph Yarborough, irrepressible conservationist that he was, began pressuring Texas State Parks and Wildlife to create a five or six thousand-acre state park on Village Creek. TSP&W did not respond to Yarborough's very public exhortations, but his repeated pleas could not be ignored indefinitely. The situation was suddenly punctuated by Congressman Charles Wilson, who urged angrily that Yarborough's proposal violated the agreement under which the Big Thicket National Preserve had been created. To make his point, he personally excluded $6.1 million of badly needed land purchase funds intended for the Preserve. Once and for all, he had put his foot down.[85]

He was soon allowed to pick up his foot. A local landowner intervened in the quarrel by informing Texas State Parks and Wildlife that he was willing to sell a sizeable tract of land on Village Creek if it could be turned into a park.[86] Senator Yarborough then stepped back from his advocacy, at least for the time being. Senator Lloyd Bentsen moved in and got the $6.1 million back into the acquisition funding. Conservationists once more relented, and let the creek flow on unperturbed.

That was still not to be the end of the affair, which began to seem unendable. In June 1986, Congressman Wilson 's aides began asking stunned conservationists if they would like to see 14,000 acres, including the Big Sandy-Village Creek Corridor, added to the Preserve. On deep reflection, conservationists decided that this would be a fine idea. So, on October 2, 1986, Wilson introduced HR 5646 to add the Village Creek Corridor (7,000 acres) to the Preserve, as well as to widen the Lower Neches Corridor (an additional 7,000 acres). A year later, on October 22, 1987, he amended his bill (now HR 3544) to include both the Big Sandy Corridor and the Canyonlands, a hilly, stream-cut area on the west bank of the Neches just below Dam B.[87]

There were to be procedural complications: a local hearing (May 21, 1988) and then, on June 4, 1988, a House hearing in Washington, D.C. By now Wilson's bill had been rechristened HR 919, and tallied exactly 13,000 acres: 6120 in the Big Sandy Corridor, 5088 in the Village Creek Corridor, and 1792 acres in the Canyonlands.[88] In July 1989, Wilson's bill passed the House. Senator Bentsen then introduced a companion bill (S 1302) in the Senate.[89] On October 24, 1989, hearings were held before the Senate Subcommittee on Public Lands. Opposition stemmed from the National Park Service (which opposed the Big Sandy Corridor) and from local landowners, who opposed losing their weekend cabins.[90]

Then, true to the Big Thicket tradition, a new complication emerged. Newly elected conservative senator Phil Gramm (R-Tex) stepped forward to oppose the Addition Bill in the Senate, arguing that though he was not categorically opposed to new land for the Preserve, he was not convinced that the idea was acceptable either.[91] Undaunted, Congressman Wilson introduced a new bill (HR 1592), which included the Big Sandy-Village Creek Corridor, the Canyonland Unit, and, in addition, the Blue Elbow Unit, later to become Tony Houseman State Park.[92] The new proposed unit enlarged Wilson's bill to 15,105 acres. Bentsen then introduced a bill identical to Wilson's in the Senate, while Gramm introduced a bill proposing a 10,000-acre addition.[93]

On November 23, 1991, the House of Representatives passed Wilson's HR 1592. The issue seemed to be moving to a conclusion when a new Senate hearing was held, with both sides agreeing to let their previous testimony reflect their views.[94] Weeks then passed before Bentsen and Gramm could get together to resolve their differences. When they did meet, the result was a 10,000-acre bill (Gramm's version) with a fateful proviso. Land taken from timber companies to create the addition to the Preserve would have to be traded for land taken from the national forests of Texas. Among other things, this meant that a remarkable degree of cooperation would have to be reached between the Department of the Interior (containing the National Park Service) and the Department of Agriculture (containing the U.S. Forest Service). No such cooperation had been achieved previously.

An ominous pause ensued. While senators held bills hostage until they could get their own bills passed, the compromise Addition Bill lay moribund in committee. On top of this impasse, senators on the committee argued over the precise character of the language in terms of which a land exchange could be managed. On October 8, 1992, after an intense letter-writing, telegram, and telephone campaign by conservationists, the Big Thicket Addition Bill was released from the Senate Energy and Natural Resources Committee and passed the Senate. A round of celebrations, all premature, ensued.

In order to make it to the president's desk for signature, the Addition Bill had to make it through an arcane mechanism termed the "consent calendar," which allows a skeleton crew of congressmen remaining in Washington while their colleagues return home to campaign, to pass noncontroversial legislation through a unanimous vote. Any congressman could, if he wished, veto a consent bill, but this had never happened in the history of Congress. That is, not until now. William Dannemire (R-Cal), a one-term congressman who had failed in his bid to run for the United States Senate from California and who told reporters that he hated Washington and everything in it, took his revenge by vetoing all seventy bills in the consent calendar, including the Big Thicket Addition Act. Dannemire left Washington, presumably never to haunt the area inside the Beltway again. The process started over.[95]

If onlookers had been puzzled over Congressman Wilson's abrupt about-face on the issue of Big Sandy-Village Creek, none could doubt his persistence in pursuing passage of the Addition Bill in Congress. Returning to Washington with greater seniority after the November 1992 elections, on January 5, 1993, he introduced HR 433, which included the Corridor, Canyonlands and, once again, the Blue Elbow Swamp. On January 21, Phil Gramm and newly appointed Senator Bob Krueger (D-Texas) introduced S 80, which contained the Corridor and Canyonlands, but not Blue Elbow. S 80 was released by the Senate Energy and Natural Resources Committee on March 3, 1992,[96] and passed the Senate on March 17.[97]

Hearings were then held in the House Subcommittee on National Parks and Public Lands on May 11 with reference to Wilson's HR 433 and the Gramm-Krueger bill S 80. Since small weekend properties on the Big Sandy-Village Creek Corridor had been excluded from all legislation, the only opposition was now from the National Park Service. Prophetically, Senator Bennett Johnston (D-La) objected to the bill's restrictive language, which required acquisition within two years.[98] Wilson's HR 433, minus Blue Elbow and identical now to Gramm's S 80, passed the House and was signed into law by President William Clinton on July 1, 1993.[99]

The president's signature may have seemed to end a remarkably long process. But it started another series of processes in motion. While it might seem a simple thing to trade land between the Forest Service and the National Park Service with the lumber companies standing as intermediaries, in practice the procedure was a complex affair. The Park Service was required to publish boundaries in the *Federal Register*, secure title evidence, and make contracts with timber appraisers. Timber cruises and fair market appraisals had to be accomplished for both timber company and national forest lands. Funds then had to be secured for surveying, title searches, and appraisals.[100] In 1995, $1.5 million were appropriated by Congress for these intermediaries.[101]

All this took time—too much time. The two-year limit against which Senator Bennett Johnston had protested was beginning to run out.[102] Congressman Wilson worked to get the extension by bringing together representatives of the National Park Service, the U.S. Forest Service, the forest products industries and the relevant House and Senate committees.[103] On December 5, 1995, the House passed Wilson's HR 826, extending the deadline of the land swap to July 1998.[104] Only a few months later (on April 25, 1996) the Senate Energy and Natural Resources Committee held hearings on HR 826.[105] On May 1, the Senate passed an Omnibus Parks Bill containing the Big Thicket Addition Act Extension.[106] All that remained was a House-Senate conference committee to iron out any differences between House and Senate versions of several pieces of legislation included in the Omnibus Bill. Struggles between congressmen and senators over these details lasted throughout the summer, holding the Omnibus Parks Bill hostage.[107]

Then, in October 1996, only minutes before the 104th Congress was gaveled into history, the Omnibus Parks Bill was finally approved. This, wrote *Dallas Morning News* reporter Nita Thurman, must surely mean that the stream corridor had been added to the Big Thicket National Preserve at last.[108] But those who have read so far—and they are to be congratulated on their stamina—must suspect that something would still emerge to stand in the way.

In the fall of 1996, Congressman Charles Wilson, after decades of service in the Texas and then the U.S. legislatures, declined to run for office. His successor, Jim Turner, also a Democrat, bravely took over where Wilson had left off, urging compromise, bringing together meetings of interested parties, even getting a thirty-day extension of the already lengthened deadline for the proposed land swap.[109] The new congressman's efforts were of no avail. Presented, in June 1997, with the requisite maps, "fair market value" and dollar amounts clearly presented, all parties walked away from the table without so much as a discussion. The Addition Act had been scuttled.[110]

Post mortem analyses of what went wrong were as numerous as speculations on tactics after a high school football game. Contract appraisers had short cut procedures while proposing questionable discounts. The Park Service was complacent when it should have been aggressive. The congressman had not done enough. Conservationists had assumed good faith on all hands when they should have been applying unremitting pressure. In the end, if there was a consensus, it leaned towards blaming the intransigence of the Forest Service, which had dragged its feet and stonewalled from beginning to end.

Whatever the causes of the exchange disaster, the results opened new possibilities—possibilities which, however, took time to be worked out. Congressman Turner pledged to continue working on the Addition Act, and to explore new avenues of approach.[111] The decision on a course of action was late in coming. Legislation to purchase the Corridor and Canyonlands "in fee simple" was explored in late 1998, but rejected.[112] On December 16, 1999, Turner convened a meeting in his Washington offices with representatives of the National Park Service, the Big Thicket Preserve, and The Nature Conservancy.[113] The subject of this meeting was never divulged. A subsequent visit by Turner with the Forest Service also failed to produce any visible results.[114] Months turned into a year, hopes dimmed, and even the remarkable patience of Big Thicket conservationists, long inured to the necessity of waiting, grew threadbare. Then suddenly, without fanfare, a solution was reached.

Sad experience had proved that it was not possible to exchange lands between timber companies and the Forest Service, and between the Forest Service and the National Park Service. Oddly enough, however, little more had been specified in the Addition Act beyond the word "exchange." Lots of things could be exchanged for lots of things, and still be within the provisions of the act. Was this really true? The U.S. Solicitor General's office responded affirmatively to queries by the National Park Service. Since the Corridor and Canyonlands had been "duly surveyed, monumented, and marked," a new exchange procedure was legal and could be undertaken. The exchangers were now to be two private conservation organizations, the Conservation Fund and The Nature Conservancy. The exchangees were to be Temple-Inland, Louisiana-Pacific, and International Paper, which had recently absorbed Champion International.[115]

Until all agreements had been finalized and all contracts signed, nothing could be said publicly about the arrangement. Meanwhile the government funding necessary to support the exchange was successfully sought with the help of Senator Kay Bailey Hutchinson (R-Tex), Congressman Turner, and the Bush administration. Three million dollars are budgeted for land purchase in fiscal year 2003, while the administration budget for FY 2004 includes five million dollars for land purchase.[116] As these words are being written, the land exchange is gradually being worked out. Those interested in the Preserve and its fortunes continue to wait for the results. Purchase of Preserve lands took 18 years. Building its trail system took 17 years. Getting a Visitor Center took 27 years. No one will be surprised if protecting Big Sandy-Village Creek were to take a few months or years more: say 29 or 30 years from beginning to end. To see "progress" in this arena seems to be largely a matter of living long enough.

What has been achieved, however, outdistances what could be expected from the efforts of a relatively small cadre of environmentalists, some sympathetic political leaders, and some stubborn local individuals. In retrospect, what has been accomplished seems unlikely, highly improbable. The Preserve exists, enlarged by small increments and to all appearances soon to be enlarged by the Canyonlands Unit and a 60-mile creek corridor. Nearby state parks and private donations, a new Visitor Center and a scientific research center attest to the extent to which the Big Thicket has become accepted not only as a monument of Texas folklore and folk history but as a region rich in educational, recreational, and scientific values. Conservationists would add, if asked, that they are proud to have been able to do so without seriously injuring the forest products industry, fundamental to the region's economy. Why not, then, celebrate?

There will, of course, be a celebration when it is finally assured that the Big Sandy-Village Creek Corridor and the Canyonlands are once and for all made part of the Preserve. There will be much music and speechmaking, and barbecue. But a shadow will preside over the festivities. For just as the struggle to save a lasting remnant of the Thicket for the future seemed to have peaked, a new challenge has emerged. Some might call it a disaster. For decades, in their arguments with conservationists, the Texas Forest Products Industry has insisted that at all costs it must save its "land base." How could it grow timber without land? Then, without warning, two of the state's three large timber companies, Louisiana-Pacific and International Paper, did a sudden about-face. That is, they stated their intention of selling vast stretches of forest in East Texas: 1,500,000 acres, to be precise. The terminology describing this immense ecological garage sale has a certain dignity. It is called "divesting." In January 2001, International Paper announced that it was divesting itself of 800,000 acres of its Texas holdings, primarily in southeast Texas. It would continue to own the forest lands in the Lone Star State that continued to fit its long-term strategies.[117] In May 2002, Louisiana Pacific announced the divestiture of 700,000 acres.[118] Suddenly, vast stretches of timberland were on the market with no one knowing who the buyers might be, or what they might do with the land.

This immense shift in land ownership could have two destructive effects. It would at least in part (perhaps a large part) destroy a set of nature preserves set up in Texas' timber country by the forest products industry since the early 1990s. And it would strip away from the Preserve the protection that timberlands had afforded the Preserve, and which ware part of the rationale for the Preserve's spread-out configuration. Both of these factors need explaining.

The corporate nature preserves have not been mentioned so far in this essay. Had things turned out otherwise, they could have been listed as jewels in the Big Thicket Natural Area, alongside the new state parks and the preserves of private organizations. As things actually have turned out, it is not clear how many of them will survive. Carefully chosen originally for their historical, scenic, and biological values, Louisiana-Pacific's "Living Legacy Lands" in the Big Thicket Area include: Steepbank Creek Palmetto Flats (269 acres), Mill Creek Waterfall (3 acres), Myrtle Prairie (210 acres), Burkeville Blackland (20 acres), Cow Creek Sandyland and Bogs (30 acres), Pocket Pine Savannah (100 acres), Sabine Swamp (1531 acres), Clearfork Baygall (50 acres), Dogwood Trail (88 acres), Rush Creek Ravines (300 acres), Neches Bluffs (100 acres), Woodpecker Hill (1304 acres), and San Augustine Ridge (94 acres). The sum total of these diverse and biologically rich lands is 4099 acres.[119]

The Champion International's "Special Places in the Woods" include Kickapoo Creek Corridor (320 acres), Blue Heron Rookery (95 acres), Battiste Creek Corridor (300 acres), Longleaf Pine Trail (317 acres), Old Bering Sawmill (10 acres), The Beaver Pond (40 acres), Carter Sand and Water Stop (14 acres), Vincent Creek Corridor (79 acres), and Prehistoric Oyster Reefs (315 acres).[120] The total acreage of the Champion International sites is 1490 acres. Sanctuary acreage of the sites of both timber companies comes to 5589 acres.

The value of these areas is very great. The Vincent Creek Corridor contains a fully developed beech-magnolia association and in its local context is credited with being a "canyon." The Blue Heron Rookery is a large permanent nesting place for not only herons but also a wide variety of water birds. Utterly unlike the Vincent Creek Corridor, the Battiste Creek Corridor is a meandering cypress swamp-stream. Its location provides it with plant and bird species from the forests to its north and from the coastal prairies immediately to its south. The Sabine Swamp is an important piece in an ecological jigsaw puzzle, connecting the newly created Houseman (Blue Elbow) State Park and Louisiana's Sabine Island Wildlife Management Area. Together these three areas would comprise a vast bottomland wilderness tangle, as valuable for botanists and zoologists as for hikers, hunters, and canoers.

Descriptions of these once-protected areas could go on and on. The question, however, is whether the areas themselves will go on and on. In "divesting" themselves of their holdings, Louisiana-Pacific and Champion International made no effort to ensure protection of the small unique places they have so recently—and with great fanfare—set aside. Long telephone conversations with executives of these corporations have left the author the barren promise that whoever bought the land surrounding them "would certainly be told" about the sanctuaries and their status. It is anyone's guess to where this might lead.

It should be added, to keep the record straight, that Temple-Inland, besides donating the Larsen Sanctuary and its creek frontage to The Nature Conservancy, continues to set aside and to protect areas valuable for their biological, archeological, and historical significance. Among these are sites with names like Beef Creek Falls, Eleven-Log Pine, Hamilton Swamp, Money Hole, Fuller's Earth Pit (a surface mine now filled with water), Silky Camellia Colony, and Wild Azalea Canyon. Similar areas are protected by Temple-Inland in Georgia.[121]

The loss of these nature preserves (in whole, or, hopefully, in part) can be described as a tragedy. If it is a tragedy, it is a tragedy of relatively small, relatively isolated areas. The sale of vast areas surrounding the Big Thicket Preserve is a loss of immense proportions. In a recent *Houston Chronicle* article, Maxine Johnston explained:

> It's the way the preserve was laid out in the first place. Rather than one big lump like the Smoky Mountain National Park or Big Bend, the Big Thicket Preserve snakes and winds over seven counties. It has nine units, most of them joined by long twisting corridors. It was designed to save as many diverse plant associations as possible, but it gives the Preserve a lot of borders. The Preserve has almost twice as many miles of border as Yellowstone Park . . . even though Yellowstone is twenty-three times larger than the Big Thicket.[122]

In the past this did not seem to be a problem. Whatever else they did, timber companies were in the business of growing trees. Having timber companies next door growing pine trees like rows of corn was one thing, Johnston stated. Having those pine plantations turn into subdivisions or five-acre tracts full of mobile homes, barking dogs, all-terrain vehicles and Chinese tallow trees would be much worse.[123]

Environmentalists concede that such situations may not appear in the short run. They add, however, that in the long run, after large acreages are purchased, these will be broken up into smaller tracts, which will then be sold at a profit by raising the price per acre. These in turn could be broken up into smaller tracts, which could be sold at a profit by raising their cost per acre. These, in turn, could be fragmented into still smaller sections, and, again, sold at higher prices per acre, thus producing a profit. And so on. Fragmentation of habitat would follow closely on the heels of fragmentation of land ownership. Subdivisions, trailer parks, strip malls, and convenience stores would replace forest. In an area in which so much has been done to preserve wilderness and the wilderness experience, the thrust towards unchecked urban and suburban sprawl comes, environmentalists state, as a needless and destructive process. For these reasons and because of the Big Thicket's "biologically sensitive" nature, the National Parks and Conservation Association has recently named the Big Thicket National Preserve one of the nation's ten most endangered parks.[124]

Conservationists feel that, having confronted a series of dilemmas that they have largely managed to resolve, they now are confronted with having to "save" the Big Thicket all over again. On their side in any such project is the fact that the land they wish to add to the Preserve, thus "buffering" it, is land put on the market by willing sellers. The problem is not that of "condemning" lands that a seller wishes to keep. It is that of finding money to fund the purchase. Congressman Jim Turner has requested that the National Park Service identify Louisiana-Pacific and International Paper land that could strengthen and protect the Preserve. The Park Service has complied, listing those parcels that would protect the Preserve from rampant development.[125] These lands involve around nine percent of the acreage currently on the market.[126] The total cost would be in the neighborhood of $116,000,000: 145,000 acres at an average of $800 per acre.[127]

Meanwhile the two large lumber companies' lands are already being sold. In early 2003 Louisiana-Pacific sold 27,000 acres in San Augustine County near Cleveland.[128] Subsequently, Louisiana-Pacific reported the sale of 43,500 acres in the "Saratoga Block" in southeast Texas. Molpus Woodlands Group has purchased two blocks of land from Louisiana Pacific, one (36,260 acres) near Oakhurst, the other a massive 145,000 acres near Corrigan.[129] More recently, Molpus has announced the acquisition of 450,000 acres: price tag $285,000,000. These lands are in Hardin, Jasper, Liberty, Newton, Orange, Polk, and Tyler Counties.[130] It will come as a relief to many that, according to corporate spokesmen, these areas are to be managed "for long term timber production," not real estate speculation.

5. Postscript to a Postscript

The present essay attempts to describe the history of the Big Thicket National Preserve, and of the Big Thicket region generally, from 1974 up to the present time (fall 2003). It must be confessed that the chronicle, though multi-sided and often weighted with particular facts, might have been much longer. This is so because other factors and other facts might have been discussed. Here are a few examples, in no particular order: 1. Lamar University has recently created a Center for the Study of the Big Thicket. It will operate in tandem with the Big Thicket Archives already in place in that university's Grey Library.[131] 2. Efforts have been made to raise the water level of Steinhagen Reservoir, on the Neches River, in the process drowning out both a rich wildlife management area and a state park (Martin Dies State Park). The goal of this is to store water to sell to Houston.[132] 3. The Big Thicket Association has recently created a Big Thicket National Heritage Trust. On the basis of this trust it has been able to purchase 45 acres at the confluence of Peach Creek and Village Creek. This purchase will be deeded to the Big Thicket National Preserve.[133] 4. A National Science Foundation grant has been awarded to the University of North Texas to study the impact of human values on the choices that will be made in the development of the region. This grant, which it is expected will be renewed, will study the Big Thicket in terms of the impact of human values on nature.[134] 5. A grant from the T. L. L. Temple Foundation has funded the University of North Texas Press Temple Big Thicket Series, of which the present book is the fourth volume.[135] 6. The Houston Wilderness, a recently founded private group, has projected a ring of parks, preserves, refuges, hiking and canoeing trails encircling Houston. This far-sighted project impinges on the Big Thicket region at two points: the western part of the Big Thicket near Sam Houston National Forest and in the San Jacinto River Basin, and the west-central part of the Big Thicket along the Trinity River, including Davis Hill State Park and the Trinity River National Wildlife Refuge. Big Thicket conservationists have joined with the Houston Wilderness to promote this venture.[136] Other developments, present and past, might have been added to these. But the present essay is long enough. To lengthen it to cover all factors that might be thought relevant would be to write not a postscript but a second book, nearly as long as the one to which it is appended.

Prof. Pete A.Y. Gunter
University of North Texas
Denton, Texas 76203

NOTES TO AFTERWORD

1. Maxine Johnston, "Twenty-five Years of Milestones: Big Thicket National Preserve," manuscript found in Big Thicket National Preserve Library, Big Thicket National Preserve, Beaumont, Texas, 1999, p. 1.

2. See above, pp. 162–64.

3. Johnston, "Twenty-five Years," 1–3.

4. "Complete the Preserve," *Beaumont Enterprise*, November 11, 1981, sec. A.

5. Joe Fohn, "Big Thicket Group Upset by Stalled Land Acquisition," *San Antonio Express*, November 26, 1982, sec. B.

6. Richard Connelly, "Out of the Thicket," *Texas Lawyer*, April 20, 1992, p. 16.

7. Steve Moore, "Title Hassles Snag Thicket Land Sales," *Beaumont Enterprise*, October 8, 1978, sec. D.

8. "Jewell Honored," *Big Thicket Bulletin*, no.11 (September 11, 1994): 8.

9. Pete A.Y. Gunter, *The Big Thicket: An Ecological Reevaluation* (Denton, TX: University of North Texas Press, 1993), 99–100.

10. Geraldine Watson, *Reflections on the Neches*, Temple Big Thicket Series 3 (Denton, TX: University of North Texas Press, 2003), 248–50.

11. National Park Service. Briefing Statement for Jennifer Yezek, aide to Senator Lloyd Bentsen, August 12, 1991, p. 5. In author's files and Big Thicket National Preserve headquarters, Beaumont.

12. "At Last! The Visitor Center," *Big Thicket Reporter*, no. 53 (September–October 2001): 1; Ann Roberts, "VC Dedication," *Big Thicket Reporter*, no. 54 (November–December 2001): 5.

13. Johnston, "Twenty-five Years," 1.

14. Johnston, "Twenty-five Years," 2.

15. Johnston, "Twenty-five Years."

16. Johnston, "Twenty-five Years," 3.

17. Johnston, "Twenty-five Years," 4.

18. Johnston, "Twenty-five Years."

19. For a detailed account of the Preserve's trails and picnic areas see Gunter, *Big Thicket*, 2.

20. Johnston, "Twenty-five Years," 2.

21. Watson, *Reflections*, 221.

22. "National Preserve Plans Prescribed Fires," *Big Thicket Messenger and Advertizer*, February 16, 1989, p. 1.

23. "County Receives $8,503 in Lieu of Big Thicket Park Taxes," *Silsbee Bee*, October 25, 1979, Sec. 1.

24. From notes taken by the author, Big Thicket Association Headquarters, Saratoga, Texas, January 25, 1992.

25. Gunter, *Big Thicket*, 164–65.

26. Linda Gilchrist, "Pinewood Citizens Tired of Floods; Conservationists Blamed," *Hardin County News*, August 15, 1979, sec. D; "Congressman to Attend Flood Control Meeting," *Hardin County News*, August 15, 1979, sec. A.

27. Bob Wolcott, "Rockland Dam Is a Must," *Hardin County News*, August 13, 1980, 1–2.

28. "Pine Island Bayou Stormwater District," *Big Thicket Reporter*, no. 25 (January–February 1997): 1.

29. Bill Jewell, "Bayous and Boondoggles," *Big Thicket Reporter*, no. 26 (March–April 1997): 4.

30. "Pine Island Bayou Boondoggle is Back!" *Big Thicket Reporter*, no. 26 (March–April 1997): 1, 4.

31. "Pine Island Bills Pass Texas Legislature," *Big Thicket Reporter*, no. 27 (May–June 1997): 1.

32. Sonya Campbell, "Flood Control Levies Return," *Hardin County News*, November 18, 1997, sec. A.

33. "Bayou Lawsuits / Election Still Pending," *Big Thicket Reporter*, no. 32 (March–April 1998): 1–2; "Bayou District Tax Election Nov. 3," *Big Thicket Reporter*, no. 33 (May–June 1998): 1.

34. "Bayou District Defeated," *Big Thicket Reporter*, no.36 (November–December 1998): 1.

35. Gunter, *Big Thicket*, 147–57.

36. Geraldine Watson, *Big Thicket Plant Ecology: An Introduction* (Saratoga, TX: Big Thicket Museum, 1975), 13–15.

37. "Neches," *American Rivers Conservation Council Newsletter*, July 1984, p. 8.

38. Betty Brink, "Letter to Bill Hallmon. President, Big Thicket Association," *Big Thicket Conservationist*, no. 6 (Spring 1983): 1.

39. Jim Walsh (Grassroots Coordinator, National Parks and Conservation Association), letter to Betty Brinks, May 12, 1983, 2 pp. Copy in author's Big Thicket Files.

40. Billy Hallmon, letter to Chief of Engineers, June 26, 1983, 2 pp. Copy in author's Big Thicket files.

41. Texas Department of Water Resources, *Water for Texas: A Comprehensive Plan for the Future* 1, June, 1984, III-6-13, III-10-15-16.

42. Theodore C. Stroup, Fort Worth District Corps of Engineers, letter to Billy Hallmon, August 6, 1983. Copy in author's Big Thicket files.

43. 100th Congress, HR 1747. Copy in author's Big Thicket Files.

44. Congressman Charles Wilson, letter to author, November 29, 1990. Copy in the author's Big Thicket files.

45. Gary Benton, "Houston, Others 'Lusting' After Our East Texas Water," *Tyler County Booster*, May 28, 1999, sec. A; "Regional Planning Group Seeks Reservoir Sites," *Tyler County Booster*, March 22, 2000, sec. A.

46. "Rockland Reservoir Keeps Resurfacing," *Tyler County Booster*, June 14, 2000, sec. A; "Reservoir Site Sparks Controversy," *Diboll Free Press*, June 15, 2000, sec. A.

47. "Region Must Balance Water, Wood Resources," *Beaumont Enterprise*, July 26, 2000; Richard Stewart, " Plan to Build Dam Threatens Wild River," *Houston Chronicle*, June 11, 2000, sec. E.

48. G. A. Begin, "Professor Opposed to Rockland Project," *Port Arthur News*, January 16, 2000, sec. A. Cf. also article by Richard Stewart immediately above.

49. "TCNR Vice Chair Canoes Proposed Wild and Scenic River," *Conservation Progress*, no. 217 (December 1999): 1. Cf. also article by Richard Stewart above.

50. "33,000 Acres Conserved on 'Middle' Neches," *Big Thicket Reporter*, no. 64 (July–August 2003): 1. Part of the source for this article is the *Deep East Texas Association Newsletter*, August 2003.

51. Gunter, *Big Thicket*, 102–3, 159–61.

52. "Temple-Inland Gift to N.C.," *Big Thicket Reporter*, no. 12 (November–December 1994): 1. Reported from *Texas Forestry*.

53. "Village Creek State Park Opened April 20," *Big Thicket Reporter*, no.8 (March–April 1994): 1; "Village Creek State Park Could Open in Two Years," *Silsbee Bee*, November 3, 1988, p. 1.

54. Gunter, *Big Thicket*, 101.

55. "Village Creek State Park," *Big Thicket Reporter*, no. 55 (January–February 2002): 2.

56. Gunter, *The Big Thicket*, 168–72.

57. Joe Liggio, "An Investigation of Plant Communities and Flora at Davis Hill State Park, Liberty County, Texas" (M. A. Thesis, University of Houston at Clear Lake, 2000).

58. "TXDOT, EPA and Blue Elbow," *Big Thicket Reporter*, no.12 (November–December 1994): 1; "Tourist Bureau/ Blue Elbow," *Big Thicket Reporter*, no. 14 (March–April 1995): 5. Lake Livingston State Park, created in 1977, might be added to this inventory. It is, however, almost entirely committed to camping, picnicking, and water recreation.

59. "Trinity River Wildlife," *Big Thicket Reporter*, no. 7 (January–February 1994): 4; "Trinity River National Wildlife Refuge Plants Trees," *Big Thicket Reporter*, no. 14 (March–April 1996): 6. Also see next note.

60. Map dated April 2002, provided by U. S. Fish and Wildlife Service. In author's Big Thicket Files.

61. Stuart Marcos, Trinity River National Wildlife Refuge manager, telephone conversation with author, September 5, 2003.

62. Gunter, *Big Thicket*, 175.

63. I would like to thank Wendy Ledbetter, Big Thicket Director, Larsen Sanctuary, The Nature Conservancy of Texas, for verifying this information.

64. "McAfee Preserve Acquired by N.A.P.A.," *Big Thicket Reporter*, no.31 (January–February 1998): 1. I would like to thank Katherine Goodbar of the

Texas Committee on Natural Resources for providing information on N.A.P.A.'s holdings in southeast Texas.

65. "Ghost Road—County Park?" *Big Thicket Reporter*, no. 18 (November–December 1995): 1.

66. "Ghost Road Committee Meets," *Big Thicket Reporter*, no. 19 (January–February 1996): 4; "Ghost Road Update," *Big Thicket Reporter*, no. 20 (March–April 1996): 4.

67. "Commissioners Approve Ghost Road County Park," *Big Thicket Reporter*, no. 28 (July–August 1997): 1.

68. Jim King, "The Ghost Road of Hardin County," *Clearance Card* 36, no.1 (1999): 1, 4–7; "Ghost Road—Who Owns it?" *Big Thicket Reporter*, no. 22 (July–August 1996): 5.

69. These areas are located and described in the websites of The Nature Conservancy of Texas, the Houston Outdoor Nature Club, and the Houston Audubon Society.

70. "Magnolia Garden Club Gift to Preserve," *Big Thicket Reporter*, no.7 (January–February 1994): 1.

71. These data have been provided by Glenna Vigil of the National Park Service Land Resources Program Center, Santa Fe, New Mexico. They include both dates of inclusion in the Preserve and plats (surveyor's maps) showing precise boundaries of all areas included. Help has also been provided by Chuck Hunter of the Big Thicket National Preserve, Beaumont, Texas.

72. U.S. Department of the Interior National Park Service Big Thicket National Preserve Briefing Statements, August 12, 1991, pp. 16–17.

73. Gerry Dickert, "Preserve Awarded Thicket Home After 16 Years," *Hardin County News*, November 14, 1990, p. 1.

74. "Big Thicket Headquarters to be Relocated at Kountze," *Silsbee Bee*, February 23, 1989, p. 1.

75. Andrea Wright, "Wilderness Treasure Puts Out Welcome Mat at Its New Visitor Center," *Beaumont Enterprise*, October 7, 2001, sec. A.

76. "Visitor Center Funding—It's for Real!" *Big Thicket Reporter*, no. 45 (May–June 2000): 1.

77. "Visitor Center Funding, "*Big Thicket Reporter*, no. 48 (November–December 2000): 3.

78. *Texas Journal of Science* 49, no. 3 Supplement, 1-189 (August 1977); *Texas Journal of Science* 52, no. 4 Supplement, 1-172 (November 2000). A third conference has met but its proceedings are not yet published.

79. "Grant Awarded . . ." *Big Thicket Reporter,* no. 39 (May–June 1999): 1.

80. "Field Research Station . . ." *Big Thicket Reporter,* no. 42 (November–December 1999): 1.

81. "Foundation Grant $1000," *Big Thicket Reporter,* no. 45 (May–June 2000): 1.

82. "Grants From Meadows and Brown Foundations," *Big Thicket Reporter,* no. 48 (November–December 1999): 1–2. A further donation from Ann Roberts is noted.

83. "Visitor Center Progress," *Big Thicket Reporter,* no. 50 (March–April 2001): 3; "First Study Groups Visit Research Station," *Big Thicket Reporter,* no. 51 (May–June 2001): 3; "Field Research Station," *Big Thicket Bulletin,* no. 53 (September–October 2001): 5.

84. See above, pp. 146–60.

85. Art Wiese, "Wilson Succeeds in Cutting Big Thicket Funds," *Houston Post,* May 25, 1978, sec. A.

86. See above in this Afterword, p. 237.

87. Gunter, *Big Thicket,* 108–9; "Big Thicket Battle Brewing Over Bill for Bigger Preserve," *Houston Chronicle,* December 13, 1987, sec. 3.

88. "Big Thicket Bill Reintroduced," *Big Thicket Conservationist,* no. 26 (Winter 1988–89): 2, 4; "Wilson Touts Thicket Bill," *Beaumont Enterprise,* February 18, 1989, p.1.

89. "Big Thicket Expansion Bill Passes in the House." *Big Thicket Conservationist,* no. 28 (Fall 1989): 1–2.

90. "Status of Senate Bill 1302," *Big Thicket Conservationist,* no. 29 (Winter 1990): 3–4; Earnest L. Perry, "Petitions Will Ask Senators to Kill Senate Bill," *Beaumont Enterprise,* July 19, 1989, sec. B; "Village Creek Landowners Issue Plea to Keep Their Property," *Beaumont Enterprise,* June 14, 1989, sec. A.

91. "House Panel Approves Thicket Expansion," *Beaumont Enterprise,* July 18, 1989, sec. A.

92. See above in this Afterword, p. 238.

93. Brandt Mannchen, "Big Thicket Bill Gets Shot in the Arm," *Big Thicket Conservationist,* no. 30 (Spring 1991): 3–4. Excerpted from *Lone Star Sierran,* April–May 1991.

94. Jennifer Dixon, "Big Thicket Might Get Bigger," *Denton Record-Chronicle*, May 21, 1991, sec. A.

95. Gunter, *Big Thicket*, 175–77.

96. "Senate Approves Thicket Addition Bill," *Big Thicket Reporter*, no. 1 (January–February 1993): 1.

97. James A. Owen, "Senate Bill O.K's Big Thicket Expansion," *Beaumont Enterprise*, March 4, 1993, sec. A; "Senate Passes Expansion Bill," *Big Thicket Reporter*, no. 2 (March–April 1993): 1.

98. "Big Thicket Addition Hearings," *Big Thicket Reporter*, no. 3 (May–June 1993): 1.

99. "Thicket Bill Passes Without Local Unit," *Orange Leader*, June 22, 1993, p. 1; "Clinton Signs Addition Bill," *Big Thicket Reporter*, no. 4 (July–August 1993): 1.

100. "Top Priority '94–'95: Money," *Big Thicket Reporter*, no.7 (January–February 1994): 1.

101. "1.5 Million for Acquisition," *Big Thicket Reporter*, no. 11 (September–October 1994): 1.

102. "104th Congress," *Big Thicket Reporter*, no. 13 (January–February 1995): 1.

103. "BTNP Addition Act—Extension Still Pending," *Big Thicket Reporter*, no.14 (March--April 1995): 1; "Extension Bill Hearings," *Big Thicket Reporter*, no. 15 (May–June 1995): 1.

104. "Extension Bill Passes House," *Big Thicket Reporter*, no. 19 (November–December 1995): 1.

105. "Senate Hearings on HR 826," *Big Thicket Reporter*, no. 20 (March–April 1996): 1.

106. "B. T. Addition Deadline," *Big Thicket Reporter*, no. 21 (May–June 1996): 1; Richard Strahan, "Preserve Land Acquisition Update," *Big Thicket Reporter*, no. 18 (July–August 1996): 1, 4.

107. "Parks Bill Held Hostage," *Big Thicket Reporter*, no.22 (July–August 1996): 1.

108. Nita Thurman, "Bigger Thicket," *Dallas Morning News*, November 10, 1996, sec. A.

109. "Addition Act Crisis," *Big Thicket Reporter*, no. 33 (May–June 1998): 1.

110. Maxine Johnston, "Forest Service Sabotages Addition Act Exchanges," *Big Thicket Reporter*, no. 34 (July–August 1998): 1–2.

111. "Turner Pledges to Complete Addition Act," *Big Thicket Reporter*, no. 35 (September–October 1998): 1.

112. "Preserve Addition Act Stalled," *Big Thicket Reporter*, no. 40 (July–August 1999): 1.

113. "Addition Act Update," *Big Thicket Reporter*, no. 42 (November–December 1999): 2.

114. "1993 Addition Act," *Big Thicket Reporter*, no. 44 (March–April 2000): 1.

115. "Addition Act Progress (Ring Around the Rosy)," *Big Thicket Reporter*, no. 55 (January–February 2002): 3.

116. "Congress Appropriates $3 Million for Big Thicket Land Acquisition," *Big Thicket Reporter*, no. 56 (March–April 2003): 1.

117. "International Paper Sells Land," *Big Thicket Reporter*, no. 49 (January–February 2001): 7. Information in this item was taken from the January 28, 2001, *Polk County Enterprise*.

118. "Big Thicket Threatened by Timber Land Sales on Adjacent Lands," *Big Thicket Reporter*, no. 52 (July–August 2001): 1–2.

119. These figures are taken from maps and habitat descriptions sent to the author by Louisiana-Pacific Corporation. Copies are in the author's Big Thicket files.

120. Gunter, *Big Thicket*, 184–85.

121. David Baxter, *Nature of the Forest: Temple-Inland's Timberlands in the Twenty-First Century* (Diboll, TX: Temple-Inland, Inc., 2002), 43–70.

122. Richard Stewart, "In the Thick of a New Fight in the Big Thicket," *Houston Chronicle*, November 18, 2002, sec. A.

123. Ibid.

124. Kate Himot, "Ten Most Endangered," *National Parks* 77, no. 3–4 (March–April 2003): 24–25.

125. "Cong. Jim Turner Asks N.P.S. to Identify Lands That Could Complement the B.T.N.P.," *Big Thicket Reporter*, no. 58 (July–August 2002): 1.

126. Ibid.

127. Stewart, "In the Thick."

128. "Speaking of Endangered Parks: It's Mayday," *Big Thicket Reporter*, no. 62 (March–April 2003): 1.

129. "More Land Sales," *Big Thicket Reporter*, no. 63 (May–June 2003): 1.

130. "Molpus Buys East Texas Timberlands," *Big Thicket Reporter*, no. 64 (July–August 2003): 1.

131. "Center for Big Thicket Studies," *Big Thicket Reporter*, no. 59 (September–October 2008): 2.

132. "Steinhagen Master Plan Draft," *Big Thicket Reporter*, no. 61 (September–October 2002,): 4.

133. "Trust to Buy Big Thicket Property," *Big Thicket Reporter*, no. 57 (May–June 2002): 1.

134. "NSF Grant for University of North Texas," *Big Thicket Reporter*, no. 59 (September–October 2002): 1, 4.

135. "T. L. L. Foundation Funds Publication Grant," *Big Thicket Reporter*, no. 55 (January–February 2002): 1.

136. Rosie Zamora and Jim Blackburn, "Path to Prosperity Winds Through City's Natural Resources." *Houston Chronicle*, July 14, 2002, sec. C.

BIBLIOGRAPHY TO AFTERWORD

Abernethy, Francis E., ed. *Tales from the Big Thicket*. Temple Big Thicket Series 1. Denton, TX: University of North Texas Press, 2002. First published 1966 by University of Texas Press.

Ajilvsgi, Geyata. *Wild Flowers of the Big Thicket, East Texas, and Western Louisiana*. College Station, TX: Texas A& M University Press, 1979.

Baxter, David. *Nature of the Forest: Temple-Inland's Timberlands in the Twenty-first Century*. Diboll, TX: Temple-Inland, Inc., 2002.

Cozine, James J. "Defining the Big Thicket: Prelude to Preservation." *East Texas Historical Journal* 32, no.2 (1993): 57–71.

Fountain, Michael S., and R. Lee Rayburn. *Impact of Oil and Gas Development on Vegetation and Soils of Big Thicket National Preserve*. Technical Report, No. 5. College Station, TX: National Park Service Cooperative Park Studies Unit, Texas A & M University, 1987.

Gunter, Pete A. Y. "The Big Thicket: A Case Study in Attitudes toward Environment." In *Philosophy and Environmental Crisis*, edited by William Blackstone, 117–37. Athens: University of Georgia Press, 1974.

———. *The Big Thicket: An Ecological Reevaluation*. Denton,TX: University of North Texas Press, 1993.

———. "Lance." *The Texas Writer* 1, no. 1 (1999): 21–24.

————. "R. E. Jackson and the Early Big Thicket Conservation Movement." *East Texas Historical Journal* 53, no. 2 (1999): 53–63.

Gunter, Pete A. Y., and Max Oelschlaeger. *Texas Land Ethics*. Austin: University of Texas Press, 1997. See especially Chapter Six, "The Big Thicket."

Johnston, Maxine, ed. *Thicket Explorer*. Saratoga, TX: Big Thicket Museum, 1972.

Johnston, Maxine, and Pete A.Y. Gunter. "Opinions: Big Thicket National Preserve Needs Your Help." *Beaumont Enterprise*, February 23, 2003, sec. B.

Liggio, Joe. "An Investigation of the Plant Communities and Flora at Davis Hill State Park, Liberty County, Texas." Master's thesis, University of Houston at Clear Lake, 2000.

Loughmiller, Campbell, and Lynn Loughmiller, ed. and comp. *Big Thicket Legacy*. Temple Big Thicket Series 2. Foreword by F. E. Abernethy. Denton, TX: University of North Texas Press, 1999. First published 1977 by University of Texas Press.

Marks, P. L., and Paul Harcombe. "Forest Vegetation of the Big Thicket, Southeast Texas." *Ecological Monographs* 51, no. 3 (1981): 287–305.

McLeod, Claude A. "The Big Thicket Forest of East Texas." *Texas Journal of Science* 23, no.2 (1971): 221–33.

————. *The Big Thicket Forest of East Texas: Its History, Location and Description*. Huntsville, TX: Sam Houston Press, 1967.

Moser, Dan. "Big Thicket of Texas." Photos by Blair Pittman. *National Geographic* 146, no. 4 (1974): 504–29.

Parker, Lois Williams. *The Big Thicket of Texas: An Annotated Bibliography*. Arlington, TX: Sable Publishing Company, 1977.

Peacock, Howard. *The Big Thicket of Texas: America's Ecological Wonder*. Boston: Little, Brown, 1984.

Pittman, Blair. *The Stories of I. C. Eason: King of the Dog People*. Denton, TX: University of North Texas Press, 1996.

"Proceedings of the First Big Thicket Science Conference." *Texas Journal of Science* 49, no. 3, Supplement (August 1997): 1–189.

"Proceedings of the Second Big Thicket Science Conference." *Texas Journal of Science* 52, no.4, Supplement (August 2000): 1–173.

Reed, James Robert. "Preservation Management in the Big Thicket." M. A. thesis, University of Texas at Austin, 1979.

Scmidly, Donald J., W.G. Norton, and Gail A. Barbara. *Game and Furbearing Mammals of Big Thicket National Preserve*. Santa Fe, NM: National Park Service, 1980.

Shafer, Harry J., Edward P. Baxter, Thomas B. Stearns, and James P. Deering. *An Archeological Assessment of the Big Thicket National Preserve*. Report No. 9. College Station, TX: Texas A&M University Anthropological Laboratory, 1975.

Sitton, Thad. *Backwoodsmen: Stockmmen and Hunters Along a Big Thicket Valley*. Norman: University of Oklahoma Press, 1995.

Suttkus, Royal D., and Glen D. Clammer. *Fishes of the Big Thicket National Preserve*. Beaumont, TX: National Park Service, 1980.

Watson, Geraldine. *Big Thicket Plant Ecology: An Introduction*. Saratoga, TX: Big Thicket Museum, 1975.

———. *Reflections on the Neches: A Naturalist's Odyssey Along the Big Thicket's Snow River*. Temple Big Thicket Series 3. Denton, TX: University of North Texas Press, 2003.

———. *Vegetative Survey of the Big Thicket National Preserve*. Beaumont, TX: National Park Service, 1982.

Wells, Joe Caulker. "Environmental Interest Groups: A Case Study. The Big Thicket Association." M. A. Thesis, University of Texas at Arlington, 1981.

INDEX

Note: *"Gallery"* refers to the photo inset following page 134.
Note: Page numbers in **bold** indicate chapters.

A